THE CONSISTENT
CONSUMER

PRAISE FOR THE CONSISTENT CONSUMER

The advantage you'll gain from reading The Consistent Consumer *is knowledge of the future—because one of the best predictors of the future is the values we hold. This is one of the most important books on customers to come out in years.*

Jim Kouzes, Coauthor The Leadership Challenge
and President Emeritus, The Tom Peters Group

Precise, witty … observations that are so dead-on that they hit you in the head like a well-aimed hammer. The Consistent Consumer *doesn't just identify what people do and how they behave, but it uncovers the why people do what they do. It's one of the smartest books you'll ever meet.*

Dan Fogarty, Keeper of the Faith, Chipotle Mexican Grill

I believe in this book. The Consistent Consumer *synthesizes politics, the arts, history, economics, and philosophy and reaches valuable conclusions. It is immensely entertaining, but most importantly to me, it is a valuable business tool. We are excited about applying its wisdom to our sales presentations.*

Neil S. Cumsky, CEO, Princeton Resorts Group, LLC

There are no limits to where you can take the information you gather from this book in improving your understanding of today's consumers. Open your briefcase and find a permanent place for this great read.

John A. Pryor, President and COO, Cousins Subs

The Consistent Consumer*'s exciting definition of generations holds together far better than the broader categories we are all used to using (such as "boomers"). The lively descriptors bring them to life in ways we can all relate to, and so in turn determine appropriate actions, as well.*

Chris Shipp, Sr. Vice President, Investment Advice and Products,
Charles Schwab and Company, Inc.

An insightful and long overdue book! Finally someone has explained clearly how to predict future behavior based on generational values. A must-read for any businessperson. Our marketing department is all over this book.

Therese Thilgen, President and Chief Content Officer,
Franchise UPDATE, Inc.

This is the book all executives need to have on their shelves if they want to understand the real issues that enable them to enhance the power of their brand, develop a viable, long-term relationship with their customers, and increase bottom-line results. Most importantly,

THE CONSISTENT
CONSUMER

PREDICTING FUTURE BEHAVIOUR
THROUGH LASTING VALUES

**KEN
BELLER**   **STEVE
WEISS**   **LOUIS
PATLER**

The Consistent Consumer
by Ken Beller, Steve Weiss, Louis Patler

Published by LTS Press

Copyright © 2005, 2007, 2013 by Ken Beller, Steve Weiss, Louis Patler

All rights reserved. The text of this publication, or any part thereof, may not be reproduced in any manner whatsoever without written permission from the publisher.

This publication is designed to provide accurate and authoritative information in regard to the subject matter covered. It is sold with the understanding that the publisher is not engaged in rendering legal, accounting, or other professional service. If legal advice or other expert assistance is required, the services of a competent professional should be sought.

This book was published in hardcover in 2005 by Dearborn Trade Publishing.
This book was republished in hardcover and softcover in 2007 by LTS Press.
This book was updated and republished in softcover and eBook in 2013 by LTS Press.

Book design by Maureen Cutajar, gopublished.com

Library of Congress Cataloging-in-Publication Data
Beller, Ken.
    The consistent consumer: predicting future behavior through lasting values / Ken Beller, Steve Weiss, and Louis Patler.
    p. cm.
    Includes index.
    ISBN 978-0-9801382-9-0
    1. Consumer behavior. I. Patler, Louis. II. Weiss, Steve M. III. Title.
HF5415.32.B45 2005
    658.8'342—dc22
    2004026173

LTS Press books are available at special quantity discounts to use for sales promotions, employee premiums, or educational purposes. Please e-mail our Special Sales Department for more information or to order books at SpecialOrders@LTSPress.com or write to LTS Press, P.O. Box 4165, Sedona, AZ 86340.

DEDICATION

To the Patriots, Performers, Techticians, Believers, Transformers and Owls...

May we all come to better understand each other and work in unison toward creating a more compassionate and peaceful world—for us and for all future Value Populations.

Contents

PART THREE

MARKETING TO VALUE POPULATIONS

PART FOUR

OPENING NEW AVENUES: MANAGING TALENT AND FINDING TRENDS

A *cknowledgments*

A book is always the result of many more people than its authors. We would like to especially thank our agent, John Willig, for bringing the opportunity to us. Michael Cunningham and the editors and staff at Dearborn Trade Publishing proved to be a wonderful matching of the minds and made this project proceed smoothly. This book benefited greatly from the excellent research and data-gathering skills of Near Bridge, Inc.'s, Ernie Baillargeon, Melinda Haseth, Laurie Masters, and Jesse Weiss.

We would also like to thank our friends and colleagues Betsy Gullickson, John Reynolds, Mike Moser, John Darling, Bob Steinbaugh, Craig Allen, Bill Daniels, Kitty Forseth, Bill Hoppin, Susan Freund, Jim Kennedy, Michael Knight, Linda Larkey, Jay Conrad Levinson, David Mills, Pat Lynch, Amy Robinson, Frank DiChristofano, Florence Stone, John Raphael, Lynn Ware, Tim Wasserman, Nancy White, Jason Saeler, Frank Chance, Jennifer Robinson, Darryl Sink, Roger Watson, Chris Shipp, Marion McGovern, Paula Reynolds, and Claire McAuliffe, who supported us early on in our efforts.

Being able to report both our research and its use in selected business settings in Part 3 of the book requires special thanks be given to our clients, who believed in the application and usefulness of our data early on: Anthony Vidergauz, CEO, California Closets; Edward Leaman, CEO, Growers & Nomads; Eric Woolworth, President, and Kim Stone, Vice President, The Miami Heat; Bernie Mullin, Vice President, The National Basketball Association; Matt Levine, President, Source USA; Dan Leese, CEO, Beringer Wineries; Linda Hudson, President, General Dynamics ATP; Craig Dewald, Global Vice President, American Express; Steve Ells, President/Founder, Jim Adams, Director of Marketing, and Dan Fogarty, Keeper of the Faith, Chipotle Mexican Grill; Phil Friedman, President, McAlister's Deli; Matt Ball and Jack Norris, Founders, Vegan Outreach; Michael Burke, Executive Director, and Lynn Rosseth, Director of Market Development, The Foodservice Packaging Institute; the Members of the United States Potato Board; Webb Howell, Publisher, Greg Sanders, Editorial Director, and Margaret Gayle, Director, Foodservice Programmes, *QSR Magazine*.

Lastly, a very special thank you to our wives—Heather, Ann, and Catherine—whose patient and endless support made this all possible.

This book has its roots in the search for consumer trends—not just any trends, mind you, but big important trends, the sort of trends that marketers, business leaders, and futurists can use to make vast pronouncements at conferences, board meetings, and cocktail parties; trends embracing really significant insights, such as "Marketing to women is increasingly important" and "People expect to have choices."

On our quest to uncover such trends, however, we discovered that the road to understanding often was muddy with inconsistent information. As we searched for ways to free ourselves from the quagmire, it became increasingly clear that the old way of trend prediction, based on continually shifting behavioral data, was essentially washed out and that the era of the multigenerational macrotrend was, in all likelihood, gone forever. Yet, as we took the time to examine the true nature of our journey, we realized that an entirely new path on the road to understanding mass consumer behavior had opened itself up to us.

It was this realization that led us to the research and title for this book. Simply put, mass consumer behavior, however apparently random it might seem, is best understood when built on a base of lasting values.

Like many who have preceded us, we could not resist the glimmer of truth that lurks in the apparent consistencies of demography. After exhaustive research into the most commonly accepted demographic attributes, including factors such as gender, ethnicity, education, income, and age, we concluded that age is the most fruitful attribute on which to focus when searching for trends. It also eventually became clear that the identification of shared formative experiences of similarly aged consumers was an effective way to uncover common values—the drivers that create trends.

Having established this understanding, we began trying to catalog the currently accepted aged-based "generational" groups, including: The Greatest Generation, Baby Boomers, Gen Xers, Millennials, and so forth. What became readily apparent was that there was little consistency or scientific reasoning behind how the beginning and ending date boundaries for each group had been chosen. The clearest beginning and ending dates we found for any group were those of the Baby Boom generation, whose boundaries were based on a boom and bust in the birth rate just after World War II (1946–1964). In general, though, we found so many discrepancies in the defining dates and descriptions of the other aforementioned generations that we began calling the existing age classifications "demographic dislocation"! (A more detailed discussion of this can be found in Chapter 3, "Understanding the Ages.")

While a boom and bust in the birth rate might define a group that behaves consistently throughout its lifetime, it is unlikely. Rather, it is reasonable to assume that a group who grew up during a boom in the birth rate would experience a considerably different environment (politically, economically, socially, etc.) than one who experienced a decline in a birth rate. With the Baby Boomers, this seems to be the case, as marketers now consistently divide this generation into Early and Late Boomers—clearly showing that this classification does not work well.

This was very apparent to us on a personal level as well. Although all three authors of this book fall into the traditionally defined Baby Boom generation, two of the authors, Steve Weiss and Louis Patler, who were born in the first half of this generation, felt they were somewhat well represented by the traditional Baby Boomer profile. On the other hand, Ken Beller, the youngest of the three, who was born at the tail end of the Boomer generation, felt that he and his age-based brethren were nothing like the Boomers—nor were they aptly described by the "Slacker" profile that is typically associated with Gen Xers. So the quest to find consistency in contemporary generational profiling began.

This posed a challenge to us. If there was such inconsistency in this field of study, what age ranges and factors would we then consider acceptable criteria for defining useful groups? How would we identify the driving forces that consistently affect consumer behavior through a group's entire life? What factors consistently shape consumer choices? Where could we look for predictive information about groups of people as they grow and mature and pass through the time-honored and inevitable "phases of life"?

During our investigation, we were drawn to a body of sociological research that suggests that broad sociocultural adaptation, which begins as early as infancy, is a strong platform for lifelong group value formation. Armed with this insight, we began the rigorous project of examining American culture with an eye toward those people, places, things, and events—*icons* as it were—that reflect and capture the zeitgeist of society at particular and clearly defined periods in history. We postulated that groups who share the same formative iconic experiences could be identified and, once identified, would constitute very powerful and consistent target markets—groups whose lifelong values, preoccupations, and pre-dispositions would be ingrained by cultural happenings and would reveal insights into likely and consistent future behaviors.

The specific research for this book spanned a three-year period, and it began by compiling an enormous database of tens of thousands of events and artifacts occurring since the turn of the twentieth century. This time frame was chosen because it coincided with the beginning of the era of mass communication—a period marking the ascension of universal soci-ocultural influences (radio, movies, television, and the Internet) over lo-cal and "tribal" influences (family tradition) as the chief catalysts of value formation in America.

Ultimately, this database of historical icons grew to include artifacts from all areas of social influence, ranging from life-altering events such as world wars and the incredible transformations of technology, to more "everyday" occurrences and artifacts culled from the realm of sports, music, television, radio, commercials, movies, books, comics, etc. In short, we tried to collect as much data on the parade of American con-temporary history as possible—everything from the Great Depression to the Golden Arches, from VJ-day to Veg-O-Matics.

Our research utilized both primary and secondary information sources. The primary information came from focus groups and interviews, while much of the secondary research came together in great part thanks to the significant amount of information that is now readily available on the Internet. Particularly rich veins of information are available through the many publicly accessible U.S. government databases, such as those of the Census Bureau and the Bureau or Labor Statistics as well as thousands of business and private Web sites. It is amazing what one can find by "Googling" anything from "women's history in America" to "commercials of the 1930s" to the "top-rated movies of the 1970s and 1980s."

Once we realized that values created by sociocultural, rather than bio-logical, forces play such an important and increasing role in defining con-sistently behaving cohort groups, we could no longer rely on the term "generation" to accurately define them, so we coined a new term: Value PopulationsTM.

In order to clearly define these Value Populations, our team began mining our database for common social and cultural themes. During this analysis, we began discovering significant starting and stopping points in those themes in American history. As we continued through this process, lines of differentiation began to emerge and groups having strong cultur-al coherence and integrity began to coalesce. Ultimately, clear demarca-tion points emerged, and within those periods we found a coherent set of lasting values.

Our research also revealed something unanticipated. Because the speed of societal change and the maturing of today's youth have both been increasing steadily since the beginning of the twentieth century, a Value Population no longer spans the tidy 20-year interval of a traditional generation and is, in fact, continually diminishing in length. Furthermore, it also became clear that value formation in later Value Populations is increasingly influenced by the multiple and very different Value Populations acting out in society at any one time.

In summary, sociocultural value formation suitably lends itself to effective consumer profiling, making it possible to not only define and understand values-based cohort groups, but to *anticipate* how they are likely to behave in future human-made and naturally occurring environments and situations. Further, because shared, common values of each Value Population last a lifetime, to the observant business leader, the benefits gained by understanding these values is significant—and can be highly profitable. From this revelation comes our perspective on *the consistent consumer.*

This book is divided into four main parts. Part 1 is intended to give the reader a better sense of the research and reasoning behind values-based demographic profiling and the method used to identify values-based cohort groups. Part 2 introduces the reader to the Value Populations and outlines the significant events, cultural artifacts, and lasting icons of the eras during their formation period. Part 3 demonstrates the application of this research within real businesses that have successfully used our Value Population research findings to increase their marketing impact and business profitability. Finally, Part 4 illustrates how values can and should be an important part of any business strategy from organizational structure, to operational excellence, to product development, to trend identification and creation.

That this material has already proven to be an aid to marketers in helping to anticipate and satisfy customers' wants and needs is something of which we are particularly proud. However, while we believe this book offers a wealth of benefits for business leaders, it also offers a plethora of understanding that is extremely useful to teachers, parents, public policymakers—anyone who can derive benefit from understanding the consistent values held within large age groups, both their own and others.

With greater insight into Value Populations, we can all better understand who we are and, in doing so, increase our understanding, mutual appreciation, and consideration for each other's perspectives. That will always be a path worth taking.

Part One

THE VALUES OF
A NATION

1

THE VALUE OF VALUES

The aim of education is the knowledge, not of facts, but of values.

—William S. Burroughs, American Writer

In the past 30 years, much has changed in the field of demographic and behavioral marketing. Significant advances in technology, coupled with easy access to data and an ever-increasing array of software tools, allow marketers to access and analyze customer transaction data in vast quantities and at an amazing rate of speed. But it seems reasonable to ask the question, "Are we getting too much measurement and not enough meaning?"

In order to help balance out this quantitative approach to measuring consumers' past behaviors and increase their understanding of "why" consumers behave the way they do, marketers regularly employ age-based generational demographics in their marketing strategies. This approach is intended to help marketers gain a better understanding of the attitudes and beliefs held by consumers; furthermore, if these attitudes and beliefs can be understood, future behavior can be better predicted and marketing strategies and advertising campaigns can be made more effective.

Interestingly, when the current methods used for this approach are closely examined, what resonates consistently throughout them is an unstated assumption that consumers' attitudes are best understood by their past behaviors. However, because behaviors are the results of deep-seated and often unconscious values, our research strongly suggests that these methods are flawed.

For marketers to be able to predict future behavior and spot future trends, a clear understanding of consumers' consistent shared values is required. Values drive behavior and can act as motivational filters through which the mass of past behavioral data becomes comprehensible and future actions predictable. For marketers, predictable behavior is what dreams are made of, because it allows them to effectively and accurately communicate with target audiences and sell more products at higher profit margins.

So, if shared values are the Holy Grail for marketers, how can values-based groups be uncovered? We think it's best done by analyzing significant historical events and cultural icons and defining their impact on the formation of group values. This analysis method yields a qualitative yet data-driven approach to understanding major and newly defined, age-based demographic markets and offers an effective way to uncover common tastes and behavioral consistencies within consumer groups.

What is important to clearly understand is that these new age-based groupings, or Value Populations, are not based on randomly chosen periods of time or on the extrapolation of past and current behaviors—as are those of the traditionally defined generational groups (Baby Boomers, Gen X, Gen Y, etc.). Value Populations, as their name implies, are groups whose consistent connection is shared values—values that were created by experiencing shared events in the cultural environment. We have identified six such groups: Patriots, Performers, TechticiansTM, Believers, Transformers, and Owls.

While the second section of this book is devoted entirely to understanding the Value Populations, a brief introduction to their formative periods and a comparison of them to the traditional and generally accepted generational cohort groups is made in Figure 1.1.

During their formative years, each Value Population is presented with unique thematic issues that they will be associated with throughout their collective lifetime. In other words, whatever a Value Population's collective and seemingly inconsistent behaviors might be, there are underlying values that will resonate consistently and continually with them throughout their lifetimes and that explain these seeming inconsistencies. Because values drive behaviors, consistent values allow astute marketers to predict behaviors and increase marketing effectiveness. It is this consistency of values that lead us to the title, *The Consistent Consumer: Predicting Future Behavior through Lasting Values*.

The foundation of this book is that experiences in our formative years create lasting values that remain constant over time. It is the recognition that every cultural time period produces art, artifacts, people, places, and things—in a word, *icons* —that seal the meaning of a moment in history. Icons embody all of the values, cross trends, and cultural currents of the time—the essence of the moment. When these icons are recognized and analyzed, they allow researchers to clearly identify the values people carry with them—throughout a lifetime. Icons offer an amazing plethora of understanding and meaning and, as will be shown in the next chapter, can be as seemingly inconsequential, or as surprising, as a child's toy.

FIGURE 1.1

Value Populations—A Redefinition of Generations

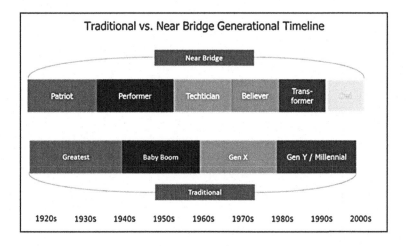

2

THE POWER OF ICONS
Mr. Potato Head

For we don't just look at icons—we resonate with them. To really take one in, some part of us must say: it is me. The more of us who do that, the more universal its acceptance.

—Douglas Rushkoff, Cultural Writer

In the history of the United States of America, it is difficult to find a more economically upbeat year than 1952. Basic American industry definitively turns a corner away from an emphasis on military goods and a shortage-stressed war economy toward an emphasis on all the things a peacetime consumer economy may desire in terms of creature comforts and corporate profits. With only 7 percent of the world's population, the United States finds itself producing 65 percent of the world's manufactured goods; the Gross National Product and disposable income soar to unprecedented levels; and the nation's 3.3 percent unemployment rate is the lowest in peacetime history.

Nearly four million new automobiles roll off assembly lines in 1952 and, even more importantly, the nation's parents produce just about the same number of new passengers. This new peak in the birth rate, which has been growing since the end of World War II in 1945 and which will be superseded every year for the next six years, is the true backbone of the nation's economic optimism about the future. Nothing, after all, supports a consumer economy like a large number of consumers.

On a more somber note, it must be appreciated that these relatively affluent 1952 babies are born into what are still hellaciously dangerous and stressful times. This is the dawn of the Cold War and atom bomb era, which some cultural commentators believe first viscerally hits home with the general American public during the 1952 Summer Olympics— the first Olympics in 40 years participated in by the Soviet Union and in which they very nearly top the victorious Americans' point total, with the outcome in doubt until late on the last day. More urgently, war with Communist forces still rages in Korea, and an enormous cloud over all future prospects is cast by America's testing of the first hydrogen bomb on the Eniwetok Atoll on November 1, 1952—30 times more powerful than the Hiroshima bomb and more powerful than all the munitions fired in World War II combined.

It is against this backdrop of material prosperity and global anxiety that Mr. Potato Head is born. Brought to the marketplace by two brothers whose company would soon come to be known as Hasbro, the original toy consists of a spike-topped plastic body on which a real potato is placed and then stuck with an assortment of plastic pin-inserted eyes, ears, noses, mouths, hats, and so forth, creating a variety of whimsical faces. Reputedly the first toy ever advertised on television, Mr. Potato Head is an immediate success and sells about four million units in its first year.

In the study of generational values, what makes Mr. Potato Head such an interesting toy at the starting point of his still-illustrious career is his role as an icon of consumption for two different generations or, more specifically, Value Populations. For the parents in 1952, all of whom were touched by the privations of world war and the material want of a global depression, what greater taboo could be broken than the injunction against *playing* with one's food? Yet here they are in 1952, apparently flush with the relief of war's end and rapidly growing material abundance, encouraging their offspring to waste food by sticking brightly colored plastic noses on real potatoes!

What does this say about this group's long-term *values?*

Also, what of the recipients of these toys? In 1952, we find them playing—endlessly playing—while the governments of hostile nations sponsor the development of new ways to eradicate the human species. Many decades later, will the values of these erstwhile tots still center around self-expression, material entitlement and, one might argue, bravery as expressed as child's play in the face of possible annihilation?

By 1964, America comes to the realization that not all of its citizens have been invited to the prosperity party. While affluence mounts for the great majority of Americans, the nation acknowledges that 20 percent of its population, situated primarily in rural areas such as Appalachia and in the ghettos of major cities abandoned by a suburbia-bound middle class, lives at or below the poverty level. Lyndon Johnson, as the focal point of his first State of the Union address, declares a War on Poverty.

Mirroring the nation's growing faith in the economic power and benefits of technology, there is a clear sense in 1964 that the solutions to vast social problems can be engineered through a combination of scientific approach and well-intentioned legislation. In addition to the aid programs of the War on Poverty, including a massive tax cut, the year witnesses the passage of the Civil Rights Act, the most comprehensive piece of antidiscrimination legislation of the twentieth century. In the public health arena, 1964 is the year of the first Surgeon General's report on smoking that establishes the link between cigarette smoking and cancer.

Despite good intentions, however, 1964 is a year in which cracks are just beginning to show in the nation's faith in its capability to outthink the future. The country is still in deep shock and mourning over the loss of its visionary president, John F. Kennedy, assassinated in November 1963. Furthermore, in response to a Vietnamese gunboat attack, the Gulf of Tonkin Resolution is passed and the Vietnam War formally begins.

The craziness that is coming to American cultural discourse is also foreshadowed by a much-noted television event. The appearance of The Beatles on *The Ed Sullivan Show* is the symbolic start of what most cultural observers mean when they talk about "the 60s." In 1964, American society is right on the verge of going a little nuts.

It is deeply consonant with the times that government regulatory agencies have a go at Mr. Potato Head. After a determination that the sharp points of the Mr. Potato Head appendages are dangerous to children, Hasbro is instructed to round off the points, which means they no longer easily pierce a real potato. Thus, in 1964, Mr. Potato Head undergoes technological reformation, becoming a plastic potato with predrilled holes.

So, what will become of the children who play with this iteration of Mr. Potato Head? Decades later, will they be inclined to some sacrifice of variety, creativity, and personal expression for the sake of safety and technological efficiency? Will they become a generation of pragmatists, a little cynical perhaps but, in the face of the enormously disruptive and capricious forces of actual life, still be convinced of the value of a rational approach to social problem solving?

In 1973, the economic fortunes of the United States of America take a turn for the worse. This is particularly unfortunate because the United States accomplishes a much-coveted social objective in this year. Although it smacks of flat-out retreat, the enormously divisive war in Vietnam ends and all American ground troops are at last brought home.

It is not unexpected that a figurative sort of cultural exhaustion might set in after the conclusion of such a prolonged society-wrenching event. But the universal energy depletion that transpires during 1973 is anything but figurative or metaphorical. In retaliation for America's support of Israel in the so-called Yom Kippur War, the member nations of OPEC induce a world-wide oil shortage that causes the price of a barrel of oil to soar from $1.50 to $11.50 in the course of just a few months.

The economic and cultural impact of this oil embargo is stamped all over American life in 1973. Not only do significant directional changes occur in the macrotrends of the once dynamic American economy, but everyday life is impacted by such factors as long lines at gas stations and the legislation of a national speed limit set at 55 miles per hour. It is a year when, as an energy conservation measure, no electric ornaments are placed on the national Christmas tree.

Sadly, the growing sense of powerlessness is compounded by a very real leadership crisis. The Vice President of the United States, Spiro Agnew, resigns in disgrace after pleading guilty to tax evasion charges. More memorably, the Watergate investigation is in full bloom, with President Richard Nixon doing little to calm the national angst when he famously tells a group of reporters, "I am not a crook."

It is against this backdrop that Mr. Potato Head is inflated, enervated, and emasculated. In 1973, the plastic Mr. Potato Head body suddenly swells to twice its original size, and the predrilled holes are replaced with slots so that the various appendages can now be fastened only in a single, physiologically "accurate" manner. Most telling, however, is that Mr. Potato Head's body and arms simply disappear (although he has had them in all product iterations to this time).

What will become of the generation subjected to such a plaything? Will they retain a lifelong fear of personal impotence seasoned with a mistrust of the clueless maneuverings of patriarchal authority? Or will they inevitably rise above it through the very experience of coping with down times, putting their hearts into empathic friendships, and believing with patient faith that things just "have to get better" in the future?

As Ronald Reagan begins his second term as President in 1985, the United States is once again feeling its collective oats. The country is in the third year of a broad economic, political, and cultural rebound that will last with few interruptions through most of the 1980s and 1990s. As the President remarks in his second inaugural address, fully capturing the mood of the moment: "In this blessed land, there is always a better tomorrow."

Arguably, it is a foreign event, the accession of Mikhail Gorbachev to the top governmental post in the Soviet Union, that best demarcates the wondrous possibilities of the era. Gorbachev's place as the last President of the Soviet Union ushers in an age of reformation and liberalization that ultimately results in the doctrinal and political dissolution of America's most feared and powerful adversary. By the end of the year, Presidents Reagan and Gorbachev are meeting face to face, earnestly discussing cultural exchange and nuclear disarmament.

Along with the sense of potential that pervades the economic and geopolitical scene, the year ushers in an important new window on tomorrow when Microsoft Windows 1.0 is introduced into the personal computer marketplace. Along with the graphical interface of the Apple McIntosh, introduced the previous year, the world embarks on a potent new era of perception, thought organization, and knowledge creation. The children of 1985, the year in which the Nintendo Entertainment System is also first brought to market, will be citizens of the interactive computer age, virtually from birth.

As with every other time in the history, 1985 does have its share of truly negative news stories. Terrorist acts and airplane hijackings are liberally sprinkled across the year's front pages. The existence of crack cocaine and the hole in the ozone layer are formally established. Rock Hudson's death from AIDS makes a high profile point about the seriousness of the news that is to come on that front.

Yet, most significantly and unlike the reaction just a decade earlier, the times just seem to be characterized by their optimistic focus. Nowhere is this more apparent than in society's return of children to a place of prominence, protection and concern in the national agenda. Typified by the creation of the National Children's Advocacy Center to combat child abuse, by Tipper Gore's appearances before Congress to warn against the alarming trends in rock music, and, for that matter, by famous rock musicians singing about taking care of the world's children in the year's noteworthy foreign aid anthem, "We Are the World," it is clear that kids are back in the cultural limelight.

While 1985 is noteworthy as the year Mr. Potato Head enters the computer age by fronting a children's software program developed for Apple, the year's really big news is that Mr. and Mrs. Potato Head become parents. Baby Potato Head, an adorable, freckle-faced plastic spud, is introduced as the feature item in the Mr. Potato Head family kit, and, quite appealingly, the whole family has bendable, permanently attached arms!

Who are the children to play with such a toy? Surely they are blessed by the simple fact that society welcomes them into the social fold. Might not such a group grow into a generation of confident can-doers? Might they not employ the nascent power of technology and their belief in the irresistibility of the collective social will to not only bend their arms in effort, but to ultimately even bend reality itself?

In the year 1996, it is hard to turn around without brushing into the emergence of a major cultural icon. Consider:

- Fox News is launched and rapidly becomes the most watched cable news television channel, appealing to its audience with right-wing ideology given equal, if not superior, status to "hard fact" in the reporting of events. From this point forward, an emotional brand of dogmatic positioning dominates every significant political contest and major social issue addressed by society.

- *Harry Potter* finds a publisher. Although author J.K. Rowling receives a mere $4,000 advance for her first book in the series about a young wizard, and the initial publishing run is only 500 copies, the *Harry Potter* series quickly becomes the most important youth icon of its age. By the time the seventh and last title of the series is published in 2007, the book sells 8.3 million copies in the first 24 hours following its release, and the notion of "magic" has become a deeply vested principle in the youth processing of the 'real' world.

- Alan Greenspan, Chairman of the Federal Reserve Board, encapsulates the economic essence of the time with the phrase "irrational exuberance." Indeed, the mid 1990s serve as a launch pad for the stock market and the technology-driven economy in general. It's a heady time for capitalists and consumers—irrational perhaps but oh so sweet while it lasts.

- The name Osama bin Laden and the terrorist organization al-Qaeda come to prominence in American affairs in the summer of 1996, as a jihad (holy war) is formally declared by the militant terrorist group against the United States. Bin Laden's activities, most fully realized in the terrorist bombing of New York's World Trade Center towers in 2001, drive both the international and many of the domestic policies of America from this time forward. Fundamentalist religion, a global oil-based economy, and military options become a truly frightening mix in the 'jihad years.'

- Science and technology yield an endless array of iconic wonders that are nothing if not mind-expanding. The year 1996 gives us Dolly the

Sheep (history's first cloned mammal), the ALH 84001 meteorite that appears to offer the first solid biological evidence of extraterrestrial life, the upgraded IBM Deep Blue computer that becomes the first computer to win a match against a reigning world chess champion, and Motorola's StarTac telephone, a mobile flip phone that ultimately sells 60 million units and becomes the prototype consumer communication device in the nascent wireless telecommunications revolution.

- The absolutely essential icon of 1996 is, of course, the Internet. It's true that, for a few years prior to 1996, electronic portals exist and it is possible for a consumer to visit the rudimentary World Wide Web. (Sixteen million do so prior to 1996.) On August 13, 1996, however, the fabric of human knowledge, connectivity and enterprise changes forever as Microsoft begins to bundle Internet Explorer with its Windows operating system and 'everyone' becomes a de facto netizen. (Actually, there are 36 million regular users by the end of 1996, a figure that doubles the following year before reaching 400 million by the end of the decade.)

- Famed Spanish sociologist Manuel Castellas publishes the first part of his trilogy, collectively titled *The Information Age: Economy, Society and Culture*, and it is clear that nothing on earth will remain unnoticed, unrecorded or unevaluated.

Even in addition to the above, it would be easy to focus on such icon-worthy happenings as the 'Mad Cow' disease crisis in the UK, the Whitewater investment scandal involving Bill and Hilary Clinton, the crash of TWA flight 800, the capture of the Unabomber, the divorce of British "royals" Charles and Diana and, oh yes, a hotly contested presidential election. Each and all of these events embrace important bits of the expansive 1996 zeitgeist. Taken collectively, they present a staunch challenge to wrap one's arms around—even if one has super-flexible arms like Mr. Potato Head's.

So, what becomes of our friend Mr. Potato Head in this eclectic and rapidly evolving cultural climate? Like almost everything else of note in these times, he undergoes a conceptual expansion. Quite provocatively in fact, Mr. Potato Head bifurcates into two distinct entities, a toy and a media personality.

With regard to the latter, the movie *Toy Story* (1995) is the career changer. Even with all his popularity through the years, nothing has as great an impact on Mr. Potato Head's cultural status as a co-starring role in a major motion picture (and its two sequels). In the mid-1990s, he becomes, among other things, a social activist (the League of Women Voters enlists the aid of

Mr. & Mrs. "P" for their Get Out the Vote campaign), a corporate spokesperson (Burger King, Cheerios), and the central character in his own eponymous television show on the FOX network.

What is quite noteworthy in a discussion of Mr. Potato Head's iconic status is the fact that he is portrayed as a rather complex psychological figure made up of equal parts cynic and romantic, accuser and apologist, curmudgeon and caretaker. This is an ambitious characterization for a toy that not long ago was judged too complicated to have plastic arms. A key insight into just how multi-layered (and funny) a potato toy can be is struck when, in the first *Toy Story* movie, Mr. Potato Head sticks his parts in the "wrong" holes and declares himself "Picasso."

Not surprisingly, the "toy" manifestation of the media persona is an enormous broadening of the product line with regard to mood and characterization. Suddenly, a light seems to go on, and it's understood that there is no definitive number of mustaches or hats a plastic potato is "allowed" to have. And if Mr. Potato Head wants to be a cowboy or a pirate, a hockey goalie or a ballerina, or a cookie jar or coin bank—well, why not?

In many ways, the children who watch, play and electronically interact with such a toy (or is "entertainment concept" a more precise rendering?) are likely closer to the essence of "play" than any Value Population that precedes them. Here, Mr. Potato Head becomes a goad to open-mindedness, imagination and an understanding that things are not always what they were intended to be. Here is where certitude about rules, roles and outcomes takes on the aspect of nothing so much as a bowl of mashed potatoes.

Or is that fried? Or baked? Or boiled? Or whipped? Or au gratin?

3

UNDERSTANDING
THE AGES

Where is the knowledge that is lost in information?

—T.S. Eliot, American Poet

While the Mr. Potato Head example was selected to tickle the imagination, it is also intended to make the point that significant social meaning and cultural understanding can be contained in cultural icons—even the permutations of a simple toy. As marketers, whom do we trust for insight? Is Mr. Potato Head telling us something much more important than quantitative analysis? Is he a legitimate symbol of the collective generational consciousness and values of an era, or is the real truth about attitudinal marketing to be revealed from our spreadsheets and computer projections? This chapter will explore these questions through critical examination of current thinking and methods related to demographic, behavioral and attitudinal information and analysis.

In an era when customer transaction data is easily and continually gathered and analyzed—from supermarket club cards that are scanned and analyzed at every register to radio frequency identification (RFID) microchips used to identify our pets—why shouldn't marketers capitalize on the burgeoning amount of computer power at their fingertips and rely heavily on expert systems to predict future behaviors?

First, transactional data deals only with the behaviors or end results of consumers' decisions, not their motivational drivers—the personal, unconscious, emotional and underlying reasons "why" they behave the way they do. As was stated earlier, past behavior does not drive or consistently predict future behavior. A previous flip of a coin has no bearing on the outcome of a future toss. Behaviors are driven by values—not previous behaviors.

Second, behavioral correlation does not necessarily equate to behavioral cause. Does a 75 percent increase in storks and a 75 percent increase in babies prove that storks bring babies? Statistically, a strong correlation can be observed—but does this correlation accurately define the cause of the increased population growth? No. Complex problems often have simple, easy to understand but incorrect answers.

Third, expert systems are best understood as "idiot geniuses." They are very adept within a narrow range of problem solving, but they are "stone stupid" at everything else. Why? Because machines cannot think, reason or gather information on their own and are therefore only as intelligent as the information that is fed into them. Trying to capture and control the millions of variables, both dependent and independent, as well as the historical, social, biological, emotional and environmental factors that go into every decision each of us makes is impossible.

To completely understand human behavior on a purely scientific basis misses the power, the thrusts, and the essence of human behavior.

So, is behavioral data useless? No, it can and should play a part in marketing and business decision making; however, a clear understanding of people's lasting values is significantly more valuable when attempting to predict future actions than extrapolating from past behaviors. While data analysis is a powerful tool that gives marketers a way of measuring the outcomes of their assumptions and predictions, it is important to remember it is only a tool—and one that is always looking in the rear view mirror.

What is interesting and will be addressed in greater detail later in this book is that the current Value Population responsible for this data analysis charge, the Techticians (see Part 2, Chapters 10, 11, and 12), is clearly drawn to this way of looking at the world—one in which everything is scientifically collected and measured. This is not to say that the Techticians and their data-crunching methods have not added many new and important ways of looking at consumer actions, it is just that their strength is also their Achilles heel—in that sometimes one can get too much measurement and not enough meaning.

So, if a purely quantitative analysis of behavioral data is not the silver bullet to finding the driving forces behind behaviors, what *causes* consumer behavior and deeply motivates choices?

For years, marketers have been looking at demographic profiling to help answer this question. Today, one would have a hard time finding even a small company that lacks insight into the age segmentation of its customers. While gender, income, ethnicity, and a host of other factors also enter into the picture, target markets are now almost invariably first referenced with regard to age and typically take one of two forms—life phase or generational.

Life phase is the term used for dividing populations into age-based groups that behave similarly at each phase of life, regardless of when they were born. Categories that are frequently used include terms such as infancy, childhood, adolescence, teens, adulthood, old age, etc.

Upon examination of these life-phase classifications, it becomes clear there are useful, valid, and consistent "marker" events often linked to certain biological truths that lead to some consistent behaviors. For example, American teens have a voracious appetite, are obsessed with looking good, don't like to hang out with their parents, and have raging hormones. Young adults, as they begin to "find themselves," often behave erratically when they "try on" new identities or "fall in love." Then there is menopause and the midlife crisis in the "middle age" group, and the loss of hearing, eyesight and taste in the elderly.

While all generations go through the same life phases, there is a significant difference between a generation and a life phase. For example, a teenager today and a teenager in the 1930s might both fight similar problems with acne, but their values and behaviors as a whole are significantly different—same life phase, different generation. So, while life phase has a place in understanding behaviors, there has to be more to capturing the lasting drivers of behavior that remain consistent with a group as it ages.

Traditionally, social scientists have used a so-called psychobiological approach in defining generational cohort groups. This approach is based upon a regularly structured and repeating pattern of human psychological and biological development, typically 20 years in duration.

But, are all 20-year generations the same? According to Strauss and Howe in their best-selling book, *Generations: The History of America's Future, 1584 to 2069,* they are—kind of. Their theory is that every generation belongs to one of four types of generations that repeat sequentially in a fixed pattern. They claim that understanding this pattern of generational repetition allows for the prediction of the future. However, with the exponential gains in technology and the ever-increasing complexity of cultural changes that have occurred over the last 500 years, it seems reasonable to question the validity of this assumption. Societies and people's values change and evolve, and to think that social behaviors will follow a consistent pattern every fourth generation for 500 years seems unreasonable.

In 1946, the great "Baby Boom" of the post World War II era "began" and "lasted" until 1964. The naming of this group in and of itself sparked a new interest and way of looking at consumers by marketers and social scientists. The thrust of consumer profiling had new life breathed into it, and consumers were now being grouped and analyzed based on specific birth periods. After the Baby Boom generation was defined, a new cottage industry was created by those laying claim to a new name for yet another "generation"—all emphasizing behavioral-based trend prediction.

Oddly enough, since the defining of the Baby Boom generation, there has been very little consensus among demographers as to the starting point and duration of future generations. The basic methodology used is to choose a time frame, give it a name, review the current and past behaviors of the group, and attempt to extrapolate past behavior into predicting future behavior.

The problem with this methodology is that human behavior is complex, nonlinear, and ever changing. For instance, take a look at the so-called "Baby Boomers." In the 1960s, they were the most "antiestablishment" generation America had ever seen, but in the 1990s Boomers became voracious capitalists. Where is the consistency in this behavior and what can account for it?

Values are like the hub of a wheel and behaviors are like the spokes. Just as all spokes originate from a hub, behaviors originate from values. In practical terms, the behavior/value connection of the Baby Boomers, illustrated by such icons as soap operas, cowboy movies, and Disneyland, yields a cohort group characterized by its dramatic and theatrical response to situations—the mining of any event for its drama, fun, and adventure—whether at a campus protest or in a corporate boardroom.

Figure 3.1 outlines some of the different generational names used by marketers to define age-based cohort groups and the range of their beginning and ending dates. Upon examination of this chart, it becomes apparent that there are some significant differences in even supposedly "consistent" cohort groupings like the Baby Boomers, who traditionally began in 1946 and lasted until 1964, but who now are often classified based on a four-year range for the beginning date and a six-year range for the ending date. That does not even take into account the splitting of the generation into "Early" and "Late" Boomers.

So, why is there all of this difference in beginning and ending date definition? Because, unlike Value Populations where a clear set of shared experiences and values-based criteria was used to define the demarcation dates of each group, the time frames for most generally accepted generational groupings were chosen somewhat at random based on past behavior instead of on lasting and consistent criteria. In Value Populations "speak," that lasting criteria is shared values.

FIGURE 3.1

Demographic Dislocations

	Beginning Range	Ending Range
Echo Boomers Generation Y Millennials Nexters	1974 - 1994	1987 - Present
Baby Bust Gen X	1960 - 1968	1975 - 1985
Boomers	1943 - 1947	1960 - 1966
Elderly Empty Nest GI Matures Parent Seniors Silent Veterans	1901 - 1928	1935 - 1952

So, what forms shared values? Before analyzing value formation, it is important to first define a value. *A value is a thematically shared and culturally based orientation, derived from significant events primarily instilled in youth and often linked to external events occurring as early as gestation.*

As was stated in Chapter 1, values are the filters through which the mass of behavioral data becomes comprehensible. In order to identify these value filters, a unique and proprietary sociocultural approach to age-based demographic analysis has been used to define consistent and lasting cohort groups. This sociocultural approach is based on the assumption that generational consciousness is created by the social and cultural environment of the time and that this in turn creates lasting values within the generation being formed. What causes behaviors in a sociological model is not past behavior, but a values response to emotions activated by the external forces or events occurring in a group's environment in the early years of life.

Prior to the twentieth century, youth experienced events and environments similar to those experienced by their parents and grandparents, so a fairly homogenous society and value-set existed. In this context, local, cultural and family conditions played a more significant role in value formation than did outside social influence. However, with the dramatic increase in mass communication, beginning with the radio in the 1920s, value formation became increasingly driven by cultural conditions that were broader and more complex—coming from across the country and around the world.

Interestingly, the increased volume and quickened rate of cultural information flow and change due to new avenues of communication such as the TV and the Internet is now shortening value formation periods. Today's youth experience far more, and grow up considerably faster, than their parents and grandparents did at the same age, making the duration of each Value Population subsequently shorter than the preceding one—and significantly shorter than the traditional 20-year cycle.

When society is analyzed from a shared-event perspective, a consistent set of lasting values can be identified and linked to a specific period in time. This period of time is what defines the beginning and ending dates of a Value Population—and the lasting values associated with this time period shape the group's behavioral and spending decisions for a lifetime. Understanding these value sets allows marketers to focus on consistent and lifelong branding and marketing strategies.

So, how are these values captured and made useful by savvy marketers? Through the use of historical icons. Icons are valuable because, among other things, they encapsulate cultural attributes and attitudes of the time. When a Value Population encounters these icons again, they emotionally resonate with them. For marketers, recognizing these emotionally consistent triggers within a target audience is crucial in creating an effective and lasting marketing campaign. An excellent example of this is McDonald's Happy Meal and the company's notion that a brand can be your "friend." This marketing icon still resonates strongly with the generation formed during the period of the Happy Meal's introduction—the Believers. (See Part 2, Chapters 13, 14, and 15.)

History tells many stories that define how social interactions and shared experiences play a fundamental role in the development of consistent and lifelong values. As distinguished Pulitzer Prize-winning author and social commentator Ellen Goodman said, "Values are not trendy items that are casually traded in." This sociocultural approach not only facilitates broad yet precise trend prediction but, by emphasizing history, opens a treasure trove of associations that can be used by the astute marketer to understand consumers' needs, wants, and desires at a core level—making it possible to elicit behavior, not just sell to it.

GETTING TO KNOW THE VALUE POPULATIONS

Part Two of The Consistent Consumer presents our research findings. It outlines the general characteristics of each Value Population, highlights the significant events associated with each value formation period, and draws conclusions concerning lasting values.

Each Value Population has three chapters dedicated to its discussion. The first chapter is intended to give the reader a cursory understanding of the broad demographic and value characteristics of the Value Population under discussion; the second chapter provides a high-level overview, or "event matrix," of the historic events that played a significant role in the value formation of the period; and the third chapter uses an analysis of contemporary cinema (the only medium that spans all of the Value Population periods, making it a strong source for comparison) as a focal point for capturing and understanding the essence of the Value Population under discussion.

The six Value Populations and their associated chapters are:

Patriots (born 1920–1937) — Chapters 4, 5, and 6,
Performers (born 1938–1957) — Chapters 7, 8, and 9,
Techticians (born 1958–1971) — Chapters 10, 11, and 12
Believers (born 1972–1983) — Chapters 13, 14, and 15
Transformers (born 1984–1995) — Chapters 16, 17, and 18
Owls (born 1996-2007) — Chapters 19, 20, and 21

It is important to note that, while the first chapter of each Value Population gives the reader an overall understanding of the Value Population's general characteristics, it is the authors' strong belief that the second and third chapters of each section are critical reading for those who truly want to understand the Value Population and put its power and wealth of historical icon associations to work.

The last chapter of Part Two, Chapter 19, "'Who's' Next?," briefly discusses the authors' views on the Value Population that is currently being formed. While the authors are not certain about when this Value Population's formation period will end, there is a clear line of demarcation from the events and cultural spirit of the Owl value-formation period to that of a new Value Population.

While Part Two contains a significant amount of information about the fundamental characteristics and makeup of each Value Population, it also offers a wonderful trip down the corridors of our collective national history and our individual memory lanes. We hope you enjoy the journey.

4

THE PATRIOTS
An Overview

POPULATION OVERVIEW

Age: Born 1920–1937
Size: 7% of the U.S. Population
Spending: $472 Billion Annually
Themes: Freedom/Fear
Values: Comfort/Virtue

Summary

It would be naïve to assume that life was easy prior to the Patriot value-formation period. On the other hand, it can be argued that life experiences were somehow more consistent, measured, local, and familiar prior to the advent of mass communication, industrialization, global depression, and world war. With the Patriots, one encounters a Value Population "forced" to collectively accept a complex, unknown, and seemingly dangerous future. While mass prosperity and cultural freedom beckon in this new age, it is the collective pain that fate inflicts on this group, primarily via economic disappointment but also through significant changes in the established social fabric, that most clearly leaves a lasting mark on their values. For this group there is a strong sense that life-changing decisions are made on their behalf—ones they do not fully participate in making, that they do not necessarily want, and that at times hurt them badly. Throughout the social commentary of the Patriot period, there is a deserved litany of suspicion regarding bankers, businessmen, brokers, and most politicians. Subjected to the grim residue of war, disease and want, Patriots, more than any other Value Population, are about exercising caution, mistrusting the motives of others, keeping their hands on their wallets, and, most of all, attending to the rules and rituals of the families, friends and social equals who validate and protect their own stash of valuables and values.

PATRIOT HISTORICAL EVENT MATRIX

Anxiety/Boom and Bust/Anxiety

Anxiety

The end of World War I (1914–1919) was largely positive for the United States in terms of its international, economic, and geopolitical standing. Yet, the postwar period, with a final wartime death toll of 5,500 fatalities per day, and a worldwide influenza epidemic in 1919, which killed 20 to 40 million additional people, including more than a half-million Americans, caused great post-traumatic stress to society.

Marked by enormous xenophobia and a clamor for cultural fundamentalism, the suddenly industrializing, immigrant-absorbing, globally ensnared, and socially/sexually liberated American society (women gain universal suffrage in 1920) breeds enormous cultural disorientation and elicits fierce counter-pressure to take things back to a more simple, familiar, and orderly time.

Boom and Bust

WWI marks the U.S. turn from a debtor to a creditor nation. The 1920s are a time of enormous economic and industrial expansion, with assembly-line manufacturing, easy credit, and rising stock prices bringing significant material prosperity into the life of the common citizen.

The Jazz Age, with its flappers and speakeasies, is perhaps the most memorable icon of the Roaring Twenties—but the real news is the introduction of socially liberating automobile travel, broadcast radio, handset telephones, and movies into the cultural fabric of modern American life.

The stock market collapse from 1929 to 1932 erases 91 percent of the value of stocks. Most of this damage is done in less than a single week during the "Great Crash" of 1929. Everything economic suddenly and desperately changes for the worse.

Anxiety

The Great Depression, which is not entirely dispelled until America's involvement as an arms seller in the early years of WWII, begins with the Wall Street crash and peaks in 1932, with 12.5 percent of the U.S. adult population out of work—and painful economic dislocation apparent in every aspect of American life. Franklin Delano Roosevelt's New Deal programs (1932–1937) play an important part in acknowledging and addressing the relief and reform challenges facing the U.S. economy. Nevertheless, there is much conservative political opposition to FDR's "welfare" programs, and a thorough watering down of the New Deal initiatives leads to another painful recessionary period in 1937.

PATRIOT POPULATION VALUES

Familiarity

- *Historical drivers.* Global conflict emerges; worldwide influenza pandemic; ethnic immigration; assembly line mechanization replacing natural agrarian rhythms.
- *Value manifestation.* Strange, disruptive, and dangerous forces in the macroenvironment lead to a high valuation of the familiar.

Creature Comfort

- *Historical drivers.* The downside of modernization balanced by an emerging consumer goods economy—first widespread availability of creature comforts, such as autos, radios, refrigerators, etc.
- *Value manifestation.* Material things take the edge off of heightened anxiety.

Wealth

- *Historical drivers.* Real ruin and deprivation after a period of enormous economic optimism (the "Roaring 20s" followed by Great Depression) pushes wealth to a primary position in the value matrix.
- *Value manifestation.* While wealth always makes the good times better, lack of it makes the bad times worse—and one should always have a little put away for the inevitable rainy day.

Affection

- *Historical drivers.* Disruption of sedentary and localized lifestyles; greater exposure to impersonal culture of mass industrialization, poverty extremes, and threatening foreign influences; the battle between the sexes as reflected in suffrage issues
- *Value manifestation.* Being liked can often provide a better psychological buffer and sense of security than being loved.

A Place in the Collective

- *Historical drivers.* War and poverty followed by the advent of social recovery programs during the FDR administration
- *Value manifestation.* The world is too dangerous for individualists, but working together we can each find our unique place while contributing to the general good of all.

Loyalty

- *Historical drivers.* The opening round in the battle between previously existing social domination and isolationist tendencies and the threats posed by multiculturalism and forces outside the system
- *Value manifestation.* In a world of suddenly conflicting and potentially dangerous ideologies, allegiance to the belief system of the collective is more than a pledge; it is sacred duty.

Virtue

- *Historical drivers.* The conflict over modern cultural evolution entails a debate over what constitutes moral integrity, especially about fundamentalist issues and events such as Prohibition.
- *Value manifestation.* A rapidly changing environment creates a strong drive to claim the moral high ground and the resultant support of an "absolute" for one's own beliefs-driven sect.

Courage

- *Historical drivers.* The difficulty in adapting to a world that is faster, more locally diverse, and more remotely dangerous than ever before
- *Value manifestation.* With so much to be truly fearful of, there is hardly a greater virtue than personal courage—particularly on behalf of the clan.

Defense and Security Systems

- *Historical drivers.* The fear of aggression from outside forces, ranging from foreign armies to germs to threatening cultures to the displacement of modern mechanized society to catastrophic financial reversals
- *Value manifestation.* A strong military presence, a vigilant police force, a tall wall around the city, good locks, some money in the bank, and a resolute belief system help to neutralize the bad guys—and there are always bad guys.

PATRIOT MACRO INTERESTS

(Life-phase considerations projected through 2012)

Public Health and Welfare Policy

It is harder to think of anything that aging Patriots are more passionate about than what they feel is a firm government promise to help support them in their old age. As children of the Depression, they witnessed the creation of a Social Security system, which they then supported all their working lives. It is now payoff time.

Loss of Partners

Possible heartbreak aside, what matters most to a Patriot is how loss of a partner will impact personal security. Insurance, a decent bank balance, and a close-knit support group are all great comforts.

Death

Generally fearful of the unknown all their lives, Patriots are wary of what may await them on the other side. They'd feel better if they could talk to someone dear who has already been there, and they would probably like to take a few dollars and a sack lunch along with them.

Legacies

Much of the economic future of the nation is tied into the inevitable reallocation of wealth that has been amassed by the Patriot Value Population. But this is a group who has no problem with putting a price on relationships. Beware the proudly displayed bumper sticker that declares, "We are spending our children's inheritance."

Grandchildren

Surely there is sentimental attachment here, but to fully understand the Patriots is to appreciate that they are always grooming members of the tribe. What's particularly interesting is that some of the grandchildren are, unlike the members of most of the in-between Value Populations, being value-formed in ways that are quite resonant with their grandparents' values.

All Things Medical

Patriots' concern with all things medical is of course obvious, but not so obvious is the Patriots' most deep-seated, and most often frustrated, expectation of the medical community. This is a group that is sold miracle pills, prognostications, and processes. Yet what they crave most is empathy and "high touch."

Military Affairs

One misses the full picture here if all one sees are grizzled veterans celebrating their own courageous survival of past wars. Yes, this group can be fierce and unquestioning in protection of the homeland, but by the same token, no group better understands that wars are political and economic enterprises with costs and sacrifices (and profits if it comes to that) which are rarely shared equally.

Comfort Food—Not Nutrition and Dietetics

Influencing the diet of the Patriots is not going to be an easy matter. This is the group who invented comfort food, and there is very little of a scientific nature that will convince them food exists for a more important clinical purpose.

Retail Function and Adaptation

Yes, more and more Patriots are likely to be drawn to the ease and personal safety of shopping on the Internet. It is nevertheless still important for retailers to understand that this is a highly social group who finds human interaction an important part of commerce.

Better Safe than Sorry

Patriots are especially motivated by safety concerns. Conspicuous signs that a parking lot is under surveillance and the presence of uniformed guards, etc., are very appealing to this group.

Relaxation for Patriots

Family gatherings (although these are so vital to personal definition, they also have heavier overtones of responsibility and conflict), picnics, block parties and other local celebrations, rooting for the home team, dining out in the neighborhood with friends, homespun humor, music, dancing, and alcoholic beverages all add to relaxation for the Patriots.

5

THE PATRIOTS
History Creating Values

T he Patriot value formation period begins at the end of World War I (1914–1919). Although largely a European event, it is an enormous and sobering historical watershed for all life on the planet. The sheer carnage of the war (8.5 million dead—600,000 at the battle of Verdun alone), facilitated by such "modern" armaments as the machine gun and poison gas, puts a chill into global human affairs that will never again fully abate. Coupled with a worldwide influenza pandemic that strikes during the final years of the war and causes the death of another 20 to 40 million people (the worst plague in recorded history until the advent of AIDS), the wartime legacy is one of deep mistrust of both "progress" and foreign involvement. See Figure 5.1.

THE ANXIOUS AFTERMATH OF WWI (1920+)

As the war ends, the United States has fewer casualties than other war participants, and the nation benefits from increased economic and political authority in the postwar period. Yet, the comprehension of what has taken place overseas and the taste of death at home (50,000 combat fatalities; more than a quarter of the entire nation afflicted with influenza, resulting in more than a half-million deaths) impact both the external and internal affairs of the nation throughout the Patriot period.

FIGURE 5.1

Casualties of World War I

Allied Powers		Central Powers	
Russia	9,150,000	Germany	7,142,558
France	6,160,800	Austria-Hungary	7,020,000
British Empire	3,190,235	Turkey	975,000
Italy	2,197,000	Bulgaria	266,919
Romania	535,706		
United States	364,800	Total Allied Power Casualties	
Serbia	331,106	22,104,209	
Belgium	93,061		
Portugal	33,291	Total Central Power Casualties	
Montenegro	20,000	15,404,477	
Greece	17,000		
Japan	1,210	Total Casualties of WW I	
		37,508,686	

Source: Spartus Education

To characterize the tone of the Patriot value-formation era as "cautious," especially regarding the acceptance of outsiders, is an understatement.

Isolationism

By the end of WWI, the United States is well on its way to becoming the world's most powerful and influential nation. American president Woodrow Wilson is particularly prominent in driving a global policy of national self-determination that radically alters the maps of Europe and the Middle East. The crown of his conception is the League of Nations, a forerunner of the United Nations, established in 1919 under the Treaty of Versailles "to promote international cooperation and to achieve peace and security." In many ways, the Patriot era officially starts in 1920 when the U.S. Senate votes against ratification of the League of Nations Covenant. (In the same year, Congress also passes legislation to sharply curtail immigration via a national quota system.) Through the next four presidential administrations, a formal government policy of noninvolvement and neutrality in international affairs prevails. Even during the early years of the FDR administration, which would eventually lead the nation's effort in WWII, separate neutrality acts are passed in 1935, 1936, and 1937.

Cultural Fundamentalism

Far more immediate and dramatic than the isolationist tone of geopolitics is the sense of extremely conservative cultural fundamentalism that dominates domestic affairs, particularly among the nation's vested Anglo-Saxon population. If death and disease are derived from foreign sources, "true" Americans must be vigilant in monitoring all that is foreign, including immigrants and homegrown defenders of exotic social beliefs. While much of this is born of an understandable fear of current events and a reasonable nostalgic longing for order, safety and conformity, there is still much real pain and repression in the course of events. Some of the representative developments of the period in this regard include:

- *The Red Scare (1920).* Nearly 3,000 communists, anarchists, and other radicals are arrested without due cause in government raids.
- *Sacco-Vanzetti Trial (1920–1927).* Two immigrant anarchist fish peddlers are tried and convicted of murders they likely have not committed and are subsequently executed. Massachusetts's governor Michael Dukakais reverses the controversial verdict 50 years later.
- *Scopes Trial (1925).* Clarence Darrow faces off against William Jennings Bryan in a battle of science versus religious fundamentalism. Defendant John Scopes is found guilty of teaching evolution in a Tennessee school and is "symbolically" fined $100.
- *Ku Klux Klan.* Advocating biblical fundamentalism, less government interference, labor pacifism, racial and ethnic purity, and a return to the values of small-town life, KKK membership grows from 100,000 in 1920 to more than 2 million in 1925. Not just a southern or rural phenomenon, the KKK has a significant presence on the city councils of Chicago, Denver, Dallas, and Indianapolis.
- *Prohibition (1920–1933).* Prohibition is a complex issue, but it is apparent that the staunchest advocates of an alcohol-free America are largely the same group who empathizes with the cultural fundamentalist agenda. Historical observers have amply demonstrated that in the postwar climate most alcoholic beverages (German beer, Italian wine, Russian vodka, etc.) are identified as immigrant products and therefore suspect on those grounds alone. Cynical political observers point out that the prohibition of liquor also particularly undermines the tax revenue and power base of politicians in industrial and ethnic-based big cities.

Boom and Bust

There is a counterpoint to the generally apprehensive tone of the Patriot value formation period—to be found in rapidly growing prospects for economic prosperity and social liberation in the mid- and late 1920s. What is often overlooked in analyses that dwell upon such factors, however, is that this state of economic and social opportunity hardly equates to a richer, more meaningful, or more secure life for all American citizens—for, although the 1920s certainly do "roar" for a time, hardly anyone makes it through the Great Depression of the 1930s unscathed or unchastened.

Economic Growth

A number of factors converge to establish the United States as a great economic force during most of the 1920s. WWI leaves the competitive economies of Europe in disarray. The development of assemblyline production principles and the wide availability of cheap urban labor allow for the mushrooming of factories. Increasing availability of electricity and communications technology facilitates the growth of production and the range of available consumer goods. A rapidly rising stock market, fueled by margin-buying and a prevailing government bias toward nonregulation of business, makes investment capital extremely cheap and most industrial expansion plans extremely practicable.

For the average American consumer, it is a time when telephones, vacuum cleaners, washing machines, refrigerators and radios (often bought on installment plans) become part of ordinary household life. Ford's Model Ts and Model As begin to roll off assembly lines and, by 1930, 77 percent of American households own a car (versus 2 percent in 1910). Indicative of the times is the rise in magazine advertising revenues, which more than triple from $58.5 million in 1918 to $200 million in 1929.

The Jazz Age

The great social icons of the 1920s include the speakeasy, the flapper, and the gangster, all generationally symbolic of new wealth, new social mores, and a youthful urge to escape the darker social and psychological repressions of the period. While the "Gatsby" life is hardly a cultural condition for most Americans, its very existence represents a prevailing desire to evade the grimness of the times. It is certainly interesting to note that many of the great heroes of the 1920s—Babe Ruth, Charles Lindbergh, Amelia Earhart, Will Rogers, and even Al Capone (an antihero but arguably more admired than reviled by a majority of ordinary citizens)—are neither political nor military heroes but are celebrated for testing the social limits of the times as well as for their noteworthy achievements.

More important than heroic icons, perhaps, is the emergence of a mass media that allows for the proliferation of new social trends. Radio storms onto the American scene, with the first commercial broadcasts taking place in 1922, and it rapidly becomes a powerful political and entertainment platform thereafter. Although the first "talkie" doesn't appear in movie theatres until 1927 (*The Jazz Singer*), the movie industry is selling $100 million in tickets per week by 1929, making it one of the largest industries in the United States.

Coupled with such factors as women's suffrage, the proliferation of handset telephones, and the rising number of automobiles (even as early as the 1920s, parents of teenagers are clucking about these "bedrooms on wheels"), American society seems ready to open up and embrace an affluent and high-spirited future.

Then—and it is this fact that must be embraced to truly appreciate the Patriot value-formation period—everything economic slams into a wall.

The Crash of 1929

Hindsight is 20/20, and there is now an ample body of scholarship that explains why the crash of the stock market in 1929 was inevitable. Too much margin buying of stocks, an overproduction of durable goods, and a laissez-faire approach toward market regulation are among the most frequently cited culprits. To fully appreciate the impact of the event is, however, to acknowledge that for the vast majority of Americans, who in 1929 are still being encouraged to invest in stocks by everyone from the President of General Motors to the President of the United States, even days before the crash begins, the devastation to come is swift and largely unexpected.

It is generally agreed that the lost value of the stock market in the first few weeks of the panic is roughly two thirds or, in 1929 dollars, $30 billion. The figure grows to $50 billion by 1932. As devastating as the economic news is, the crash is also a crippling blow to the American spirit, as the rise in stock market value has largely become the key symbolic indicator of the nation's improving emotional well-being. See Figure 5.2. In short, the national mood is devastated, and suddenly all those previous anxieties about modern life seem quite validated.

FIGURE 5.2

Dow Jones Industrial Average

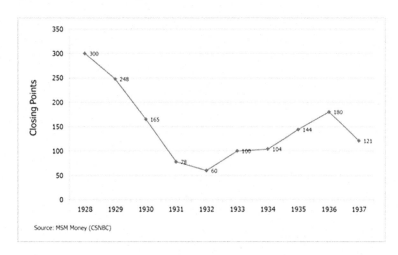

Source: MSM Money (CSNBC)

THE GREAT DEPRESSION (1929–1939)

It is hard to capture a decade-long period of abject suffering and misery in just a few sentences. Suffice it to say the 1930s are a time never to be forgotten by those who lived through them. The raw numbers—12 million unemployed adults in 1932, representing about 12.5 percent of the American workforce—can't paint the picture harshly enough. Nor do they immediately convey images of bread lines, soup kitchens, communities of makeshift shacks, the roving unemployed, the institutionally displaced, or the thousands of farm families unable to sell (and because of mercilessly bitter climate patterns, often unable to grow) their crops.

Even for those who manage to survive this fierce period, there is an erosion of confidence in institutions that stamps the Patriot value-formation period forever. The common man becomes aware that most of the wealth of the nation is concentrated in the hands of the very rich (in 1929, the top 1 percent of Americans have a combined wealth 650 times greater than the bottom 11 percent), who have little intention of recovery spending or investing during unpromising economic times. Further, politicians, especially those who advocate a hands-off policy toward domestic financial regulation, are *de facto* tools of the relatively small pool of very rich capitalists, whose companies control the wealth of the nation. (In 1929, the 200 largest American corporations controlled 50 percent of the nation's business wealth.) The politics of the era are laced with far more political scandal than dedicated public service.

Ultimately, the Great Depression leaves its mark on a Value Population that grows up suspicious of authority that represents its motives as anything other than financial. Yet even the resentment of such authority pales in the wake of the devastation of the period. The real value lesson of the Great Depression is that being among the haves is a great gift of grace. Ethical questions may be raised regarding the acquisition of fortune, but the glitter of gold is nothing less than the light of salvation.

PREWAR ANXIETY (1933–1937)

The New Deal

Running on a promise to deal with the problems of the Depression and to repeal Prohibition (it is worth noting that, to the Patriot generation, alcoholic beverage consumption is a symbolic political act as well as a form of escapist behavior), Franklin Delano Roosevelt is elected in 1932 to the first of four presidential terms. The massively aggressive social agenda of Roosevelt's pre-WWII terms in office includes a host of "New Deal" public relief measures, such as the Civilian Conservation Corps and the Works Progress Administration (programs that put 8.5 million Americans to work building the nation's infrastructure of roads, bridges, public facilities, and airports). Additionally, there is far-reaching fiscal policy legislation, such as banking reform (including the establishment of the FDIC), a variety of measures to rein in "excessive corporate profits," agricultural commodities support, an aggressively graduated income tax (1934), pro-labor legislation (the Wagner Act of 1935 protects the rights of unions to organize and strike), and the institution of Social Security (1935).

Championing the cause of the "forgotten common man," the FDR administration once and for all establishes the principle that government has a broadly proactive, and perhaps even paternalistic, obligation to the welfare of the masses.

The fly in the ointment is that much of this progressive initiative and outlook, not to mention the high taxes and deficit spending in their wake, is bitterly opposed by the "economic royalists," FDR's term for the wealthy capitalists who control the finances, and therefore wield much of the political power of the nation. Using the considerable means at their disposal to mitigate FDR's initiatives, the New Deal programs are significantly compromised by 1937—a year that ushers in a painful new recession. Ultimately, while FDR's programs cannot be underestimated in their salutary effect on the morale of the nation, the real death of the Great Depression comes only as a result of a new global war.

The Age of Dictatorship

It is essential to keep in mind that however desperate the conditions in the United States become during the Patriot value-formation period, they are consistently much worse in economically devastated Europe and Asia. With promises of salvation to their politically disenfranchised, psychologically scarred, and economically desperate countrymen, Italy's Mussolini (assumes dictatorial power in 1922), Russia's Stalin (1924), Japan's Hirohito (1926), and Germany's Hitler (1933) offer radical plans for economic recovery and renewed national pride. Tragically, these visions are entwined with some of the most unspeakable acts of mass terrorism ever perpetrated upon humanity and are the forerunner of a military expansionism that will lead to a second global war.

As mentioned earlier in this analysis, the prevailing American response to these ominous rumblings is largely a policy of foreign neutrality and isolationism (although it is interesting to note that American membership in the communist party, reflecting an infatuation with socialist economic theory, peaks in 1935). American economic policy, particularly with regard to international trade tariffs, is extremely restrictive and in fact helps to fuel the breakdown of world trade and the resultant global financial crisis. As late as 1937, FDR is promising the nation that American boys will never again be sent to fight in a foreign war.

Americans are still dragging their heels and digging in as the Second World War in Europe begins. Unavoidable confrontation is massing on the horizon, but with it will come a new Value Population, the Performers, who, unlike their immediate predecessors, the Patriots, will be as outward looking and universally involved as any generation in history.

6

THE PATRIOTS
Cultural Expressions of an Era

I can't help what I do! I can't help it. I can't.
—Peter Lorre as M (1931)

MONSTERS AND MADMEN

The movie industry, in any modern sense, begins during the Patriot era—and perhaps with no other Value Population does cinema provide such an unguarded look into an era's very soul. Even a casual observer will readily note how many of the earliest commercial films are extremely dark and humorless "horror" movies. In terms of the era's guilt, doubt, pain, and fear of the unknown, it is not a very big leap from Hollywood to the headlines.

A heartbeat removed from full-out psychological confession, the films of the period swarm with truly evil and scary monsters dwelling in terribly creepy and surreal habitats. From Dracula's first appearance in *Nosferatu* (1922) through *Dr. Jekyll and Mr. Hyde* (1931), *Dracula* (1931), *Frankenstein* (1931), *Freaks* (1932), *King Kong* (1933), and *The Bride of Frankenstein* (1935), to name just few well-known films, one gets a suggestion that the protagonist of the Patriot value-formation period is a very uncomfortable resident of a nightmarish land brimming with secret terrors, noxious spirits, and unhealthy impulses. "Demonic urge" movies like *M* (1931) and *The Invisible Man* (1933) are similarly full of uncontrollable dementia; the former featuring a child-murderer so possessed by evil that other criminals pitch in to help catch him; the latter portraying a victim of a rash experiment whose side effect is an evil desire to take over the world. See Figure 6.1.

FIGURE 6.1

Top Ten Horror Films of the Patriot Era

1. *Nosferatu (1922)*
2. *Bride of Frankenstein (1935)*
3. *Kabinett des Doktor Caligari, Das (1920)*
4. *King Kong (1933)*
5. *Frankenstein (1931)*
6. *Freaks (1932)*
7. *The Invisible Man (1933)*
8. *The Phantom of the Opera (1925)*
9. *Dracula (1931)*
10. *M (1931)*

Source: As voted on by the members of Internet Movie Database, Inc.

With little subtlety, the message is delivered that God has abandoned the world and the devil has indeed taken up residence within the flock. It is worth noting that in some of the era's films—*King Kong* and *The Bride of Frankenstein* come to mind—the title monsters are portrayed with a modicum of sympathy, seen as somewhat innocent victims of a foul human manipulation rather than as perpetrators of original sin. Indicative of the era's tone is the fact that the single most popular boxoffice star of the 1930s is Boris Karloff, who as Frankenstein in *The Bride of Frankenstein* mutters to his would-be spouse one of the era's most revealing and poignant closing lines, "We belong dead."

Privilege and Pain (It Hurts Only When I'm Hungry …)

> *The state's promise did not mean anything. It was all lies! They just wanted to get me back so they can have their revenge. Why, their crimes are worse than mine, worse than anybody's here. They're the ones who should be in chains, not we!*
>
> **—James Allen, I Am a Fugitive from a Chain Gang (1932)**

> *You know, the Parkes were never educated to face life. We'd been puppets for ten generations. Boy, did I feel sorry for myself. I wandered down to the East River one night thinking I'd just slide in and get it over with. But I met some fellas living there on a city dump. Here were people fighting it out and not complaining.*
> *I never got as far as the river.*
>
> **—William Powell, My Man Godfrey (1936)**

Patriots do not come into the world looking to be preoccupied by trouble and sorrow—they are too busy looking for work or attempting to hold on to what they have. Revolutionary economic and political fervor, stirred up by charismatic military dictators, might be on the menu elsewhere in the world, but the temptations and tribulations foisted upon foreign populations are hardly the focus of the American culture (or perhaps they represent a showdown too painful to contemplate).

Much of this period's cinematic portrayal of the rich and powerful, at least of the domestic variety, is as bemused as it is critical—a fact that likely says something important about the Patriot value-formation period. In blockbuster flicks of the era such as *Platinum Blonde* (1931), *Dinner at Eight* (1933), *The Thin Man* (1934), *Top Hat* (1935), and *My Man Godfrey* (1936), one gets the clear impression that the primary function of the upper class is to preserve the social spirit of the Roaring 20s by hosting parties, imbibing alcohol, dancing, and exchanging witty banter. Even when the rich are portrayed as elaborately egotistical and are raked over the coals for their personal duplicity and social pretentiousness, it is somehow also clear that it wouldn't be such a terrible thing to have one's place among them.

Despite the prevailing mellow tone, however, it would be wrong to dismiss the abject want and frustration that does come across in some of the period's popular art. In movies such as *Metropolis* (1927), *All Quiet on the Western Front* (1930), *I Am a Fugitive from a Chain Gang* (1932), and Charlie Chaplin's immortal *Modern Times* (1936), the desperation of the masses and the perceived "soullessness" of the political, economic, and social leadership that would manipulate them from war to unrewarding work to want are all too painfully apparent. It cannot be too strongly observed that this is a generation in which danger, desolation, and deprivation permeate the atmosphere, and it is small wonder that this Value Population, in its adulthood, so unashamedly embraces a peaceful life of tract housing, Sunday dinners, and all the glories of a consumer economy.

Group Hug (Families and Other Personal Belongings)

Once in the gang, you know the rest.
—Joe, *Little Caesar* (1930)

Alone bad. Friend good.
—The Monster, *The Bride of Frankenstein* (1934)

A message that is not always in the forefront of this era's movies, but that obviously represents a value so ingrained to this value-formation period that it is almost incessantly in the background, is the importance of belonging to a group in which everyone holds similar, if not identical, values. Not to put too fine a point on it, but a generation racked by war and poverty obviously feels that survival is vested in loyalty to a clan that will help support them in the bad times and watch their backs in the good. Generally, one's "allegiance to clan" consists of family, close friends, and/or culturally similar neighbors, rather than a dogmatic following of political, social, or economic philosophy or institutions.

Interestingly, the first "talking" picture ever made, Al Jolson's *The Jazz Singer* (1927), deals with a son who betrays his father's expectations. (Like his father, he's supposed to become a cantor in the synagogue, but he wants to sing jazz instead.) The movie's uplifting ending is an affirmation of traditional values. The son sings in the synagogue, and there is reconciliation.

Although Patriots are generally characterized as strongly devoted to their children, movies of the late 1920s and 1930s rarely feature children. It can be argued that this stems from the group's view of children as fertile perpetuations of the clan, rather than strong and highly individualized members of society. In the immensely popular "escapist" Shirley Temple films of the mid- and late 1930s (Temple is America's most popular box-office attraction between 1935 and 1938) it is interesting, and perhaps a bit ironic, to note how often this oddly precocious thousand-watt singing and dancing phenomenon is portrayed as an orphan. In other words, who could possibly be her parents?

Arguably, the cinematic phenomenon that best captures the visceral sense of the clan is the ubiquitous gangster movie. Although they most often approach matters from the criminal side, there's no denying that films such as *Little Caesar* (1930), *The Public Enemy* (1931), *Scarface* (1932), *Manhattan Melodrama* (1934), and *Angels with Dirty Faces* (1938) are testaments to the principles of allegiance to a code, respect for a hierarchy founded upon a meritocracy (the meanest and shrewdest gets to be the boss), physical and mental toughness, and life-and-death loyalty in service to the brotherhood. Not only are such principles attractive to movie audiences of the time, they are also more than a little useful as "instructional guides" when the generation is conscripted to fight a war.

Misogynists, Misanthropes, and Money (Love for Sale)

We're fighting for this woman's honor, which is more than she ever did.
—**Groucho Marx as Rufus T. Firefly in Duck Soup** (1933)

"Haven't you ever met a man who could make you happy?"
"Sure, lots of times."
—**Cary Grant and Mae West, She Done Him Wrong** (1933)

Angel, ha! She's a female! And all females is poison!
They're full of wicked wiles!
—**Grumpy, Snow White and the Seven Dwarfs** (1937)

It was beauty killed the beast.
—**Reporter, King Kong** (1933)

Perhaps men and women have always mistrusted and/or misunderstood each other's motives, but in an era of unguarded speech, occurring decades before the days of political correctness, there's no mistaking the rift. Some of the boy/girl tension in the films of the Patriot value-formation era is no doubt an expression of sexual frustration in a less sexually free time. Yet, in this era, women are also for the first time becoming real participants in the worlds of commerce, politics, sports, science, and exploration—and men react by creating a popular culture full of sexual objectification.

In reviewing literally dozens of popular movies of the era, such as those quoted above, one gets the reasonable, if artistically exaggerated, impression that to the Patriot man, the contemporary woman is basically irrational, insincere, and headstrong (not to mention quite often a trollop). To the Patriot woman, the contemporary man is basically dumb, duplicitous, and disposable—not to mention extremely sex starved.

A lot of this is, of course, intensified by a crippled economy in which the practice of gold-digging is presented as an understandable, even if also hurtful and morally wanting, survival strategy. It is joked about in movies, such as 1933's *Duck Soup* (Margaret Dumont: "I don't think you'd love me if I were poor." Groucho Marx: "I might, but I'd keep my mouth shut."); *Dinner at Eight* (Jean Harlow: "If there's one thing I know it's men. I ought to. It's been my life's work."); and *She Done Him Wrong* (Mae West: "I wasn't always rich. No, there was a time when I didn't know where my next husband was coming from."); but the humor doesn't entirely mask the visceral knowledge that there is real want in the world. In all, relationships entered into for the sake of material security are hardly ill-advised or unfortunate.

In the context of all of this, it is particularly interesting to consider Frank Capra's *It Happened One Night* (1934), an immensely popular movie that is the first ever to win all five major Oscars. In this good-natured story, a love match develops between a working class reporter (Clark Gable) and a willful little rich girl (Claudette Colbert). It is generationally significant in that there is so much appeal to a story in which simple, shared events and a little animal magnetism lead to love and to triumph over class differences. Still, it is hard to ignore the long-term value implications for Patriots when the reporter scores a major coup with his future father-in-law by observing (about the man's daughter): "What she needs is a guy that takes a sock at her once a day whether it's coming to her or not."

The Patriot Ideal

If you lose this war, don't blame me.
—**Buster Keaton in *The General* (1927)**

I'll do it. We'll get a home even if I have to work for it!
—**Charlie Chaplin as The Little Tramp, *Modern Times* (1936)**

I'll wash and sew and sweep and cook!
—**Snow White, *Snow White and the Seven Dwarfs* (1937)**

He's got goodness, Mabel. Do you know what that is?
No, of course you don't.
We've forgotten. We're too busy being smart alecks. Too busy in a crazy
competition for nothing.
—**Jean Arthur as Babe, *Mr. Deeds Goes to Town* (1936)**

The idealized Patriot is a combination of Buster Keaton, Charlie Chaplin, Snow White, and Gary Cooper. This is not necessarily who a Patriot is, but it is who he'd figuratively like to be.

In *The General* (1927), Buster Keaton is informed that he is of no use to the confederacy as a soldier in the Civil War, and subsequently his girlfriend rejects him. He instead becomes a train engineer and, of course, saves the girl and almost single-handedly wins the war for the South. Courage and humor are part of the package, but the real Patriot virtue manifest here is accepting the unsought role and turning it into a benefit for oneself and the greater society.

In the remarkable *Modern Times* (1936), Charlie Chaplin's Little Tramp character comes up against every imaginable dehumanizing attribute of industrialization, job-hunting, and deprivation in an era of economic depression. Through a combination of simplicity, goodness, resilience, and indomitability, he never suffers a loss of what can only be described as happiness. (Many critics have pointed out the similarity between the Little Tramp and Mickey Mouse.) In the movie's famous final scene, the Little Tramp walks down the road with his sweetheart—there's only trouble behind them, but there is an amazing feeling of hope regarding the future.

The feminists of later Value Populations might take exception to Snow White's "some day my prince will come" take on life in *Snow White and the Seven Drawfs* (1937), but that doesn't change how Patriots look at it. Keeping up spirits and managing the domestic life of the clan (Snow White first assumes she has stumbled upon an orphanage, not a den of dwarves) is just another example of accepting a role that works for the good of the many. It is not just the courage it takes to escape the wicked queen, charm the knife-wielding woodsman, or survive a life with Dopey and Grumpy in an enchanted forest—it is the lack of complaint.

Ultimately, one finds the total Patriot wish-package in Gary Cooper's portrayal of Longfellow Deeds, the title character in Frank Capra's Academy Award-winning *Mr. Deeds Goes to Town* (1936). A tuba-playing greeting card poet in a relentlessly folksy New England village, Deeds becomes heir to a $20 million fortune (a truly astounding sum in 1936) left by a distant uncle. Though targeted for exploitation by attorneys, by a female reporter who eventually falls in love with him, by "opera lovers," and by a host of other shrewd operators, Deeds foils everyone's plans by simply being democracy's model common man—kind, courageous, funny, subtly sagacious, and very aware of whose hand is in his wallet.

Because Deeds first has the audacity to state that he doesn't need the money (there must have been an audible movie audience gasp) and then decides to use the entire amount to underwrite a fund for poor family farmers, he is of course made to stand trial for his sanity. This concern with "sanity" is a meaningful echo of the themes introduced throughout the Patriot value-formation period—when monsters and madmen roamed the movie screens, hacking through the audience's sense of self-worth. It must have felt more than comforting when the Deeds' trial judge announces his finding that this quintessentially good everyman is simply "the sanest man I've ever met."

7

THE PERFORMERS
An Overview

POPULATION OVERVIEW

Age: Born 1938–1957
Size: 21% of the U.S. Population
Spending: $1.81 Trillion Annually
Themes: The Atomic Age/Personality
Values: Freedom/Drama/Adventure

Summary

If Performers sometimes seem unduly self-absorbed and self-indulgent, one must first consider the conditions of their value-formation period before passing too blithe a judgment. Born during and just after global war, and being heirs to the advent of "we will bury you" communism and its consistent threat of nuclear annihilation, the offspring of the Patriot Value Population—most notably characterized by caution and an obsessive allegiance to the prevailing practices of the clan—might well have emerged as a tribe of crushed gray spirits quivering in the darkest corners of their own repressive nightmares. But be it a matter of fate, fortune, or their own sheer numbers, the Performers take the exact opposite generational tack—that of lighting their own inner flames rather than cursing the darkness.

There are always exceptions to these broad generalities, but no other Value Population quite compares with Performers for their lust after life's sheer drama—for the belongings, feelings, and events that make an individual feel unique and very much alive.

PERFORMER HISTORICAL EVENT MATRIX

Hope/War/Prosperity

Hope

Although the New Deal legislation of the FDR administration is eventually disqualified by the courts, the economy appears healed from the Great Depression and headed in the right direction, as evidenced by steeply growing employment, national minimum wage legislation (1938), and a broadly recovering stock market.

A comprehensive and coherent vision of a materially-flush consumerist future takes shape at the New York World's Fair of 1938. At the same time, there is a great opening up of the possibilities of the human creative spirit via the birth of television and the proliferation of Technicolor movie epics (e.g., *Wizard of Oz* and *Gone with the Wind*).

Despite ominous political and military developments in Europe, there is still ample faith that policies of isolation, appeasement, and neutrality will prevent direct U.S. involvement in a broad military conflict.

War

World War II (1941–1945), with global military and civilian fatalities numbering upwards of 45 million people, brings death and destruction to humanity on a scale that can barely be contemplated.

Essential historical icons for the era are the genocidal German concentration camps and the Japanese cities of Hiroshima and Nagasaki, whose populations are instantly devastated by atomic bombs.

The threats of military dictatorship and nuclear weaponry, and the fragility of human life in their shadows, linger long after WWII and throughout the Korean (1950–1953) and "Cold" Wars.

Prosperity

The end of WWII ushers in a period of unprecedented economic growth, particularly reflected in the rise of automobiles, suburbia, disposable consumer goods, and the overall growth of the middle class.

The United States becomes the world's foremost nation, and New

York City becomes the center of economic, political, and cultural civilization—the cornerstone for the United Nations building is laid in New York City in 1949.

Children are born to returning soldiers and their wives in the greatest historical numbers ever (i.e., the Baby Boom); and these children soon become the focus of American culture.

PERFORMER POPULATION VALUES

Personal Freedom

- *Historical drivers.* Survival of WWII and the Cold War; the cultural pendulum swings away from restrictive "collective" doctrines of the Patriot period; parental indulgence; automobile culture.
- *Value manifestation.* Vastly educated and incredibly affluent by historical standards, this entitled Value Population appropriates the right to freedom of belief, expression, affiliation, location, and life change. Wealth and power are desirable facilitators, but these are means not ends.

A Place in the Sun

- *Historical drivers.* Popular culture (soap operas, movies, kid-centric television, Disneyland) and historical events (war and nuclear annihilation) conspire to present life dramatically, urgently, and in fairly strict terms of heroes and villains.
- *Value manifestation.* The quest is not necessarily for a center-stage spotlight or real glory (although that might occasionally be nice) but for a place where one is recognized, respected, and ultimately rewarded for one's unique attributes and contributions—and if it is fun, all the better.

Courage and Adventure

- *Historical drivers.* The true war hero and the cowboy myth; the national highway system; the psychological survival imperative of an A-bomb burdened age.
- *Value manifestation.* Life is too short to let fear be the boss. A happy heart is a racing heart. Experience is life's greatest treasure.

Creativity

- *Historical drivers.* An enormous influx of variety in goods, services, and diversions; a pendulum swing away from the closed-off and self-protective insularity of the Patriots.
- *Value manifestation.* The urge to produce, express, or accomplish something unique—artistically, intellectually, athletically, socially, politically, financially, and so forth—is powerful. Child bearing and raising is definitely included here.

Youthfulness

- *Historical drivers.* From *The Wizard of Oz* to Disneyland to *Leave It to Beaver* to *The Catcher in the Rye* to Dr. Benjamin Spock, the child becomes, for the first time in American history, the consistent center of cultural preoccupation and commentary.
- *Value manifestation.* The hope, self-infatuation, energy, and resilience of Performers are best suited to the young and young-at-heart. Unsurprisingly, this Value Population puts a premium on parental encouragement of, and identification with, their own young.

Romance

- *Historical drivers.* The intensification of relationships against the backdrop of war—the agony of loss, the joy of discovery and return; the *Casablanca* myth.
- *Value manifestation.* Flirtatious, sexual, and/or everlasting romance is the perfect blend of reward, excitement, and essential validation of one's worth. In all endeavors, the ultimate adventure is the adventure of the heart.

Glamour and Style

- *Historical drivers.* The vivid colorization of life, ranging from movies to food to cars to clothes to household appliances; Hollywood is brought into the home via television.
- *Value manifestation.* There is a deep affection for all things that help to transcend the ordinariness of life, from fashion to fine dining to luxury automobiles to exotic vacations to the work of a good plastic surgeon.

Headlines, Summaries, and Generalizations

- *Historical drivers.* Global historical events of extreme urgency meet the dawn of the television age; proliferation of dramatic formats yields expectation of sudden changes; President Eisenhower introduces the one-page summary to government reports.
- *Value manifestation.* Details are deemed too sticky. There is a preference for broad generalizations that can be summarily rallied behind or easily dismissed. Performers hate not being able to have or change a personal opinion.

Friendship

- *Historical drivers.* Empowerment at an early age leads to unique youth affiliations; increased suburban population and "playing" become important social trends.
- *Value manifestation.* Here friendship is uniquely fashioned as a relationship between kindred spirits associating on the basis of freely chosen beliefs, empathies, and experiences, rather than on the basis of heritage or hierarchy.

PERFORMER MACRO INTERESTS

(Life-phase considerations projected through 2012)

Business Problems

In terms of the old ant/grasshopper fable, Performers have had their share of being ants, but they have really been much more disposed toward being grasshoppers. Brought into the world in a time of economic optimism and growing material affluence, they were counseled about rainy-day savings, but inevitably they seemed to get a shiny new toy before the lecture was over. Now in their middle age, they are confronting the reality that economies do grow soft from time to time, that markets change, that new hard-to-learn technologies and other required job skills emerge, and that good jobs and entire industries sometimes go away forever. The insecurity such changes breed often seems to become a terrible fly in the ointment of their self-satisfaction. This group really never expected to run out of resources or the ability to recover—but now?

Children

With the youngest of Performers now in their mid-50s, Performers are generally confronting that time in their children's development cycle when college, careers, and their children's own families are looming large on the horizon. Issues of resources are of great importance in all these endeavors, but so is the matter of their offspring's success and creative fulfillment—which, most Performers strongly feel, reflects on their own life's accomplishments.

Credit Problems

Taken as a whole, the Performers' credit "abuse" is not as striking as those of younger Value Populations, but their situation is certainly serious enough; stock-market fickleness, an unkind job market, and a general propensity to be less savings-conscious than their parents are catching up with Performers—an enormous problem for a group that is not into self-denial.

Education

Performers need no prompting to understand the link between a child's education and his or her success. However, this concern with education is also true of their own development, as the Performer generation prepares to live, work, and "grow" longer than any preceding generation in history.

Heart Disease and Other Ailments

Although medical science continues to make remarkable strides, the deck still seems stacked against middle-aged men (and many women) when it comes to serious health issues, including heart disease, the leading cause of death in the United States. Even beyond genetic risk, many of the stress-causing and health-impairing conditions of modern life are minimized by a generation whose tickers have been tocking for a good long while now.

Pleasure and Fun

Although they are aging, Performers seem little inclined to dispense with activities performed for pure pleasure. This group is not likely to retreat gracefully to the front-porch rocker, though they may have to take up the issue of endurance with their hearts and backs. Look for this group to seek active fun, including travel, for as long as they can stand it—and social stimulation when they can no longer even stand.

Personal Passions

Even more than pleasure and fun, Performers are indelibly imprinted with a desire to feel and express their essential life urges—this may mean a passion for writing poetry, collecting stamps, cooking, performing charity work, or flying stunt airplanes. It is also likely to manifest in a substantial increase in the tens of millions of prescriptions that have already been written for Viagra. Performers need to do more than live—they need to feel alive.

Property Appreciation

They might not care to admit it to their own parents, but the Performers have been convinced by the vagaries of market investment that there is no asset like a real one and no real asset like a home. Indications are already strong of a spate of second-home buying by this Value Population, which is looking to turn retirement into both a pleasure and a sound financial plan.

Public Morality

Morality is a very interesting area with regard to Performers who, frequently during their maturation process, have dismissed as "square" many of the socially "uptight" customs and concerns of their elders. Now, though, the mantle of gray is on the heads of Performers, and one can only wonder if their tolerance will be tested as they now become the collective voice of experience.

Risk-Taking

Whether it is a trump card or a trouble spot, Performers have historically been adventurous and risk-tolerant. How this may manifest physically, socially, and economically in an aging population is a matter of uncharted territory—but it pays to flatter Performer courage.

Relaxation for Performers

Performers enjoy just about any public spectacle or display (participatory or spectator), including concerts, theatrical presentations, sporting events, glamorous parties and social occasions, escapist vacations, romantic outings and getaways, club and organization social events, as well as elective classes and workshops.

8

THE PERFORMERS
History Creating Values

Most modern demographers consider the World War II era almost exclusively as a phenomenon of the Patriot Value Population who actually fought the war and then celebrated victory. We certainly agree that the war era itself was a manifestation of the values of the adult population of the time. However, in a key departure from standard analysis, our primary emphasis regarding these events is on the youthful segment of the population whose values were formed during and in the close aftermath of this worldwide test and reorganization of political, economic and social realities.

When one gets beyond birth-rate demography and the reasoning that events have validity only for the adults who are acting them out, an alignment of history according to something other than the "common wisdom" occurs. With this in mind, one of the most fascinating insights into Performers is that much of this group's value-formation story is thematically foreshadowed in the brief period between 1938 and 1940, just prior to the U.S. entrance into war. The war itself does, of course, become a key part of the story, but the earlier period gives a valuable look into the value-formation themes of the period as a whole.

VULNERABILITY TO DANGEROUS
GLOBAL FORCES

At the beginning of the Performer period, there is still hope that isolation and appeasement can be successful strategies to halt the spread of tyrannical global imperialism. In 1938, France and England sanction Nazi Germany's annexation of Austria and dismemberment of Czechoslovakia, and in 1939, the United States formally declares neutrality with regard to "the war in Europe." Also in 1939, however, Germany's armed invasion of Poland forces France and England to declare war. In Asia, an expansionist Japan occupies Indochina in 1940, and the bombing of Pearl Harbor and the U.S. entrance into world war take place the following year. The mood of this period is characterized by a growing and desperately oppressive awareness that the world is a fiercely dangerous place where every man, woman, and child is at risk and where burying one's head in the sand is no longer a viable option—and never will be again.

UPWARDLY MOBILE ECONOMY

It may sound almost inconsequential in light of the above, but at the New York World's Fair of 1938–1939, an economically recovering global civilization gets its first look at the future as conceived by capitalist forces confronting the desperate "want" experienced during the global depression. The fair's central exhibit is General Motors' Futurama, a prescient vision of the United States "in 1960" as a society dominated by automobiles, urban skyscrapers, suburbs, and kitchen appliances. Although the World's Fair is temporarily disrupted by hostile global developments and ends badly (mostly sold as scrap materials for the war effort), postwar society would largely fulfill this vision of a consumer-centered, highway crisscrossed civilization into which the generation of Performers would be born.

INDIVIDUALS VERSUS SOCIETY

It is an issue soon swallowed up by the collective practical necessity of building an army, but John Steinbeck's *The Grapes of Wrath*, published in 1939, and Richard Wright's *Native Son*, published in 1940, eloquently argue that America does not just practice discrimination against its poor and its racial minorities, but that the rights and opportunities of all "common" individuals in the American "system" are tenuous at best when opposed to the interests of the rich and powerful. The issue is to grow much more significant and divisive after the war, particularly when war "heroes" return to lives at the lower end of the social spectrum. This coming to terms with the injustices of the "system" stamps itself upon the very soul of Performer value formation.

TRANSITION TO THE TUBE AND TECHNICOLOR

In 1939, President Franklin Delano Roosevelt becomes the first U.S. President to appear on commercial broadcast television when he gives a short speech at the reopening of the New York World's Fair. The very next day, RCA introduces its first television sets to the buying public and announces a broadcast schedule on its NBC subsidiary. The new technology is adapted slowly (only 9 percent of U.S. households own sets as late as 1950) and does not reach sophistication or saturation until the end of the Performer period—but, the early eager development of this world-changing new entertainment-oriented medium and the youthful population born in its wake go hand-in-hand.

Along with this milestone in television development, movies in 1939, according to many film historians, had their single greatest year ever. Among the now-classic movies released in that one year are *The Wizard of Oz, Gone with the Wind, Mr. Smith Goes to Washington, Stagecoach, Destry Rides Again, Wuthering Heights,* and *The Hunchback of Notre Dame.* While the specific thematic relevancies of many of these movies will be explored in the next chapter, it is well worth noting that this veritable all-at-once explosion of intense and artfully crafted movies reflects an essential shift of perception that will dominate this value-formation period. With the Performers comes the evolutionary moment in which media itself become transcendent—first through movies and then along with television—via the creation of stories and technologies that not so much capture reality, but in all ways dramatize and enhance it.

WORLD WAR II (1939–1945)

A nuanced discussion of the effects of war in general, and of World War II specifically, might rightfully run to encyclopedic length. But, as has already been indicated, the issue in this discussion is the effect such an event has on the value formation of a population just coming into being at the time of the event. What, in other words, is the impact of such an all-consuming and deathly dangerous conflict on the children being born in its shadow?

In the manner of nursery stories, one encounters a classic mythology (albeit populated by real people performing real acts) of heroes and villains. Especially as filtered through the adults acting out the story, one gets the most compelling and clear-cut sense of a war between good and evil. Drama is everywhere in such a tale, and it is this drama as well as an innate expression of knowing what is right (even when this is entirely subjective) that becomes a keynote of the Performers as they mature.

Ultimately, from the perspective of American Performer value formation, the most important fact of the war may be that it concludes in victory for the American side. One must assume such an outcome engenders many desirable virtues in an emerging population, from courage to optimism to a prevailing sense that time and fate, and perhaps even God, are on one's side.

Even allowing for the sweet psychological fruits of victory, there's little denying that World War II opens up a Pandora's box of evil that permeates the climate of global affairs and generational consciousness during the entire Performer value-formation period. The cost of victory, if one counts the world's total military and civilian casualties during the WWII era, is an incredibly demoralizing 45 to 50 million lives. In the United States alone, more than a million soldiers are listed as killed, injured, captured, or missing in action.

Assuredly, the post-war discovery that six million people have died in concentration camps because of their religious and ethnic affiliations may have left some sort of scar on the collective psyche of Performers. But perhaps even more devastating is the image of the mushroom cloud over Hiroshima that carries away 200,000 lives during a few moments in August of 1945. Forever afterward, and quite manifestly in the politics and culture of the Performer value-formation period, the possibility of the annihilation of the human race in a brief exchange of button pressing is to hang over humankind.

Quotes from Leaders of the Performer Era

As long as I live I shall think only of the victory of my people. I shall shrink from nothing and shall annihilate everyone who is opposed to me

...

I want to annihilate the enemy!

—Adolph Hitler, *German Chancellor* (1938–1945)

A single death is a tragedy, a million deaths is a statistic.

—Joseph Stalin, *Russian Premier* (1941–1953)

Bombs do not choose. They will hit everything.

—Nikita Khrushchev, Russian Premier, *Time Magazine's* Man of the Year (1957)

The object of war is not to die for your country, but to make the other bastard die for his.

—George S. Patton, *U.S. General* (1941–1945)

COLD WAR (1945+)

New Enemies for Old

Had WWII resulted in a clear and absolute victory for the forces of democratic capitalism, it would be possible to put a less guardedly upbeat spin on the implications of the event. Quickly, though, it becomes apparent that there is a powerful new brand of despotism abroad in the world. The Soviet Union, a former ally possessed of its own fearsome nuclear capabilities, reveals that the challenge to Western dominance has simply changed its color (to communist red) not its stripes. The everything-at-risk tension between superpowers is to grind away at global society for the next half-century.

New Enemies at Home

Names such as Alger Hiss, Ethel Rosenberg, and Joe McCarthy grab a fair share of the domestic headlines between 1949 and 1953. The issue here is the sometimes real, more often imagined, threat of communist infiltration into the domestic, political and cultural affairs of the nation. As a vocal and powerful faction of the Patriot generation uses "witchhunt" tactics to insulate itself against perceived enemies of the state, the Performers begin to grow up in a world where there is fuzzy delineation between the just operations of democratic law and the belligerent designs of a lynch mob.

KOREAN WAR (1950–1953)

More War

In a world clearly grown weary of war, the American-led United Nations police action fails to capture the patriotic spirit of the era's previous conflict and is essentially fought to a draw. Still more communists, this time Chinese, become dangerous enemies of the United States. During the same period, Jews and Arabs engage in armed hostilities in Palestine, and the division of India and Pakistan also leads to thousands of refugee deaths. In short, world war has ended, but dangerous and deadly world turmoil has not.

AMERICAN PROSPERITY (1940S AND 1950S)

Consumer Goods Heyday

The silver lining that nearly blots out the mushroom cloud is the remarkable affluence of America's postwar economy. At the end of WWII, America goes on a celebratory production and spending spree that involves, according to one commentator, "an awesome and bewildering array of stuff." Coupled with continuing mammoth expenditures on defense, the American gross domestic product (GDP) grows 51 percent in the decade after the war. See Figure 8.1. More Americans join the middle class than at any time in history—a threefold increase from 1940 to 1960. The United States, with 6 percent of the world's population, becomes the producer and consumer of one third of the world's goods.

It is worth noting that the emergent American passion for material goods, and the culture that champions them, attract mostly ardent support. But the same culture also quickly engenders a "movement" of influential, articulate, and passionate critics of the bland uniformity that a consumer society engenders. In addition to the prodigious outpouring of the anti-materialistic and antiestablishment "beat generation," key commentaries of the period include John Kenneth Galbraith's *The Affluent Society*, William H. Whyte's *The Organization Man*, Sloan Wilson's *The Man in the Gray Flannel Suit*, and Ayn Rand's *Atlas Shrugged*.

Although adult Performers are often criticized for their materialism, it is essential to acknowledge that the conspicuous consumption frenzy and the middle-class homogenization of the postwar period are essentially Patriot (Performer parents) phenomena. Performers grow up in an environment where material comfort is bestowed upon them as the most loving act of a generation brought up in an economic depression (and to this day, it is fair to say that Performers often respond to material goods as a return to mother's milk). But they also grow up in a culture that probingly questions the value of all this "stuff" and cultural sameness, and whether the acquisition of goods is a rewarding and interesting enough premise upon which to build a worthwhile life. Performers, who tend to embrace the clash of opposites, the very soul of drama, have always derived much of their value character from the "war" of this material ambiguity in their natures.

FIGURE 8.1

U.S. Gross Domestic Product (GDP)

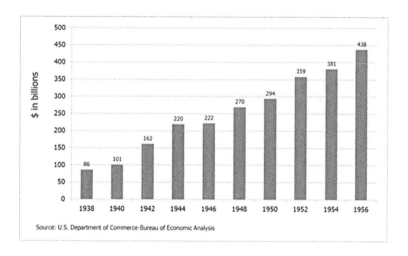

Source: U.S. Department of Commerce-Bureau of Economic Analysis

Although adult Performers are often criticized for their materialism, it is essential to acknowledge that the conspicuous consumption frenzy and the middle-class homogenization of the postwar period are essentially Patriot (Performer parents) phenomena. Performers grow up in an environment where material comfort is bestowed upon them as the most loving act of a generation brought up in an economic depression (and to this day, it is fair to say that Performers often respond to material goods as a return to mother's milk). But they also grow up in a culture that probingly questions the value of all this "stuff" and cultural sameness, and whether the acquisition of goods is a rewarding and interesting enough premise upon which to build a worthwhile life. Performers, who tend to embrace the clash of opposites, the very soul of drama, have always derived much of their value character from the "war" of this material ambiguity in their natures.

Automobiles and Suburbia

Central to the postwar economy is the automobile. By the mid-1950s, automobile sales in the United States average around 9 million new units per year. Government money pours into highway construction during the Eisenhower administrations, reaching its apex with the passage of the Federal Highway Act of 1956 that essentially creates and funds the nation's interstate highway grid. The Performer generation is the first to grow up with the car trip as its birthright.

The rapid development of suburbia reinforces and justifies the need for additional automobiles, highways, and domestic consumer goodies. Built between 1946 and 1951, the tract homes of Long Island's Levittown become a national icon of the future of U.S. domestic civilization. By 1960, the U.S. housing supply has increased by 25 percent from the 1950 total, and 30.5 percent of the entire national population lives in suburban communities.

NEW YORK CITY AT THE CENTER OF THE UNIVERSE

After WWII, America is at the summit of global civilization, and New York City is, from that indelible moment of victory celebration in Times Square, at the summit of America. The great symbolic crowning of the City as the world capital comes with the opening of the United Nations in 1952. As previously ethnic residential neighborhoods are bulldozed, New York City commits itself to commerce and the skyscraper. In the last eight years of the 1950s, more new office space is created in New York City than exists in the entire city of Chicago. During the Performer period, "the city that never sleeps" becomes the world's foremost center for trade, culture, style, and information. Its "bright lights and Broadway" and its advertising mecca, Madison Avenue, become for the Performer generation symbols of what "making it" is all about.

THE SOCIAL COST OF URBAN RENEWAL

With the postwar federal government developing highways, sponsoring highrise real estate development (Title 1), and giving attractive tax breaks to suburban mortgage holders (Title 2), major cities become less demarcated by the vibrant ethnic neighborhoods and street life that has defined them in the past. Groups who can afford it flee to the new suburbs, taking a good portion of the tax base along with them. Less upwardly-mobile populations—particularly blacks and Puerto Ricans—find themselves, while already reeling from the disruptions of war, increasingly uprooted, "ghettoized," distanced from familiar support networks, denied civic services, and forced into menial jobs. This metropolitan-based cauldron of poverty and disenfranchisement is to come to a full boil in the era of the Techticians, but the heat starts here.

CHILDREN—SEEN AND HEARD

What deserves special emphasis here is the unique historical nature of the Performer perspective itself: Performers are the first modern Value Population that imposes a strong and unique point of view on its society from the time of its early youth. Although many reasons for this influence on society can be debated, such as the sheer number of young Performers, a doting adult generation, the need for atomic escapism, or something like fate, it is nonetheless a powerful influence.

Assuredly, general affluence, a strong educational system, and the advent of television enable Performers to form what may be called "generational consciousness" faster than preceding Value Populations. There are countless icons of this phenomenon, but surely nothing like the vision of Disneyland—a child-centered vision of the U.S. "dream culture" opened in July of 1955 (with an astounding 90 million people watching on television)—could or would have been rendered into reality at any preceding moment in history.

Although the exact dates of value-population demarcation are arguable, the mid- to late 1950s are a profound turning point in history, because by then young people begin to fully emerge with an independent and often predominant cultural perspective and voice—a voice that will exist in conflict with the Patriot value culture and from which the next Value Population, the Techticians, will largely be formed. Indicative of this timing are three landmark 1957 television events: the first national telecast of *American Bandstand,* the famous "waist up" appearance of Elvis Presley on *Ed Sullivan,* and the airing of the first episode of *Leave It to Beaver,* the first television series to tell its story from the point of view of a child protagonist.

It is interesting to note that while most demographers consider the Baby Boom to have lasted through 1964, the absolute peak year in U.S. births is 1957, with just over 4.3 million live births that year. See Figure 8.2. After 1957, the number of live births steadily declines while the cultural acting out of a fully formed Performer Value Population moves to center stage and begins influencing the formation of Techtician values.

FIGURE 8.2

U.S. Total Birth Rates

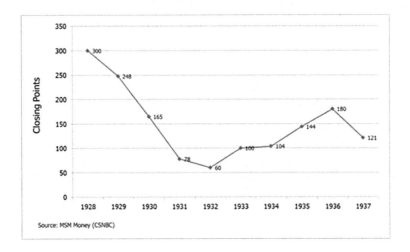

Source: MSM Money (CSNBC)

9

THE PERFORMERS
Cultural Expressions of an Era

*Your choice is simple. Join us and live in peace or pursue your present
course and face obliteration. We shall be waiting for your answer. The
decision rests with you.*

—**Klaatu, *The Day the Earth Stood Still* (1951)**

WORLD WAR AND ITS
COMPLICATED AFTERMATH

For an unprecedented number of
Americans, victory in WWII ushers in an era of economic and social up-
ward mobility. In fact, most superficial sociology and trends analysis de-
rives its understanding of Performers as a product of Chevrolets on the
road, Donna Reed in the kitchen, and good times at the malt shop. It is
argued here, however, that while the material blessings of the postwar
period are coveted and enjoyed by the Patriot generation acting out its
own values, to Performers, there is a much darker tone to the times in
the midst of their value formation.

An important basic truth of the Performer era is: "Just because a war
ends does not mean its influence goes away." The angst, anxiety, sadness,
and loss that linger after WWII are hugely magnified by the Cold War
and the revelation of the destructive capacity of atomic weapons. Movies,
more than any other media of the era, give a frightening vision of what
is forming in the collective psyche of the Performer generation.

If there is a cinematic "establishing shot" for Performers, it is the
panoramic display of human carnage—the destruction of the Confederacy—in *Gone with the Wind* (1939). For the next 20 years, thoughts and
visions of meaningless and terrifying destruction hang over movie-house
fare like an invading army from hell. War images, massacres, crowd vio-

lence, personal violence, and murders by the bushel become the staple of the silver screen. Eventually, these enemies of mankind's survival are joined by legions of monsters, such as the giant mutant ants in *Them* (1954) and the intergalactic bad boy *Godzilla* (1956)—products of atomic radiation and a future almost too terrifying to contemplate.

In addition to the images of violence and doom, the psychological somberness of the period is reflected in at least the following four major recurring themes: disaffection; mistrust of vested and powerful interests; the western way; and death, an interesting neighbor.

DISAFFECTION

I'm not an officer and a gentleman anymore.
I'm just another soda jerk out of a job.
—Fred Perry, The Best Years of Our Lives (1946)

Many movie buffs might have a hard time identifying the most commercially and critically successful American movie made between *Gone with the Wind* (1939) and *Ben Hur* (1959). That movie is *The Best Years of Our Lives* (1946), which tells a torturous tale of back-to-normal adjustment for returning heroes—American soldiers who are attempting to fit back into the families, the jobs, and the social order they left behind when they headed off to war. It is a "sobering" saga of battered relationships and crushed economic expectations punctuated with binge drinking.

In many of the great iconographic films and books of the Performer era—*Catcher in the Rye* (1951), *Shane* (1953), *On the Waterfront* (1954), and *Rebel without a Cause* (1955)—it is the disaffected antihero, the person who simply can no longer pretend to fit into the prescribed order of things regardless of the personal consequences, who captures our attention and, most frequently, our sympathies.

MISTRUST OF VESTED AND POWERFUL INTERESTS

"Why should I?"
"Patriotism."
"That word gives me a pain. No thank you. I don't go for patriotism, nor patriots."
"I could dispute that with you."

"Waving the flag with one hand and picking pockets with the other.
That's your patriotism. Well, you can have it."

—**Ingrid Bergman and Cary Grant, as Alicia and Devlin, *Notorious* (1946)**

Considering how real and painful the blacklisting of actors, writers, and directors was to become during the so-called "communist witch hunts" of the McCarthy era, it is particularly impressive to note the number of popular films of the era that take at least some jabs at the nation's most cherished social, political, and economic ideals and institutions. The particular target in many films is the stereotyped fat-cat businessman who prospers in good times and bad, and who seems little inclined toward gratitude, generosity, or the rules he endorses for the rest of society. The greatest of these antientitlement statements is made in *Citizen Kane* (1941), but the sentiment is echoed throughout the era, particularly in its many great Westerns.

THE WESTERN WAY

A man has to be what he is, Joey. You can't break the mold. I tried and it
didn't work for me.

—**Alan Ladd as the title character, *Shane* (1953)**

It is useful to think of the great Westerns of the Performer era— including *Stagecoach* (1939), *Destry Rides Again* (1939), *My Darling Clementine* (1954), *Shane* (1953), *The Searchers* (1956), and countless others—as compelling hybrids of a private psychological dreamscape (famed Western director John Ford's great visionary insight was that the actual Monument Valley was no less a fantastical setting than Oz) and an eminently public meeting on the town square. Here is the artistic genre that, via its examination of the conflict between a human being as a heroically free individual and the land as a communally exploitable resource, truly does provide the mythological context for an examination of postwar America.

In the Western, one gets a bare-knuckled examination of what sort of person—the cowboy or the capitalist—should hold the purse and the political power. See Figure 9.1. The genre consistently presents compelling drama and dialogue regarding the appropriate shape of the national future, accomplishing this in part by always putting death on the line. It is the Western that asks (and dramatizes the answer as a life-and-death matter) whether a society is best served by courageous individualism or whether safety, stability, and prosperity are obtained through allegiance to a more politically orthodox and socially responsible collectivism, a profoundly relevant postwar discussion.

FIGURE 9.1

Top Ten Western Films of the Performer Era

1. *High Noon (1952)*
2. *The Searchers (1956)*
3. *Red River (1948)*
4. *The Ox-Bow Incident (1943)*
5. *Stagecoach (1939)*
6. *My Darling Clementine (1946)*
7. *Shane (1953)*
8. *Destry Rides Again (1939)*
9. *Winchester '73 (1950)*
10. *She Wore a Yellow Ribbon (1949)*

Source: As voted on by the members of Internet Movie Database, Inc.

As in a good fight, heavy blows are given and taken in all aspects of this complex ideological exploration. Remarkably, and with sincere appreciation of the difficulty of what is being examined, there really is no clear-cut answer. Yet it is hard not to notice that John Wayne, Henry Fonda, Jimmy Stewart, and Alan Ladd (and then TV's Hopalong Cassidy, The Lone Ranger, Gene Autry, Roy Rogers, etc.), rather than the settlers or capitalists, always seem to be among the courageous individualists—even when they wear badges. This is a glamorous fact certainly not lost on the young toy-gun-toting Performers.

DEATH, AN INTERESTING NEIGHBOR

In Italy for 30 years under the Borgias, they had warfare, terror, murder,
and bloodshed, but they produced Michelangelo, Leonardo da Vinci, and
the Renaissance. In Switzerland they had brotherly love; they had 500
years of democracy and peace; and what did they produce?
The cuckoo clock.
—Orson Welles as Harry Lime, *The Third Man* (1949)

Is there no exemption for actors?
—Erik Strandmark as Jonas Skat, in response to Death coming for him, *The Seventh Seal* (1957)

The prevailing sentiment of movies during the Performer value-formation era (especially after the war) is that war and death are rarely good for society or the individual and should be avoided if at all possible. However, because some argue that, at times, wars are morally justifiable, then it becomes necessary to produce soldiers who are willing to die for a cause. Thus, a fair number of Performer movies talk up the nobility of death for a worthy objective. Assuredly, John Wayne's bravery in the fight against Indian "savages" provides spiritual fuel for some Performers who will later fight in Vietnam.

Beyond the "worthy cause" point of view, it is useful to note the memorable Performer-era movies that further address war and death as some sort of complex, not-always-unsatisfactory answer to an extremely difficult question. One thinks of Hamlet's "To be or not to be" soliloquy, which is actually delivered by Doc Holiday in *My Darling Clementine* (1946)—perhaps the strangest scene ever filmed in an American Western. There is also the compelling *From Here to Eternity* (1953) which, although a postwar movie, presents the start of the war, even with its certainty of death and crippling injury for some, as a somehow satisfactory resolution to many of the difficult relationships and situations in which the movie's main characters are embroiled.

Perhaps one should not make too much of these philosophical meanderings. But, to the emergent generation of Performers, war and potential personal annihilation occupy much the same role as poverty does to the Patriots. To a large portion of the Performer population, the threat of death is not some abstract condition of life but an enormously present and persistent influence on value formation. How could anyone be surprised when, in their late adolescence and early adulthood, a significant portion of the newly minted middle-class Performer population turns its backs on materialism in a symbolic gesture of life affirmation and their hearts towards a peace movement?

LIFE AS SOAP OPERA

By gad, sir, you are a character. There's never any telling what you'll say or do next, except that it's bound to be something astonishing.
—Kaspar Gutman describing Sam Spade (Humphrey Bogart), *The Maltese Falcon* (1941)

A person doesn't always get what she deserves. Remember it. If there's anything in life you want, go and get it. Don't wait for anybody to give it to you.
—Mrs. Thornton, *Peyton Place* (1957)

Perhaps the most noteworthy and remarkable observation about Performers is that they do not immediately, collectively, and permanently retreat right back into the womb. Traditional interpretation attributes this not to some amazing generational survivalist response but to the fact that this event era has parents who indulge their children in all possible ways, with the result that these children become insufferably cocksure and egomaniacal. But that, besides being arguable, is almost a comical slight when one considers the ferocity with which this generation has tried to work out its relationship with the world.

Leaving the ultimate "why" to the sociologists and psychologists, there is just no avoiding the truth that the "typical" Performer life manifests, from the perspective of the individual Performer, as a soap opera wherein he or she is the star. According to the Museum of Television and Radio, soap operas (a radio phenomenon of the 1930s brought to television in 1952 with *The Guiding Light* and established as an essential television form in 1956 with *As The World Turns*) are characterized by an intense and dramatic preoccupation with birth, death, marriage, romance, current social issues, and villainy. At their very core, soap operas are relentless multiyear, sometimes multi-decade, character studies that explore the helpful and harmful nuances of every emotion, thought, value, relationship, and capacity for transformation that can occur within an individual's lifetime.

The reason it is so hard to describe, sell to, or manage the Performer generation is that one is dealing with people who see themselves not only as individualists, but also as individualists who zealously reserve the right to grow, change, change back, make things more interesting, and, as suits them, perform as brilliantly as master artists or as self-destructively as drunken sailors. This is a generation that apparently operates on the principle that an ego must be both strong and flexible to survive. Ultimately, the only description that really comes close to capturing the Performer personality is one that recognizes their capacity for willfulness and self-styled complexity.

Cinematic examples of this character complexity in Performer movies are many: Rhett Butler does not join the Confederate army until its cause is obviously and totally hopeless *(Gone with the Wind);* Jimmy Stewart intends to "clean up" the West's most degenerate town as a pacifist sheriff *(Destry Rides Again);* Humphrey Bogart's motives and machinations are so convoluted that even the screenplay's author admits he doesn't know who actually commits one of the film's murders *(The Big Sleep);* and too numerous to mention are the films where the reformed prostitute and the town drunk are the characters of true ethical superiority. Particularly interesting considering the stereotypical notion of his dramatic persona is the character complexity that is written into so many of John Wayne's best "heroic" roles (stretching from *Stagecoach* in 1939 to *The Searchers* in 1956), in which he is variously an outlaw, a racist, a tragic loner, and a very morally ambiguous soul.

For all of the above, though, there are some themes and preoccupations that do consistently cycle around in the films of the Performer era. Taken collectively, they seem to address characteristics that are important in a philosophy made of equal parts intensity, individualism, and survival.

LOVE BETWEEN SOUL MATES

Maybe if I told you a story, you'd change your mind about the dead coming back. Maybe you'd know, as I do, that there is a force that brings them back, if their hearts were wild enough in life.
—Ellen, Wuthering Heights (1939)

The stories of Heathcliff and Catherine, Rhett and Scarlett, and Rick and Ilsa are so well known that often neither their last names nor the movies wherein they appear need be identified. But even in less-famous romances of the period, there is frequently something powerful and larger than life in the apparently fated pairing of these couples. These matches rarely end happily but, thanks to the intensity of the match, there is always the hope of the next life—or a next meeting in Paris. One should never underestimate the Performer preoccupation with love and romance as some sort of key to eternity.

DRAMATIZATION AND STYLE

I don't want realism. I want magic!
—Vivien Leigh as Blanche DuBois, A Streetcar Named Desire (1951)

If one wants to identify the exact instant when the Performers come into being, it is at the moment in *The Wizard of Oz* (1939) when Dorothy's house drops on the wicked witch and everything goes from black and white to Technicolor. To understand Performers is to appreciate their desire to have things vivid. This can and often does refer to character and plot points, but it just as frequently refers to style. The shadows of film noir, the warbled story lines and crazed costuming of musicals, the wide-screen panoramas in Westerns, and the drama of war stories are compelling not because they capture reality but because they enhance mood. Such dramatic overdoing and aggressive preoccupations with style have generally continued to appeal to Performers, as they help make life a bit more vibrant and perhaps also constitute a little laugh at death.

CHEMICAL MOOD ENHANCEMENT

It shrinks my liver, doesn't it Nat? It pickles my kidneys, yeah. But what it
does to the mind. It tosses the sandbags overboard so the balloon can soar.
—**Ray Milland as Don Birnum, *The Lost Weekend* (1945)**

Judging solely from the breadth of its appearance in the popular movies of the era, it would be virtually impossible to overestimate the adult Patriot population's preoccupation with boozing. And despite the strong antidrinking message of the Academy Award-winning film, *The Lost Weekend,* quoted above (which the American liquor industry is reported to have tried to suppress by offering to buy the negatives), one can only come to the conclusion that drinking is something generally done by the good guys. In film after film of the Performer value-formation era, alcohol not only helps to deaden the pain of a bad situation, it makes people absolutely pleasant, funny, cool, spontaneous, and, not infrequently, wise.

In *Casablanca,* the impossibly urbane Rick Blaine (Humphrey Bogart) observes that he doesn't trust people who say "when" if they are being poured a drink, because that means they're dishonest and don't trust themselves being drunk. In *Harvey* (1950), drinking clearly helps the pleasantly addled James Stewart to be both imaginative and kind. This tolerance for alcohol (perhaps "endorsement" is actually the right word) is even extended to the early television era in "charming" skits, such as Lucy's bout with Vitameatavegamin (an alcohol-laden vitamin drink) and Brett Maverick's quotes from "my old pappy," such as "Never cry over spilt milk—it could've been whiskey."

Perhaps the most interesting observation regarding alcohol's influence in the Performer's formative years is that of Margot Fontaine (Bette Davis) in *All about Eve* (1950), when she comments that infants would "get drunk if they knew how." This prescient comment simply fails to take into consideration that Performers were being formed to have their mood alteration and mind expansion take place on the more stimulant rather than depressant end of the spectrum. How could Patriots ever have been shocked when their kids got into pot and LSD? And why would we be surprised that this generation looks for new miracle pills and additives (the Vitameatavegamin without the alcohol) to enhance their lives today?

FATALISM AND A SENSE OF HUMOR

I'm not only a philosopher sir, I'm a fatalist. Somewhere, sometime, there may be the right bullet or the wrong bottle waiting for Josiah Boone. Why worry where or when?

—Doc Boone, *Stagecoach* (1939)

There's a tone to the movies of the Performer era that can only be called philosophical. Unlike the preceding Patriot generation which pretty much collectively knew what it wanted from life (work, security, somewhere to belong), the Performers' intense preoccupation with the individual twists and turns of life against a backdrop of potentially broad and personally inevitable annihilation lends little in the way of common generational goals. It doesn't make a marketer's life any easier, but to understand Performers is to acknowledge the insight that one's personal outlook is everything—and the selection of that outlook is a birthright.

This message comes through in various expressions and appreciations of life's ephemeral nature made throughout the movies of the era. But it is even more apparent in the era's comedy, which at its best is a wry appreciation of how fate and chance can so easily and suddenly turn situations for the better or worse.

Consider the scene in *The Best Years of Our Lives* in which Butch the bartender counsels a young soldier who has returned from the war with prosthetic hands (a role played by an actual war hero who received a special Academy Award for his work in the movie): "Give 'em time kid. They'll catch on. You know, your folks will get used to you, and you'll get used to them. Then everything will settle down nicely, unless we have another war. Then none of us have to worry because we will all be blown to bits in the first day. So cheer up, huh?"

A KID'S LIFE

If you really want to hear about it, the first thing you'll probably want to know is where I was born and what my lousy childhood was like and all that David Copperfield kind of crap, but I don't feel like getting into it, if you want to know the truth.

—Opening lines, J.D. Salinger's *Catcher in the Rye* (1951)

So much is made of the Performer childhood, of the life of material goods, and of the behavioral permissiveness furnished by a generation of doting parents—Patriots—who had just gone through a depression and a war. But even though there is little denying the self-involvement of Performers, the "spoiled brat" analysis is a story told by the Patriot generation, not by Performers themselves. What the Patriots believe to be parental purpose—"produce 'em, feed 'em, school 'em, church 'em, give 'em a nice bike on Christmas, and then they'll hang around to plant the crops, procreate the tribe, and protect the traditions when they're grown up"—is eventually challenged by Performers, not without some reason, as a form of manipulation by a generation with its own shortcomings.

One could call it ingratitude but, unlike Patriots, young Performers are not that interested in the past (especially the recent past with its gas chambers, global war, and nuclear detonations). It is sometimes leveled as a criticism of Performers that they live too much in the moment (and indeed they have not prepared well for retirement, if the truth be told) but from their perspective, neither the past nor future holds anywhere near as much promise, allure and credibility as an interesting, fulfilling and, pun intended, manifested present.

When Performers start having the story told from their point of view in books such as *Catcher in the Rye* (1951) and movies such as *Rebel without a Cause* (1955) and *Blackboard Jungle* (1955), not only is there a lot of poignancy in the protagonists' alienation from the values of the society into which they have been born, but there is also a relentless observation that no adult really listens to them. Rock and roll soon comes along to get the Performers "heard" of course, but the parental response to this "noise" is generally even more outrage and denial. But if one wishes to truly appreciate the more solemn side of growing up as a Performer, one might do well to fully attend to the following bit of dialogue from *Rebel without a Cause:*

> *Planetarium narrator:* "In all the immensity of our universe and the galaxies beyond, the earth will not be missed. Through the infinite reaches of space, the problems of man seem trivial and naive indeed, and man existing alone seems himself an episode of little consequence." (There is a reddish burst of fire, and the show ends.)
>
> *Jim* (James Dean to Sal Mineo, who is hiding under a seat): "It's all over, the world ended."
>
> *Plato* (Sal Mineo, whose busy parents are rarely around except to dole out money): "What does he know about man alone?"

THE PERFORMER IDEAL

With enough courage, you can do without a reputation.
—**Clark Gable as Rhett Butler, *Gone with the Wind* (1939)**

Kiss me. Kiss me as if it were the last time.
—**Ingrid Bergman as Ilsa Lund, *Casablanca* (1942)**

I'm impatient with stupidity. My people have learned to live without it.
—**Klaatu, *The Day the Earth Stood Still* (1951)**

My pa did it the old way and I'm gonna do it the new way.
—**Jimmy Stewart as the pacifist sheriff Tom Destry, *Destry Rides Again* (1939)**

Once more, it is unnecessary to go much further than Oz to understand the ideals that are most precious to Performers. (Interestingly, when *The Wizard of Oz* was released in 1939, it was critically acclaimed but *not* commercially successful. Ahead of its time, the film did not reach "phenomenon" status until young Performers could watch it on television.) The key elements that *Oz* introduces, and which are to hold sway over Performer value definition in movies ranging from *Casablanca* to *Alice in Wonderland* for the next 20 years, include the following:

- *Leaving Home.* There is the familiarity and safety of all the things associated with home. Opposed to these is the call to adventure. Adventure invariably entails danger and sometimes ends badly but, given a sense that life is fleeting and there is much evil to be defeated in the world, the call to adventure wins.
- *Adventure Survival.* Life is an adventure, and the three qualities an individual needs to survive an adventure are: courage, a heart, and a brain. Personal qualities are essential—pedigree is not.
- *Vivid Stimulation.* The land of adventure is invariably more stimulating than one's familiar turf. It is likely to be in Technicolor, and it may very likely include singing munchkins, flying monkeys, mad hatters, or the Gestapo. Stimulation by the vivid and the exotic is a sure sign that you are alive.
- *Fellowship before Authority.* The world is full of scarecrows who deserve closer attention and snake-oil salesmen who pretend to be wizards. Fellowship is always to be valued. Authority is always suspect. Some way, somehow, everyone is interestingly and uniquely acting out a part.

Certainly, Dorothy does come to the tacked-on, Patriot-induced conclusion that there's "no place like home." Yet, the greater Performer truth is revealed in her look of wonder and the excitement of her impending adventure when she realizes she's finally made it "somewhere over the rainbow." To a Performer, Kansas will always be a little disappointingly black and white.

10

THE TECHTICIANS
An Overview

POPULATION OVERVIEW

Age:	Born 1958–1971
Size:	20% of the U.S. Population
Spending:	$1.89 Trillion Annually
Themes:	Science/Speed/Service
Values:	Self-Reliance/Pragmatism

Summary

Techtician (technician + tactician) values derive from a complex mix of social idealism and world-weary cynicism. Born into a world flush with scientific, social, economic and personal potential, some of which did manifest in very positive ways during their value-formation period, the Techticians were ultimately subjected to a degradation of events. President John F. Kennedy invoked outer space as a metaphor for man's unlimited potential for advancement. Unfortunately, advancement did not occur, and the times instead declined in the forms of political assassinations, violent generational confrontations over moral attitudes, and the ethical calamities of the Vietnam War and the Watergate scandal.

While simultaneously disposed toward altruistic acts of service and a cautious, if not cynical, approach toward swallowing too much of anyone's pitch, Techticians now seem to be marked by nothing so much as their pragmatism. They accept few absolutes—relying mainly on "the facts" and a rational process for stringing them together for the benefit of some greater, albeit conditional, good.

> *We choose to go to the moon. We choose to go to the moon in this decade and do the other things, not because they are easy, but because they are hard, because that goal will serve to organize and measure the best of our energies and skills ...*
>
> **—John F. Kennedy**

TECHTICIAN EVENT MATRIX

Hope/Hyperdrive/Chaos and Exhaustion

Hope

The specter of global war fades from cultural prominence as WWII and the Korean War recede into history. Society comes to accept that "peaceful" nuclear standoff between the United States and the Union of Soviet Socialist Republics (USSR) is a far more desirable scenario than no-win mutual destruction.

The energy, enthusiasm, and idealism of youth become the keynotes of U.S. culture, as the post-war babies surge into their adolescence, teen years, and early adulthood. Peace and love have their cultural heyday—in concept anyway.

Idealistic future-oriented political leadership surfaces, particularly during the "Camelot" period of the Kennedy administration (1960–1963). Even after Kennedy's assassination, the Johnson administration continues the "Great Society" drive toward a humanitarian social agenda and a space agenda that lands a person on the moon in 1969.

Hyperdrive

The scientific research advances of military and space technology begin to flood into the private sector. Satellite communications, integrated circuit technology, and commercial jet travel are just some of the developments that alter the speed and orientation of the world. In an historical eye blink, the "Age of Information" is rooted.

Progressive social agendas flood the cultural landscape. The Techtician period witnesses the true birth of the civil rights, antipoverty, feminist, environmentalist, consumer, and peace movements.

Running huge deficits to fund the war in Vietnam, the government spurs the gross national product (GNP) to its greatest period of historical growth ever (a 50 percent increase between 1961–1969). A 15 percent real rise in wages and the advent of revolving credit also aid the rapid economic expansion.

Chaos and Exhaustion

The assassinations of the idealistic and inspirational leaders, John and Robert Kennedy and Martin Luther King, Jr., lead to a feeling of chaos and unrest.

The Vietnam War becomes an enormous political, social, and ethical morass that deeply divides the nation, largely along generational lines (Patriots versus Performers).

The Richard Nixon administration is burdened by a deteriorating postwar economy, and its own sorry ethical stance in the Watergate break-in scandal, ending in Nixon's "I am not a crook" speech.

TECHTICIAN POPULATION VALUES

Self-Reliance

- *Historical drivers.* Self-involved emotional confrontations between Patriots and Performers during Vietnam era; assassination of capable and charismatic leaders such as John F. Kennedy, Robert Kennedy, and Martin Luther King, Jr.
- *Value manifestation.* It is unwise to count on anyone else to make *your* well-being his or her priority. Even the best leaders may let you down.

Service

- *Historical drivers.* The JFK "what you can do for your country" legacy; an era of broad social activism regarding civil rights, environment, consumer protection, etc.; the beginning of the service economy.
- *Value manifestation.* The world is a difficult place in need of improvement. Active commitment to a cause, or just sheer helpfulness, trumps lip service.

Pragmatism

- *Historical drivers.* Inevitable response to the Vietnam War and the cultural excesses of the 1960s; the appeal of the real science underlying the dreams of the space age.
- *Value manifestation.* Results are far more impressive than motivations. One should make the best practical use of people, places, and things, avoiding unnecessary excess if it is not useful.

Data and Logic

- *Historical drivers.* For the first and only time in contemporary history, science is esteemed as a servant of mankind and not just some extension of military affairs; an era of engineering begins to produce marvels throughout society.
- *Value manifestation.* The single most desirable apparatus at one's disposal is a sound piece of information processed by an orderly mind.

Time

- *Historical drivers.* The advent of the Age of Information, commercial jet travel, and the space age.
- *Value manifestation.* What is worth doing probably needs to be done now ... and quickly.

Skill

- *Historical drivers.* The doctrinal certainty of the Patriots and the dramatic self-valuation of the Performers seem too lightly won; contrast to the first landing on the moon—a miracle of preparation and precision.
- *Value manifestation.* Words are cheap. Life is not a dream—practice and heavy lifting are usually required.

Technology

- *Historical drivers.* Satellites, commercial jets, interplanetary probes, moon landings, heart transplants, miracle drugs, microprocessors, etc.
- *Value manifestation.* Techticians were born to be the creators and stewards of the technology boom of the 1990s. "Personal computer" is an apt description of the individual Techtician, reflective of much that is valued here.

Alienation

- *Historical drivers.* Inner cities in turmoil; growing extremes in wealth and poverty; assassination; lack of victory and perceived meaning in Vietnam; technology.
- *Value manifestation.* Beyond the survivalist's awareness of the need for self-reliance is the debate over the existence of God versus the absence of God. Techticians reserve the right to move between the extremes of belief and nonbelief while questing for a sort of objective personal perfection.

Nature

- *Historical drivers.* An enormous upsurge in ecological activity as reflected in phenomena like Earth Day and Rachel Carson's classic book, *Silent Spring;* the cultural balance to technology.
- *Value manifestation.* In many ways, nature becomes the essence of Techtician spirituality, and stewardship of the biosphere the most spiritual of all acts. Natural law is ultimately accepted as a reflection of God's perfection.

TECHTICIAN MACRO INTERESTS

(Life-phase considerations projected through 2012)

Base-Building

Because Techticians understand that a strong building begins with a strong foundation, they are likely to be literal base-builders in terms of employment, income and property ownership, working hard to create long-term foundations for mature life.

Domesticity

Techticians are often ambiguous about traditional family relationships, especially parenting, which frequently strikes them as an irrational "roll of the dice." When considering their roles associated with home life, they tend to think in terms of improvement of people, places, and things.

Issues with Authority

One of the sobering aspects of maturity is learning that you rarely get to be in charge. Ironically, Techticians are mostly disposed to being okay with this because their orientation toward service makes them excellent functionaries in the execution of someone else's larger vision. Nevertheless, Techticians tend to be frank in their estimation of an authority figure's shortcomings, and the outcomes of this social dynamic will be most interesting to see, as will the sort of leadership this Value Population produces.

Living Conditions

In their homes, Techticians appreciate pragmatic conveniences such as electronic compatibility of appliances, office and workshop areas, and good insulation. Natural settings are also usually a plus.

Parents

Rarely disposed toward sentimentality about the plight of the aged, Techticians confronted with the needs of their own aging parents tend nonetheless to be pragmatic and loyal.

Private Life

With maturity often comes an inner-directedness that makes the stresses of dealing with the public world tolerable. Gravitating toward self-improvement activities—from bodybuilding to book clubs, from tap dancing to transcendental meditation—helps Techticians maintain their sanity and stay grounded.

Property

Techticians tend to value the tangible and are likely to want to own "real" property in their maturity. Their adulthood could easily coincide with an upsurge in hard assets rather than financial instruments.

Public Enemies

The fact that an adult generation must confront its common antagonists is often a struggle for Techticians, as they tend to have "value trouble" with moral and ethical absolutes and may tend to see villainy in shades of gray. By the same token, they have little sympathy for self-promoters and self-righteous perpetrators of pain, who are absolutely certain in their cause.

Security—Physical and Spiritual

While broadly reflected in some of the preceding issues, the Techtician propensity for finding reassurance in the rational, the tactile, and the factual bears repeating. One of the emerging macrotrends in today's world is the bridge building going on between science and religion, with scholars on both sides attempting to prove that the hand of God is obvious in the precise mechanics of the natural world. This is a comforting proposition to most Techticians and is useful in understanding what makes the average Techtician feel safe and secure.

Accountability and Accommodation

Another principle of maturity is that one becomes fully accountable for one's decisions and actions. Hoping for the best and expecting the worst may have the ring of truth for the Techticians, who may thus be blessed with an appreciation of, and an accommodation for, life's up and down cycles.

Relaxation for Techticians

High-tech gadgetry, self-improvement projects, reading, physical exercise, activities in nature, domestic projects, walking the dog, games of skill, intelligent conversation, etc.

11

THE TECHTICIANS
History Creating Values

A NEW DEMOGRAPHY

Born between 1958 and 1971, the Value Population we named the Techticians is unique in the field of modern demography. Although major works on generational analysis most often acknowledge that the children of the 1960s arrived during a period unparalleled in its social eccentricity, these works rarely ascribe to this group a value matrix that is uniquely their own. Due in part to the common sociological ideology that a generation is reproductively decreed to last for 20 years, the Techticians are seen either as a second wave of Baby Boomers or as a first wave of Gen Xers.

This unique group, while in some ways an odd hybrid of the selfactualizing Performers and the disenfranchised Believers, is really not best characterized by an understanding of their predecessors or their successors. Along with the Performers, it is one of the two largest Value Populations (hardly a generational afterthought!), the Techticians share among themselves so much more than the vivid self-absorption of the Performers or the hope of rescue that describes the Believers. Ironically, it is the very fact of a society sped up by emergent mass communications, technology, and radical social change that begins to define the Techticians and call into question the appropriateness of double-decade value formation analysis.

SCIENCE, SPEED, AND INFORMATION

One fails to properly understand the Techticians if one fails to emphasize the importance that science and technology play in the era of Techticians' value formation. See Figure 11.1. This Value Population began with an unprecedented bright hope of scientific and social potential. While admittedly the Techtician value-formation story does not have a particularly happy ending, the rush to combine the Techticians' failures and frustrations with that of the following generation as their prevailing keynote, completely and inappropriately diminishes an understanding of the Techticians' real virtues—their pragmatic devotion to accomplishments via rational, detailed, fair-minded, efficient and rollup-your-sleeve endeavors that ultimately seek to facilitate and serve some greater good.

FIGURE 11.1

Scientific and Technological Breakthroughs of the Techtician Era

---

1958 — First transatlantic jet passenger service begins.

1959 — Navy Launches Vanguard Satellite; first integrated circuit s developed by Texas Instruments.

1960 — First working laser is built; Digital Equipment Corporation builds the first microcomputer.

1961 — First American man goes into space; contraceptive intrauterine device is developed.

1962 — First Interplanetary probe reaches Venus; first industrial robot is introduced.

1963 — Quasars are discovered; first liver transplant is performed; sedative Valium is developed.

1964 — U.S. Surgeon General affirms cigarette smoking causes cancer.

1965 — First commercial communication satellite is launched; first American walks in space.

1966 — FDA approves "the Pill" safe for human use; DNA code is fully deciphered.

1967 — World's first successful human heart is transplanted; Pulsars are discovered.

1968 — Largest American petroleum reservoir is discovered in Alaska.

1969 — Scanning Electron Microscope is developed; first humans walk on moon.

1970 — Floppy disk is introduced; bar codes are developed for retail and industrial use.

1971 — Microprocessor is introduced; Mars is orbited and photos reveal its surface.

Source: Family Education Network, Inc.

THE SPACE RACE

With Russia's launch of Sputnik in 1957 and the U.S. launch of Explorer in 1958, the space race was on in earnest. What began as another expression of Cold War competition quickly morphed into something more hopeful—a sense that humanity was living in infinite space and possessed the genius to unlock the productive secrets of technology and push its domain toward the stars. The Mercury and Apollo space programs were important driving forces of the Techtician era, and confidence culminated with the first human landing on the Moon in 1969. This sense of expanding domain also had a political correlative in the granting of statehood to Alaska and Hawaii in 1959.

CIVILIAN JET TRAVEL

At virtually the same historical moment those early satellites were being launched, airlines introduced international and domestic jet service, and the demolishing of New York City's Penn Station in 1963 was the symbolic end of the long-distance passenger rail age. Besides helping to foster the sense that science and technology were capable of lifting people above their earthly limitations, widespread jet travel also stamped this emergent event era with one of its most salient defining characteristics—the need for speed.

Similarly, popular culture began to change its own primary soundtrack from country and pop ballads to the jet-fueled beat of rock and roll. The landmark jet-fighter-inspired tail fins of the 1957 Chevrolet Bel Air are legendary to this day.

INFORMATION TECHNOLOGY
AND THE SERVICE AGE

In 1959, Texas Instruments introduced the first integrated-circuit technology. In 1960, Digital Equipment Corporation built the first minicomputer, and the U.S. Department of Defense literally invented the earliest version of the Internet. In 1962, the first communications satellite was sent into orbit.

These events and other early iconic rumblings of the electronic Age of Information went largely unnoticed by the general population of the time. However, it is important to note that, by as early as 1957, the number of managerial, clerical, and service jobs in the United States had surpassed

FIGURE 11.2

U.S. Service-based Employees Versus Production-based Employees

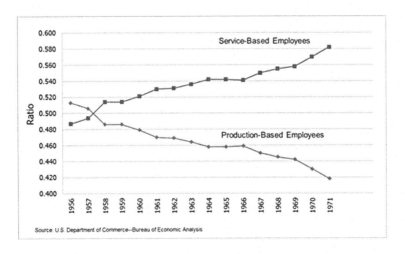

production-based blue-collar jobs. See Figure 11.2. This marked the Techtician era as truly the dawn of the information and service ages.

What did not go unnoticed by the general public was a mass communications device called television. Whereas in 1950, only 9 percent of American households had televisions, by 1960, the household penetration had reached an astounding 87 percent, with the average household set turned on more than five hours per day. See Figure 11.3.

FIGURE 11.3

Average Time Per Day Television Is Turned On and Percentage of Households with a Television Set

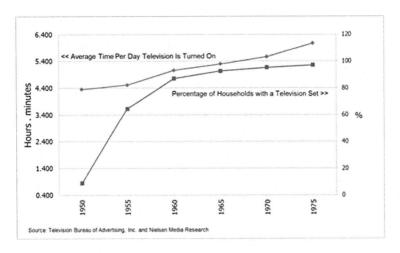

Virtually unavailable at the end of the 1950s, color televisions were in more than half of American households by the end of the Techtician era in 1972. What began as an entertainment novelty quickly became a social force, with the often-cited turning point being the televised 1960 Kennedy/Nixon presidential election campaign debates. Inarguably, among all its other impacts, this new mass medium forever changed the world by speeding up the time frame and vastly broadening the scope of information and experience delivered to the human race.

SOCIAL TURMOIL

Symbolized by the inspired and inspiring leadership of individuals such as John F. Kennedy and Martin Luther King, Jr., the Techtician era began with a profoundly idealistic sense of human potential. It soon became apparent that society's growing infatuation with speed, coupled with the broad access of conflicting interest groups to a mass-media pulpit, was going to severely challenge comprehension and change in U.S. contemporary culture. Ideas, expectations, and agendas were suddenly flying around much faster than people could respond or adapt to, with the result being a severe fracturing of the social mass exemplified by a sad inclination toward acts of confrontation and violence. See Figure 11.4. Although it was a difficult time, it is also important to acknowledge that much vitally important social legislation was enacted during this era.

FIGURE 11.4

U.S. Crime Index Rate

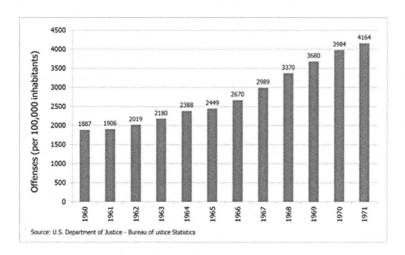

Source: U.S. Department of Justice - Bureau of Justice Statistics

CITIES IN TURMOIL

The broad political and economic policies of the 1950s, which developed highways, encouraged the growth of middle-class suburbs, and directly funded the development of office-tower urban centers and highrise apartment projects, had a devastating effect on the nation's cities. With the destruction of traditional neighborhoods, the decline of the tax base, and the diminishment of municipal services, the poorer classes found themselves deeply disenfranchised drones in the "American Dream." This story has other important aspects, but the bare facts are incontrovertible: riots in Los Angeles' Watts neighborhood caused 34 deaths and $200 million in damages (1965); riots in Newark led to 26 deaths, 1,500 injuries, and 1,000 arrests (1966); riots in Detroit killed 40, injured 2,000, and left 5,000 homeless (1967). And every other major city in the United States was a proverbial powder keg—barely short a match.

Civil Rights

Beyond the poverty and the overcrowding, there was the gut-level issue of racism itself. In the period between the court-ordered integration of schools in Little Rock, Arkansas, at the end of 1957 and the 1963 March on Washington, where Martin Luther King delivered his famous "I Have a Dream" speech, hundreds of thousands of primarily young blacks and whites participated in peaceful protests for racial tolerance and equality. Despite the passage of the Omnibus Civil Rights Bill and significant War on Poverty legislation in 1964, it was not much of a "timestep" from peaceful protest to the radical Black Panther movement, race riots, and the ultimate iconic in-your-face megalomania of "The Greatest," Muhammad Ali.

To society's less liberal members, it seemed as if more than a hundred years of social order was to be eliminated—violently—in the space of a season, and this was more than many could tolerate or accept.

Feminism

In the same year as the March on Washington (1963), the publication of Betty Friedan's Feminine Mystique launched the feminist movement. A contentious and confrontational exploration of perceived sexual inequities and gender-based entitlements, this early feminist activism eventually led to the 1972 passage by the Senate of a constitutional amendment barring gender-based discrimination; however, it was never ratified by the full

Congress. While the real feminist movement would peak during the next Value Population era, that of the Believers, here is where the seeds of the movement that would forever change sexual roles and relationships, perhaps not entirely to anyone's satisfaction, were sown.

Environmentalism

In the same way that Betty Friedan's book launched feminism, Rachel Carson's *Silent Spring*, a polemic against the environmental harm of pesticides, inaugurated the environmentalist movement in 1962. The Techtician era is when humanity realized that population growth and industrial practices were manifestly at odds with ecological survival. A reflection of how important this issue was becoming (some commentators contend that it has always been the single most historically important social issue of the 1960s) was the celebration of Earth Day on April 22, 1970, by 20 million Americans and the subsequent creation of an aggressive Environmental Protection Agency later that same year. It is worth noting that consumerism also got its start in the 1960s, with the publication of Ralph Nader's *Unsafe at Any Speed*, an indictment of the automobile industry, published in 1965. Many of the issues of the consumerists proved to be environmental issues, and the two causes became politically allied.

Vietnam

In terms of Value Population analysis, the Vietnam War was the focal point for a desperate collision between the most fundamentally incompatible values of the Patriots (sacrificial allegiance) and the Performers (sanctity of individual life). Although there is no way that the importance of this conflict (both the real war abroad and the ideological conflict at home) can be over-expressed in the history of the era, the point here is to understand the influence this remote (albeit televised) and confusing war, and the related student protest movement, might have had on the value formation of the Techticians.

Techticians were born into a world where "hawks" (bombastic, cold, manipulative, and clearly materialistic group, arguing an unconvincing "love of country" ideology in the face of enormous American casualties) were opposed by "hippies" (stoned-out, smug, self-indulgent, and anarchical, arguing that "feeling groovy" is the divine law of life). In its negative extreme, the war was not an issue likely to produce any heroes or meaning to an emergent generation, who perhaps best appreciated that the United States did not win this war, honor its participants, or even celebrate its end.

Leadership and Moral Ambiguity

I do not believe that any of us would exchange places with any other
people or any other generation. The energy, the faith, the devotion which
we bring to this endeavor will light our country and all who serve it ...
and the glow from that fire can truly light the world.

—John F. Kennedy, 1963

Without making it sound like too much of a polemic, the fact is the Techtician era begins with the emergence of John F. Kennedy and the immense hope for the future of mankind and concludes with Richard Nixon's humiliating resignation over Watergate, a botched political burglary. Historical perspective has smoothed out the evaluations of these two presidents (Kennedy down some in stature, Nixon up some), but the experience, as lived and as reported on contemporary television, was hardly an uplifting story of human progress.

It is well worth noting that, because of the proliferation of television and the intense image scrutiny it allowed, the mass population had never before in history been so close to its leaders or current events. Partisans of the true social dreamers of the era, most notably John F. Kennedy, Martin Luther King, Jr., and Robert F. Kennedy, lost far more than agenda advocates when these leaders were assassinated; they lost very real presences that stood for hope in their daily lives. In addition, the traits of leaders who were less "telegenic," or less well-spoken, or who simply endorsed less-populist agendas, were magnified into something bordering upon evil.

Having established this, an important part of the story of the Techticians is how the events and dealings surrounding the leaders of their developmental period seem so consistently dishonest and/or tragic. The Warren Commission Report (1964), which found the assassination of John F. Kennedy to be the work of a solitary gunman, was highly suspect even at that time—with even less convincing stories emerging after the murders of Robert Kennedy and Martin Luther King, Jr., both in 1968.

Almost all government-released information related to the war in Vietnam seemed a bit too neatly fabricated, a suspicion that was justly proved in many respects by subsequent historical studies. A recent book on the Lyndon B. Johnson White House reports that, during a discussion of the Gulf of Tonkin incident, a deadly naval confrontation that was the prime justification for the escalation of American troops from "advisor" to "combatant" status in Vietnam in 1964, Johnson is captured on tape as remarking, "For all I know, our Navy was shooting at whales out there."

Ultimately, when it comes to the people in charge of selling or defending their take on events, Techticians tend to find it all a little suspect. In their value-formation period, good leaders came to bad ends, bad leaders came to bad ends, and the assumption of authority, moral or otherwise, is never to be entirely trusted. On their bad days, Patriots may be described as fearful of authority, and Performers can be characterized as contrary for the fun of it, but Techticians really seem to have little choice about authority but to doubt it.

Economic Ambiguity

In terms of gross domestic product, the period between 1961 and 1969 was, on a percentage basis, the strongest growth period in the history of the modern U.S. economy. See Figure 11.5. Not only did real, adjusted-for-inflation, economic output grow by more than 50 percent during these years, but real wages increased by 15 percent. Vietnam may have been an ethical morass, but the huge debts the federal government incurred to fund the war effort, while simultaneously holding the line on new taxes, not to mention the extra stimulative kick given by the advent of the revolving-payment credit card in 1966, proved to be very good for the broad economy.

FIGURE 11.5

U.S. Gross Domestic Product and Percent Annual Change

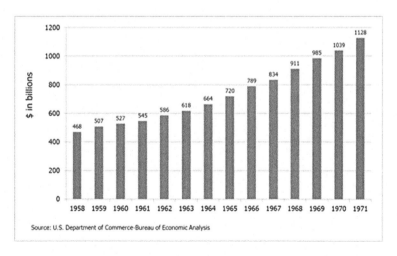

Source: U.S. Department of Commerce-Bureau of Economic Analysis

Nevertheless, by the end of the Techtician period, it was apparent that inflation was likely to become an enormous problem. Initially resistant to devaluation of the dollar and to wage and price controls, in

1971, the Nixon administration finally acquiesced to the issue, but by most accounts, it was too late. What went up in the 1960s was going to come down hard in the 1970s. Although most of the decline is part of the story of the Believer era, Techticians are defined in part by great prosperity turning into gloomy economic writing on the wall.

Perhaps it is fair to surmise that the Techticians primarily have a pragmatic sense that wealth is a facilitator of independence, a tool of personal growth, and an aid to causes, rather than as a guarantor of security, a tool of indulgence, or an emblem of social status (although there is likely some appeal to wealth as a measure of one's "smarts"). To a Techtician, ultimately, financial stability may not be "easy," but it is certainly something to work on.

12

THE TECHTICIANS
Cultural Expressions of an Era

This world is so full of crap, a man's gonna get into it sooner or later,
whether he's careful or not.

—Paul Newman as Hud Bannon, *Hud* (1963)

SOCIETY AND THE INDIVIDUAL:
BEYOND ALIENATION

The single most important difference between the art of the Techtician period and that of its predecessors, the Performers, is that the Techticians' heroes and heroines are represented as much more uncertain about the role of individual passion and personal preference in the affairs of the real world. It is not that Performers are always successful or well integrated into their circumstances, but the solution to social disenfranchisement in Performer terms is generally an acting out of a stronger or different facet of one's personality. What is essentially accepted as self-actualizing drama in the Performer world view, though, veers very close to social pathology in the faster, exponentially more complex, and morally ambiguous universe of the Techtician.

Perhaps the most common protagonist of the Techtician cinema is the social pariah, the individual whose consciousness, characteristics, and/or circumstances make participation in the affairs of "normal" society an unimaginable impossibility. A short list of these indelible Techtician-period characters include the following:

- Norman Bates, *Psycho* (1960), a momma's boy as a homicidal maniac.

- T.E. Lawrence, *Lawrence of Arabia* (1962), a successful warrior but also a dangerous desert madman who sees himself as a latter-day Moses.
- Raymond Shaw, *The Manchurian Candidate* (1962), a brainwashed war hero who is set up by his politically powerful mother to assassinate a presidential candidate. (As an interesting aside, this movie so eerily foreshadowed the Kennedy assassination and its surrounding sense of political subterfuge that the movie's release was suspended and the star, Frank Sinatra, bought all the rights to ensure the movie would not see general release for decades.)
- The Man with No Name, *A Fistful of Dollars* (1967), the ultimate morally ambiguous gunfighter.
- Rosemary Woodhouse, *Rosemary's Baby* (1968), Satan's unwitting concubine and mother of the Antichrist (another ominous foreshadowing, as the film's details of a pregnant woman tortured by a cult came horrifically true for the film's director, Roman Polanski, whose pregnant wife, Sharon Tate, was tortured and murdered by the Charles Manson "family" the following year).
- Captain America, *Easy Rider* (1969), whose decision to drug-deal his way to easy money and drug-take his way to easy enlightenment ends in personal and social tragedy.
- Yossarian, *Catch-22* (1970), a bombardier of questionable mental competence who attempts to flee the insanity of WWII in a rubber raft.
- Alex DeLarge, *A Clockwork Orange* (1971), a murderous sociopath delinquent who is psychologically conditioned (ultimately unsuccessfully) to avoid violence.

For the most part, these characters are not merely romantic loners or alienated outsiders, but individuals who are cast out by the established social framework in the same way that a healthy body rejects a foreign pathogen—violently and frequently with deadly effect. Even when society appears not to have driven the characters to mental incapacity, there is so often an irredeemable incongruity between the values and/or circumstances of the central figures and the societies in which they must perform. Consider Dustin Hoffman as both Ben in *The Graduate* (1967) and as Ratso Rizzo in *Midnight Cowboy* (1969), the doomed lovers Tony and Maria in *West Side Story* (1961), the archetypal bug-squashed "Organization Man" C.C. Baxter in *The Apartment* (1960), or even the wrongly convicted Dr. Richard Kimble of television's *The Fugitive* (1963).

Techticians seem to be not so much interested in the creative power of the ego as they are in its vulnerability to complex social conditions. They are not essentially hopeful and do not believe everyone escapes in the final reel.

Ultimately to Techticians, society may have its positive moments, but, given tendency and enough time, it has an alarming tendency to drive even the strong individual toward insanity, corruption, violence, or despair.

LEADERSHIP AND DOCTRINE: MAY THE FARCE BE WITH YOU

World domination. The same old dream. Our asylums are full of people who think they're Napoleon. Or God.
—Sean Connery as James Bond, Dr. No (1962)

We have to shoot and kill and destroy. We represent everything that's wholesome and good in the world.
—Don Adams as Maxwell Smart, Get Smart (1965)

Ample mention of the Techticians' mistrust of political leaders and their self-serving, socially menacing tactics and agendas has been made earlier in this book, so the point will not be overly elaborated upon here. It is worth mentioning, however, that certainly one of the richest thrusts of the popular art of the Techtician period is the excoriation of political leaders, their methods, and their doctrinal beliefs. This is sometimes handled with thoughtful sensitivity in such great historical dramas as *Inherit the Wind* (1960), *A Man for All Seasons* (1966), and *The Lion in Winter* (1968), but the typical tone of the period is satire and farce.

Indicative are movies such as *One, Two, Three* (1961), *A Funny Thing Happened on the Way to the Forum* (1966), and *The Producers* (1968), the latter two starring Zero Mostel in the originals and both enjoying successful Broadway revivals with the Techtician audiences of today. Much popular television fare at the time employed satire and farce, including *F Troop* (1965), *Get Smart* (1965), *Hogan's Heroes* (1965), *The Monkees* (1965), and particularly, the BBC's *Monty Python* (1969). Perhaps the greatest work ever in this thematic vein, however, is Stanley Kubrick's *Dr. Strangelove* (1964), a dark comic treasure trove of over-the-top leaders and knuckleheaded statesmen whose actions resulted in the destruction of the world via a largely mechanical nuclear-retaliatory disaster.

In summary, Techticians have reservations about society at large—reservations that naturally extend to the individuals who seek to govern that society. For those whose interests run toward organizational dynamics and/or mass marketing, it is worth keeping in mind that the Techticians may not be the first to embrace the wisdom emanating from the executive suite or the first to raise their hand in a salute to the flag—any flag.

THE DOMAIN(S) OF DHARMA

There's nothing wrong with you Ray; your only trouble is you never
learned to get out of spots like this; you've let the world drown you in its
horseshit and you've been vexed ...

—Jack Kerouac, *The Dharma Bums* (1958)

Just because Techticians often feel they are denied meaningful personal integration into a "crazy" world created by their predecessors in no way automatically implies they have abandoned the search for personal peace and enlightenment. On the contrary, although the search often comes at a cost in social terms, many Techticians are concerned (consciously and unconsciously) with finding their *dharma*—roughly translated as one's appropriate place and sustaining characteristics within the totality of the universe.

It is remarkable that Jack Kerouac, the same author who so forcefully captures the spiritual essence of the Performers in his book, *On the Road* (written in the early 1950s, published in 1957), is so elegantly attuned to the different spiritual vibration of the Techticians in his 1958 work, *The Dharma Bums*. The former work is an exuberant tribute to the intoxicating glory of the unfettered ego let loose in an immense physical and spiritual realm of personal creative freedom. The far more devotional and precise second work suggests that the least among us, even if literally bums, may fulfill a spiritual duty greater than our own by surrendering their "vexed" egos to appropriate places of peace and performance within the immensity of consciousness.

As abstract and esoteric as this may sound, it is very helpful in appreciating the quest of Techticians to find some places of peace—and actually, there turn out to be a few.

NATURE

The human beings believe everything is alive. But the white man believes
everything is dead.

—Old Lodge Skins, *Little Big Man* (1970)

The hippie "flower people" sometimes made an appreciation of nature seem saccharin and dopey as heck, and the budding environmentalist movement sometimes made nature seem like just another battlefield. However, there is also an important spiritual aspect to this awareness of nature's primacy that serves Techticians to this day. In a value system so heavily influenced by technology and the urge to speed things up, and amidst general cultural commotion, it is not surprising that many Techticians would grow up to find a restorative sense of peace, righteousness, and order in nature. In the seminal movie *Easy Rider* (1969), a very downbeat vision of an American youth/drug culture that had cashiered its idealism, the only genuine admiration expressed is for the people who are working the land. And it is in a small cabin on Desolation Peak that the protagonist of *The Dharma Bums* eventually finds ecstasy through immersion in the nature all around him.

THE LOGICAL MIND

In a child's ability to master the multiplication table, there is more holiness than in all your shouted hosannas and holy holies.
—**Spencer Tracy as Henry Drummond, *Inherit the Wind* (1960)**

"Thank heavens!"
"Mr. Scott, there was no deity involved. It was my cross-circuiting to B that recovered them."
—**Exchange between Scotty and Mr. Spock, *Star Trek* (1966).**

They're awful hard to buy for. Besides it was something they could use.
—**Don Knotts as Barney Fife (explaining why he bought his parents a septic tank as an anniversary gift),**
***The Andy Griffith Show* (1960)**

From the most mundane daily activities to the most abstruse technological challenges, pragmatism and rational thought provide the average Techtician great comfort and strength. Brought up in an era that seemed to be spinning off its axis in so many literal and figurative ways, the Techticians have generationally embraced functionality and its helpmates, efficiency and precision. Even while people, events, abstractions, and causes were failing and perplexing them, the Techticians discovered that physical principles remained comfortingly constant and good old "two plus two" could reliably be counted on to equal four.

In general, the popular art of the Techtician value-formation period exhibits great admiration for science and technology. This ranges from lighthearted amusement with gizmos and inventions in movies, such as *The Absent-Minded Professor* (1961) and *The Nutty Professor* (1963), to a fond appreciation for stirring science adventure in movies like *Journey to the Center of the Earth* (1961) and *Fantastic Voyage* (1966), to deep fascination with the complex technical gadgetry and plots of the James Bond movies (which premiered with *Dr. No* in 1963), to absolute devotion to the amazingly thoughtful, ambitious, and influential *Star Trek* (first released on television in 1966 and still running strong today). Other technological "fascinations" of the period range from Scientology, a highly structured, mind-based religious system that had its first great burst of prominence during the Techtician value-formation period, to the so-called "Marvel Age of Comics" in which comic book genius Stan Lee explored (via characters such as Spider-Man and The Hulk) both the awesomeness and the angst of technology-based superhuman transformations in "normal" people.

While hardly an unmitigated endorsement of a technological and rational value system, the movie *2001: A Space Odyssey* (1968) deserves a brief mention here. When it first came out, the contemporary (Performer) audience largely rejected it as aloof and cerebral, complaining that the only fully developed character was Hal, the supposedly "infallible" computer that adapts human self-preservation traits and murders most of the crew on its space mission. What is interesting is that the movie eventually achieved its enormous popularity in a series of re-releases between 1975 and 1982, when the Techticians were movie-going teenagers.

SERVICE

Ask not what your country can do for you, ask what you can do for your country.

—John F. Kennedy (1961)

Ah chrysanthemums. Such serviceable flowers.

—Maggie Smith as Jean Brodie, *The Prime of Miss Jean Brodie* (1969)

Of all the overlooked virtues of this overlooked generation, likely the most significant to the world's well-being is the Techticians' willingness to perform service. In many demographic analyses, Generation X either receives sympathy or catches mild disdain for being drafted into the worker-bee positions of the service economy. However, it is the Techticians' value conditioning that makes them well suited to the acknowledgment that self-sacrificing service is an unimpeachable good.

Unlike Patriots (who may give blindly loyal service to the causes of their clan), or Performers (who may render service for the glory),

Techticians possess a sense of service that is more situational and coolly efficient. Their innate sense of empathy for personal dilemma allows them a special gift for recognizing the need for unconditional help. Pragmatic by nature, they give service as, and in the amount, it is needed.

If this sounds overly abstract, remember that the popular art of the Techtician value-formation period rewards those who give remarkable service with special powers and protections. Such is the case with the "practically perfect" *Mary Poppins* (1964), the odds-beating, town-saving *Magnificent Seven* (1960), the always-surviving galactic "good scouts" of the Starship Enterprise, and the world's ultimate, world-saving Secret Service agent, James Bond.

Perhaps the most memorable example of the true heart of spiritual and selfless service appears in the documentary *A Night to Remember* (1958), when the officers of the Titanic, facing certain personal doom, do their best to load the lifeboats, while equally dedicated chamber musicians play to their deaths in a gesture of peace amidst panic and despair.

RELIGION

Almost at the moment he died, he said, "Father forgive them, for they know not what they do." Even then, and I felt his words take the sword from my hand!

—**Charlton Heston as Judah Ben-Hur, *Ben Hur* (1959)**

This is madness, my Lord. Don't do it. I could not serve both God and you.

—**Richard Burton, as Thomas Becket (advising the king not to make him archbishop),**

***Becket* (1964)**

I'm not a beatnik. I'm a Catholic.

—**Jack Kerouac, in a *New York Times* article—Joseph Lelyveld, October 22, 1969.**

There is evidence of a meaningful religious urge in the Techticians. They exhibit not so much an involvement with the mysteries of faith or divine love but rather a profound intellectual appreciation of God's manifest perfection. In a world so full of compromised leadership, moral equivocation, false doctrine, selfish materialism, and general tribulation, God remains for many Techticians the only conceivable source of truth, authority, and enlightenment.

Needless to say, this does not always bode well for society, as the human corruption that manifests itself in the name of God is often the most pernicious of evils. This is amply demonstrated in the brilliant 1960 movie *Inherit the Wind,* in which religious fundamentalism faces off against science in a confrontation that still fascinates Techticians to this day. Nevertheless, one shouldn't overlook the Techticians' urge to understand and serve some greater good. Compelling movies of the Techtician value-formation period, including *Ben-Hur* (1959), *Spartacus* (1960), *Barabbas* (1962), *Becket* (1964), *Godspell* (1971—Broadway; 1973—movie), and *Jesus Christ Superstar* (1971—Broadway; 1973—movie), demonstrate that there is no greater good to serve than God.

WHAT'S LOVE GOT TO DO WITH IT?

I find the moment that a woman makes friends with me, she becomes jealous, exacting, suspicious, and a damned nuisance. And I find the moment that I make friends with a woman, I become selfish and tyrannical. So here I am, a confirmed old bachelor, and likely to remain so.

—Rex Harrison as Professor Henry Higgins, My Fair Lady (1964)

Women! I could have conquered all of Europe, but I had women in my life!

—Peter O'Toole as Henry II, The Lion in Winter (1968)

"You're NOT a girl! You're a GUY!
Why would a guy wanna marry a guy?"
"Security."

—Tony Curtis and Jack Lemmon as Joe and Jerry, Some Like It Hot (1959)

Traditional romantic love comes in for fairly shoddy treatment in the value system of the Techticians, Doris Day notwithstanding. This was exemplified by the rise of feminism, the contemporary overthrow of many social traditions and cultural taboos, the conflicting demands and options of modern life, and the commercial need for cinema to differentiate itself from family-oriented television.

Further examination of social issues, among them the simple truths regarding love, sex, and relationships, reveals the Techticians' view that just because something is biological doesn't necessarily make it logical. See Figure 12.1.

Notwithstanding romantic love, some of the breakthrough "romantic" preoccupations of the Techtician-era cinema include the following:

- *Homosexuality: Some Like It Hot* (1959), *Spartacus* (1960), *The Boys in the Band* (1970)
- *Incest: Lolita* (1962)
- *Impotence: Bonnie and Clyde* (1967)
- *Mixed marriages: Guess Who's Coming to Dinner* (1967), *Harold and Maude* (1971)
- *Prostitution: Midnight Cowboy* (1969) (the only X-rated film to ever win the Best Picture Oscar)
- *Confirmed bachelorhood/spinsterhood: My Fair Lady* (1964), *The Odd Couple* (1968), *The Prime of Miss Jean Brodie* (1969)
- *Adultery: The Graduate* (1967), *Bob & Carol & Ted & Alice* (1969), *Carnal Knowledge* (1971)

In addition, several mother-son relationships of the era seem to have been taken from a term paper on Freud and written by Satan (or vice versa). *Psycho* (1960), *The Manchurian Candidate* (1962), *The Birds* (1963), *Bye Bye Birdie* (1963), *My Fair Lady* (1964), *Who's Afraid of Virginia Woolf?* (1966), with its imaginary son, but no less powerful for that, and *Harold and Maude* (1971), among others, are all films that feature mothers who intend to keep a stranglehold on their sons' lives, most particularly their romantic interests. Although explaining this should truly be the work for a psychiatrist, not social-trends historians, it is hard to ignore the cinematic proliferation of would-be emasculating mothers in the Techtician value-formation era.

FIGURE 12.1

U.S. Divorce Rates

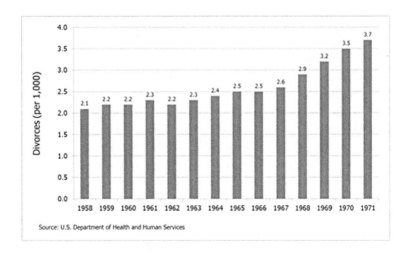

Source: U.S. Department of Health and Human Services

Finally, it is hard to resist mentioning the television introduction of *The Newlywed Game* (1966). The show's major draw was the tension that developed between competing and frequently belligerent newlyweds who discovered all the comical (to the audience) ways in which they were emotionally incompatible and clueless about one another. This popular, long-running show demonstrates clearly the Techticians' largely dispassionate perception of Cupid.

COMMERCE: THE NECESSARY EVIL

It's real hard to be free when you are bought and sold in the marketplace.
—Jack Nicholson as George Hanson, *Easy Rider* (1969)

He's got 92 credit cards in his wallet. The minute anything happens to him, America lights up.
—Walter Matthau as Oscar Madison, *The Odd Couple* (1968)

There was a time when I used to get lots of ideas. I thought up the Seven Deadly Sins in one afternoon. The only thing I've come up with recently is advertising.
—Peter Cook as The Devil, *Bedazzled* (1967)

By now it should be clear that Techticians are both pragmatic and wary of the prevailing socioeconomic system. Furthermore, as discussed earlier, their values formed in an era of remarkable debt-financed affluence, albeit one that eventually spiraled into painful inflationary recession. See Figure 12.2. Many Techticians, therefore, experience inner conflict when it comes to the notion of amassing wealth. The obvious benefits of good material fortune in terms of personal autonomy in the present and future play off against the broad spiritual and social costs of collectively worshipping a demonstrably mean and fickle golden idol.

As a brief aside, it is extremely useful to note that many, if not most, of the individuals who saw their options-laden/day-trading ships about to come in during the technology boom of the 1990s were Techticians. Then this same group watched these vessels sink as the tech bust suddenly hit with the fury of a typhoon. A useful defining characteristic of the realist Techticians is their "what goes up must come down" attitude toward this turn of events. This same storm manifested as panic in the Patriots and heroic poise in the Performers.

Although judgments regarding matters of commerce are not all negative in the popular art of the Techtician-formation period, the most singularly consistent and arresting trend of this period is a pronounced and growing sympathy for the criminal adversaries of capitalism, i.e., thieves. They may reach bad ends, but everyone in the theatre roots for, or at least admires, the crooks in movies such as *Bonnie and Clyde* (1967), *The Producers* (1968), and *Butch Cassidy and The Sundance Kid* (1969). In other movies, including *How to Steal a Million* (1966) and *The Thomas Crown Affair* (1968), not only are the thieves cool, they also get away with their crimes!

FIGURE 12.2

U.S. Real Weekly Wages

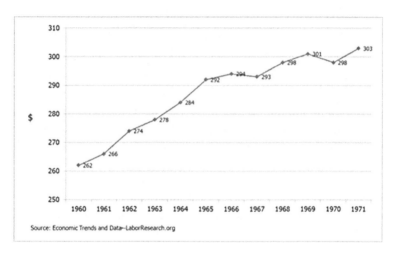

Source: Economic Trends and Data—LaborResearch.org

That this trend toward rooting for the bad guys is an antisocial attitude is not lost on the Techticians. Nevertheless, the notion of "antisocial" is as much a dark comic thought as a cause for concern to the Techticians. Surely, a group as assaulted by moral ambiguity, social chaos, and failed leadership in their value-formation period is not entirely above the belief that ends justify means—a notion worth keeping in mind if one's own commerce involves them.

THE TECHTICIAN IDEAL

Anything can be great. I don't care, brick laying can be great if a guy knows what he's doing and why, and if he can make it come off.

—Paul Newman as Fast Eddie Felson, *The Hustler* (1961)

There are some men in this world who are born to do our unpleasant jobs
for us.
Your father's one of them.
—Maudie Atkinson, *To Kill a Mockingbird* (1962)

Let me help. A hundred years or so from now, I believe, a famous novelist
will write a classic using that theme. He'll recommend those three words
over 'I love you'.
—Capt. James T. Kirk, *Star Trek* (1966)

I am putting myself to the fullest possible use, which is all I think that any
conscious entity can ever hope to do.
—Hal the Computer, *2001: A Space Odyssey* (1968)

To be blunt, there probably is no such thing as a Techtician ideal. An ideal is an abstraction that implies absolute principles, and there is something about a belief-based system that repels Techticians more than any other Value Population. Rendered virtually incapable of reconciling a smooth fit between the fulfillment of the individual and the conditions of society, Techticians are most likely to accept that the system is flawed and that they don't comfortably "fit in."

Having established this conditionality, however, there is no denying the Techticians' high regard for individuals who do their personal best under whatever circumstances they happen to find themselves. Many of the "outsider" roles of Paul Newman come to mind, including that of the pool hustler in *The Hustler* (1961), the convict in *Cool Hand Luke* (1967), and the train robber in *Butch Cassidy and the Sundance Kid* (1969). In all of these characters, no diminishment of will or skill occurs in the face of harsh personal conditions and an unjust authoritarian society. To the Techtician, that's exactly what makes a good guy.

Although there is often a hint of vivid Performer egoism about them, the fictional heroes of the Techtician value-formation period most often derive their essential essences from performing their actions, often at mortal risk, for the benefit of someone or something other than themselves. James Bond gets the cool toys and the babes; Capt. Kirk and Mary Poppins both get to fly; Spider-Man gets web throwers, a neat-looking suit, and superpowers. The key to their heroic drives is that they all are in service to human needs greater than their own personal happiness or survival. The fact is rendered even more poignantly in Gregory Peck's Atticus Finch in *To Kill a Mockingbird* (1962). Here, the defense of an unjustly accused black man puts a white Southern lawyer's own family at mortal risk. Of course, those brave, doomed officers and musicians on the Titanic in *A Night to Remember* (1958) will always come to mind.

Although films such as *Dr. Strangelove* (1964), *2001: A Space Odyssey* (1968) and *A Clockwork Orange* (1971) demonstrate that science is not the cure-all for the world's problems, Techticians firmly hold the belief that reasoned analysis abetted by technology have to be ultimately more helpful to mankind than the crazed ambiguities of life on the planet as it now stands.

In many ways, the Techtician ideal is best summed up by Charlton Heston as George Taylor in *Planet of the Apes* (1968): "I'm a seeker too. But my dreams aren't like yours. I can't help thinking that somewhere in the universe there has to be something better than man. Has to be."

13

THE BELIEVERS
An Overview

POPULATION OVERVIEW

Age: Born 1972–1983
Size: 16% of the U.S. Population
Spending: $1.24 Trillion Annually
Themes: Withdrawal/Watergate/Women
Values: Relationship/Diplomacy

Summary

It is tempting to dismiss Believers as victims of a bad patch of history and to simply offer generational condolences. Certainly, Believer value formation takes place in an era of broad political, economic, and social dissolution, and there is hardly a more representative phrase than "power outage" to describe the general tone of the times. But to be frank, the term "power outage" is a common aspect of the characteristic Believer personality. What makes the Believers such a fascinating group, however, is an appreciation of the skills they develop to cope with and survive the issues posed by such a low-wattage value-formation period. Along these lines, some of the defining qualities of Believers include empathy, patience and, perhaps most importantly, the faith that rescue may be near at hand. To some observers, the idea that things are simply going to get better of their own accord may seem rather naïve and escapist, but the overriding "truth" of the Believer value-formation period is that, at its darkest hour, the Ronald Reagan administration comes along and things suddenly do get better. Grace, Believers seem to inherently know, can arrive only if one makes room in the spirit for its possibility.

BELIEVER EVENT MATRIX

Exhaustion/Downturn/Rescue

Exhaustion

America's effort to extricate itself from the Vietnam War finally succeeds with withdrawal of ground troops in 1972, but the result of retreat is fatigue, anxiety, and cultural malaise, rather than relief and celebration.

The OPEC oil embargo of 1973 highlights a historically unprecedented year of energy shortage problems punctuated by brownouts, restrictive fuel allocations, service-station gas-pump lines, and rapidly escalating oil prices—this coupled with "defeat" in Vietnam reveals extraordinary U.S. vulnerability to external powers.

A decade-long political leadership vacuum is initiated by the Watergate scandal in 1972 and Nixon's resignation in 1974.

Downturn

After the boom of the 1950s and 1960s, the Believer period is marked by a weak economy, including recessionary gross domestic product (GDP) periods, a flat stock market, historically high loan defaults, and "stagflation" (high inflation with little job growth).

Social dysfunction becomes systemic with huge rises in abortions, unwed mothers, divorces, latchkey kids, and school dropouts. Concurrently, the so-called "Me Generation" is symbolized by a debauched club-and-cocaine culture and a pervasive attitude of self-righteous self-gratification.

Adding to this downturn is "America Held Hostage," CNN's relentless coverage of the Iranian hostage crisis, when 63 U.S. citizens are held for 444 days (11/1979–1/1981) at the U.S. embassy in Tehran, and all negotiations and rescues fail.

Rescue

Ronald Reagan's persona, perhaps more than his policies, symbolizes the return of the absent father to a society in need of a strong hand on the social rudder.

Although the economy weakens during Reagan's first years in office, inflation finally abates, unemployment peaks in 1982, and a turnaround begins in 1983. Deficit spending, lower interest rates, and a tax increase to preserve social security are an odd mix of "fixes," but they work.

The Iranian hostages are released and the country takes heart from feel-good news, such as the first launch of the space shuttle (1981), the first woman U.S. Supreme Court Justice (1981), and the first woman in space (1983)—and on a symbolic level, a military victory in Grenada (1983).

BELIEVER POPULATION VALUES

Friendship and Love

- *Historical drivers.* Crushing social trends related to the family including rising divorce rates, abandonment by fathers, and unwed mothers; drug usage; difficult economic times for many; children given short shrift in public policy.
- *Value manifestation.* The best way to emotionally navigate dark times is with empathic friends in the same boat. Love between kindred spirits is life's ultimate reward.

Suspicion of Leaders

- *Historical drivers.* The Nixon, Ford, and Carter administrations cast doubts on motives and effectiveness of traditional leadership; negative father-image trends.
- *Value manifestation.* You may have to accept the bosses, but you don't have to believe they know what they are doing.

Feminism

- *Historical drivers.* The 1970s represent the move of feminist principles from theory to practice; politics, business, the arts, and many traditionally male-dominated fields experience an influx of female talent and leadership; *Ms. Magazine; Roe v. Wade;* Charlie's Angels.
- *Value manifestation.* Never send a man to do a woman's job.

Peace and Diplomacy

- *Historical drivers.* The post-Vietnam era ushers in a period of conflict avoidance; Anti-Ballistic Missile Treaty with Russia; trade relations with China; Carter-led Israel-Egypt peace talks.
- *Value manifestation.* The world periodically wearies of war—it causes great pain and doesn't promise much of a future. Peace seems so much easier and talking less messy.

Comfort and Ease

- *Historical drivers.* Resource deprivation is a reality throughout society; inflation and job growth stagnation dominate the downbeat economic feeling of the times; crime-riddled New York City—the great symbol of capitalism—declares bankruptcy.
- *Value manifestation.* It is not the same as the abject material want of the Great Depression, but the deprived state of the Believer value-formation era fosters a healthy respect for having enough ... and for locating a nice place to enjoy it.

Justice

- *Historical drivers.* The resignation of Richard Nixon over the Watergate scandal; landmark Supreme Court women's rights cases and the appointment of the first woman Supreme Court justice; peace and arms control treaties instead of armed conflict.
- *Value manifestation.* Peoples rights are important. Tyranny is the use of force when fairness is not even considered as an available option.

Patience

- *Historical drivers.* Energy shortages and gas lines; 55 mph national speed limit; 444-day "America Held Hostage" crisis in Iran.
- *Value manifestation.* Sometimes problems are resolved overnight, but probably not this night.

Grace

- *Historical drivers.* Eventual release of the Iranian hostages; uptick in emotional milieu and economic fortunes during the Reagan administration; presidential pardons of Nixon and Vietnam draft dodgers.
- *Value manifestation.* One must never lose hope and faith, for rescue may be near at hand, and it would be a shame not to have left a light on.

Art

- *Historical drivers.* Tough times breed a strong strain of hopeful *Star Wars/Superman/Raiders of the Lost Ark* escapism; design trends move away from modernism towards humanism; love as redemption becomes a central theme in literature; dancing and the romantic ballad make a return.
- *Value manifestation.* Creativity can be a type of hopeful transcendence. It gives mankind the ability to write happy endings, even if they just occur in the imagination.

BELIEVER MACRO INTERESTS

(Life-phase considerations projected through 2012)

Children

Believers have a complicated generational outlook regarding kids. Having had their values formed in an era of broad parental and social dysfunction, many Believers will decide that life has far more satisfying and less stressful purposes than parenthood. By the same token, many Believers could decide that their greatest personal achievement might be an enlightened and enthusiastic attitude toward offspring (their own and others). Stay tuned!

Communication

Believers' emergence into adulthood has ramifications for both the form and content of communications in our society. On a very obvious level, this is a population that has been exposed to interactive computer-driven electronic media from a very early age and seems to prefer participation to passive reception (e.g., chat rooms to newspapers). The key is communication that breeds active community, even if narrowly defined as pertaining only to Believers themselves.

Local Gathering Places

Believers, who prize community, are entering the gathering places of the adult world with a fair amount of enthusiasm. They appear to like the courtship places (restaurants, clubs), the cultural places (museums, theaters), the consumer places (malls, contemporary metro centers), and anywhere they can collectively kick back and be comfortable. While style definitely does matter, environments that appeal tend to emphasize ease over edginess.

Ideas and Learning

To hear some college professors tell it, Believers are a uniquely uninspired and uninspiring group of scholars. But one must consider: 1) Believers formed their values in an era of political, social, cultural, and economic enervation that has led to a generational indifference toward the potency of institutional wisdom; and 2) Believers have a fondness for the sort of learning that allows things to seem better than they are. Call it "art," but the real key is that too much reality, rationalism, and regulation tend to poison the potential of a good rescue fantasy. In all, Believers are far less likely than Techticians to worship at the altar of scientific empiricism.

Neighbors

As Believers move into their first apartments and starter homes, it is interesting to observe how inherently wary many of them are of neighbors. Capable of being quite sociable and respectful of community, Believers are nevertheless very protective of their own need for recuperative privacy and dislike being vulnerable to the implicit aggression of neighbors whose music is too loud, whose cooking smells too pungent, or whose demands for Scout cookie sales is too incessant. Whatever their personal behavioral tastes, Believers, more than any other Value Population (except maybe Patriots), need to be among like-minded and like-valued neighbors.

News

Value Populations entering adulthood suddenly come to realize that news is something that involves them on a participatory and reactive basis, rather than just being something that pertains to their parents and other adult populations. Yet, despite the difficult situation of the world today, Believers may be very value-inclined to not pay too much attention to "hard" news, preferring to keep an illusion of equanimity through a devotion to the features aspects (celebrities, fashions, entertainment, etc.) of the news. This could be their Achilles' heel, but Believers have faith that it won't be.

Offices and Office Workers

Believers tend to bring a very particular set of personal requirements to the workplace, especially regarding a preference for order, peace, and harmony in the environment. Ironically, this is sometimes frustrating to managers of other Value Populations, who view business as a battlefield and are far more willing to prize urgency and competitiveness over tranquility. But such managers should be wary of jamming their Believer colleagues' very sensitive radars.

Restlessness

For a Value Population that had the enormous economic promise of the late 1990s as a background to its school years, the less generous reality of the early twenty-first century is quite the disappointment. Given their smaller numbers and the boom in the economy, Believers were brought up believing that their hardest choice would be which great job offer to take. Unfortunately, after they had a few years of work under their belts, they were confronted with a national malaise similar to that of their birth years, and the specter of dissipation again looms.

Independent Contractors Not Company People

Entering the workforce, Believers offer their employers an odd mix of artistic entrepreneurism and an ability to fit comfortably into an orderly environment. Even though they bring a lot of potential grace to impersonal institutions, polls of Believer college students indicate they are not interested in joining those large organizations, which are, after all, too impersonal.

Vehicles

Just as media started to become less "mass" and more individually interactive with the advent of Believers, the reign of the American automobile industry was challenged by a slew of foreign imports selling individual feature benefits rather than vested brand loyalty. While Believers can sometimes follow a fashion with the best of them, it is with this generation that the notion of loyalty to a particular automobile brand is likely dead as an Edsel.

Relaxation for Believers

Believers enjoy activities of courtship and socialization, both in person and electronically. All work and no play make Jack a dull boy—or at least not part of the in crowd. The desire to maintain personal peace and equilibrium often manifests in the desire to go off by oneself to pursue some reflective personal pleasure or to just tune out.

14

THE BELIEVERS
History Creating Values

Traditional Generation X analysis tends to lump the value-formation events of the 1960s and 1970s together. Certainly, issues of failed leadership and broad social disruption are common to both eras. However, there are key and crucial differences to these periods that are not easily glossed over by traditional reliance on a 20-year generational cycle that begins at the end of a birth rate boom and bust cycle.

POWER OUTAGE (1972–1982)

First and foremost, it is not simply an abstraction to point to the widely dissimilar—actually *opposite* is not too strong a term—energy levels of the two periods. Whereas the dynamic Techtician era is characterized by an enormous amount of intellectual, political, and societal engagement with breakthrough technological advances and economic robustness, the far less vigorous Believer period is a time of limited energy (both actual and political), flagging economic hope, and a pervasive sense of social ennui and isolation. It is as if a switch is turned off at the beginning of the Believer period (symbolically, in 1973, the White House decides not to light the national Christmas tree as an energy saving measure), and the nation embarks on a restless national nap in which the cultural emphasis switches from "save the world" to "save anything you can."

The two events that most dramatically demarcate entrance into the Believer period are Watergate (1972–1974) and the withdrawal of all combat troops from Vietnam (1972). While the impact of both events as challenges to political and ethical consciousness have been discussed as part of the Techticians' value-formation time frame, the significance of these events is different for Believers. In the case of Watergate, the federal government's immersion in the political scandal, which culminates with the resignation of President Nixon (1974), precipitates an era in which the United States is beset with extremely ineffectual leadership (including the Ford and Carter administrations which *seem* somehow absent in office). In regard to military withdrawal, the country discovers that the costs, both financial and psychological, of involvement in Vietnam are largely to be felt as debt, apathy, and alienation in the war's aftermath.

The sense of the times as "running on empty" is not at all abstract or far-fetched in light of the very real resource shortages related to an OPEC oil embargo (1973), an OPEC price manipulation that doubles the price of a barrel of oil (1979), the perceived failure of nuclear energy (most dramatically evidenced by the partial meltdown of a reactor at Three Mile Island in 1979), and a worldwide food production crisis (lasting most of the 1970s).

ECONOMIC WOES: THE LIMITS OF GROWTH AND STAGFLATION (1972–1983)

In the landmark book, *The Limits of Growth* (1972), an influential team of economic, environmental and population scholars argue that there is no way the world economy can sustain a boundless rate of development. The "prophecy" seems to come true almost immediately, as energy shortages and recession curb growth around much of the globe. In the United States, the period, further exacerbated by the debt of the Vietnam war and a reduction in military spending, is punctuated by recessionary decreases in the real GDP (1974, 1975, 1980, 1982), a virtually flat stock market (1965–1982), the loan default of America's capitol of capitalism, New York City (1975), and, quite important symbolically, the establishment of a national 55 mph speed limit (1974).

While economic historians are still arguing over who deserves the blame for the darkened economy (as well as who deserves the credit for the eventual recovery), the key economic reality of the Believer period becomes stagflation, a confusing and pernicious period of rising prices unexpectedly coupled with little or no job growth. The Misery Index (a sum of the inflation rate and the unemployment rate) breaks 11 for the first time in post-World War II history in 1973, rises rapidly to a peak of 20.7 in 1980, and does not return to under 12 until the first year of the Transformers' value-formation period in 1984. At their worst, interest rates hit 20 percent in 1980, and the unemployment rate jumps to 10.8 percent at one point during 1982. In 1979, the consumer price index jumps 13.3 percent, the largest one-year rise in more than three decades. See Figure 14.1.

The economy, like the public mood, is simply overwhelmed and exhausted.

THE IRONY OF PEACE

The Believer Value Population is the first modern generation to live through a value-formation period in which the United States does not have a significant number of troops involved in a military conflict abroad. In fact, it can be persuasively argued that the most outstanding accomplishments of the Believer era, certainly as far as the United States is concerned, are its contributions to conflict containment and world peace. During the Nixon administration, the war in Vietnam ends (in 1972 troops are withdrawn, and in 1973 bombing stops), relations are "normalized" with China (1972), a strategic arms limitation treaty is signed with Russia (1972), and the military draft is eliminated (1973). Jimmy Carter's landmark Middle East diplomacy leads to the Camp David accords and a Nobel Peace Prize for Anwar al-Sadat, the President of Egypt and Menachem Begin, the Prime Minister of Israel (1978).

Despite these considerable accomplishments, the national feeling seems to be one of anxiety and vulnerability rather than calm control. In addition to the emotional aftermath of Vietnam, America's first lost war, the nation learns how vulnerable its economy is to foreign interests as the Arab-Israeli conflict leads to the Arab Oil Embargo in 1973. The feeling of powerlessness crests with the taking of 63 hostages at the American Embassy in Tehran by militant Iranian students, an event made especially dispiriting by a failed military rescue attempt and the incessant media coverage. ("America Held Hostage" is ABC's label for a relentless dose of depression dished up throughout the 444-day ordeal that lasts from November of 1979 through Ronald Reagan's inauguration day in January of 1981.)

National confidence does not seem to reemerge until Ronald Reagan sends a small force of U.S. marines to liberate the island nation of Grenada from a Marxist regime apparently buttressed by a few hundred Cuban "construction workers" in 1983, renovating the notion of a Communist "menace."

FIGURE 14.1

The Misery Index (Inflation Rate + Unemployment Rate)

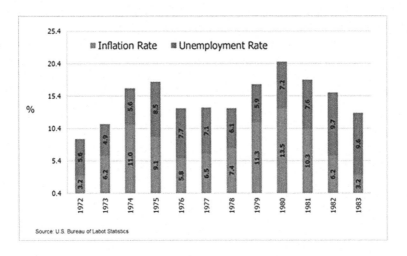

Source: U.S. Bureau of Labor Statistics

SOCIAL DYSFUNCTION AND WOMEN'S RIGHTS

Much of the research on Generation X focuses on the social dissolution that becomes most apparent in the 1970s. Indeed, there is more than enough aberrant behavior to cluck over and no shortage of demoralizing statistics with which to tar a generation. But in all honesty, Believers are no easier to capture with grand generalizations than any other generation or Value Population.

To understand Believers, one must acknowledge the undeniably harsh social truths of the Believer value-formation period, particularly those related to family life and child-rearing. This rightfully starts with a nod to the Supreme Court findings in *Roe v. Wade* (1973), which greatly facilitate legal abortions. Arguments of ethics, religion and social responsibility will be left to other forums, but there is little denying that the *timing* of this event in the context of broad social disruption appears significant.

BELIEVER-ERA SOCIAL TRENDS

- *Birth rate decline.* Some commentators select the year 1972 as the opening demarcation of "Generation Y" (which they extend, we believe mistakenly, all the way to 1995), because it is the year that the U.S. birth rate slips below the population replacement rate. Interestingly, in this same year, the Rockefeller Commission, a joint presidential-congressional effort, tacitly approves this trend when it issues a report that concludes, "We have not found any convincing argument for continued population growth."

- *Rise in abortions.* In 1972, the number of legal abortions represents 13 percent of all known pregnancies. By 1976, that figure has grown to 21 percent and by 1980 it has reached 25 percent.

- *Rise in births to unmarried mothers.* In 1969, 10 percent of all live births in the United States are to unmarried mothers; by 1985, that figure has more than doubled to 22 percent. See Figure 14.2. The last year that a majority of black children are born into married two-parent households is 1975.

- *Rise in divorces.* Divorce rates climb steadily throughout the 1970s, peaking from 1979 to 1981 when 22.8 of every 1,000 married women over the age of 15 got divorced each year—double the rate of the mid-1960s.

Additional troubling statistics, particularly related to education, religious practice and child welfare, paint a generally glum picture of society's regard for children and family. When the 1970s are referred to as the "Me Decade," it is adults turning away from a child-first doctrine that is most damning in the eyes of traditional family-value supporters. The facile abandonments by fathers, the well-chronicled nightlife scene, the drugs, the glib profaning of conservative institutions, and the libertine sexual experimentation make it hard to grant a sympathetic spin to this story, even as historical artifacts.

FIGURE 14.2

U.S. Birth Rates to Unmarried Mothers

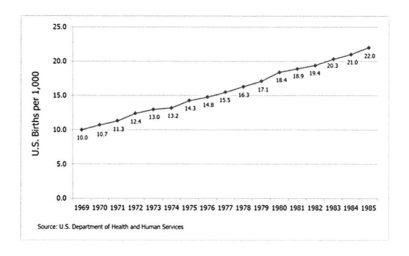

Source: U.S. Department of Health and Human Services

Yet, one should not entirely mistake the caricature for the reality. First, amidst all the hue and cry over *Roe v. Wade,* it is sometimes conveniently forgotten that this seven-to-two majority decision of the Supreme Court is a profound acknowledgment of women's rights. It may be seriously argued that if the number-one overlooked achievement of the Believer era is its relative military peace, then the creation of a climate allowing the empowerment and individuation of women is the second. More than just a time of abstract feminist philosophy, the 1970s usher in a mainstream change in the perception of women's roles and their influence on society. The first year of the Believer period, 1972, is noteworthy for such developments as the launch of *Ms. Magazine;* the total domination of popular culture—especially music charts and awards—by women artists such as Helen Reddy, Carole King, Carly Simon, and Aretha Franklin; and the passage of Title IX legislation that puts women's educational activities, especially intercollegiate sports, on an equal government-funding footing with men's activities.

Arguably, most of the era's women remain in traditional roles or choose not to push the envelope much farther than the fictional career women on the *Mary Tyler Moore Show* (1970–1977). But suddenly there is at least the implied "right" to fantasize about becoming a crime-fighting Charlie's Angel (1976–1981)—or to actually become a revolutionary, like Patty "Tania" Hearst (apprehended in 1975), or a Supreme Court Justice like Sandra Day O'Connor (1981), or an astronaut like Sally Ride, the first woman in space (1983). And if failure more often becomes reality, as is so sadly illustrated by the abortion and divorce statistics quoted above, well at least there is now a right to fail. Intriguingly, the Believer era ends on a rising tide of "family values," with the U.S. Congress voting against the Equal Rights Amendment in 1982.

Ultimately, it should be acknowledged that there is often a conservative bias in much of the social analysis done on the Believer period. The aim here is not to judge the analysts or to approve of socially deviant behavior but simply to suggest that there is more to this "Me Decade" stuff than cocaine and contraception. For just as individuals from other event eras form unique value attributes to deal with economic challenge, war, or even mass prosperity, Believers have grown to develop values that work in the context of social dysfunction and economic malaise.

Ultimately, and maybe a little ironically, one cannot help but notice that many of the values that "work" for both men and women in this period are values that are associated with traditional feminine virtues. Among these are nonviolence, creativity, personal empathy, patience, faith, and an orientation toward accepting assistance. Maybe the truth is best expressed by Cyndi Lauper by the title of her sassy 1983 hit, "Girls Just Want to Have Fun."

RESCUE

A terrible year by most anyone's standards, 1980 is plagued by a horrible economy; a hostage crisis; a deterioration of the relationship with the Soviet Union (because they invade Afghanistan), which results in a suspension of the SALT agreement; a U.S. boycott of the Moscow-based Olympics; the reinstitution of draft registration; the murder of John Lennon; and the legend-ending destruction of Muhammad Ali at the hands of Larry Holmes. America is badly in need of an economic and emotional boost.

That lift arrives in the person of Ronald Reagan who, preaching the gospel of lower taxes, business-friendly deregulation, American military might and especially conservative family values, becomes the strong American father-figure who has been absent for the better part of a traditional generation. There is little arguing that Ronald Reagan's election as U.S. President in late 1980 has a profound impact on the mood of the country.

The reason the early years of the Reagan administration are included in the Believer analysis is two-fold. First, although many books, articles, and doctoral theses have been written about the economic maneuverings of this period, the truth is that the economy actually worsens during the early years of the Reagan presidency. (As mentioned earlier, unemployment soars to 10.8 percent at the end of 1982.) Second, both in terms of its revivification of spirit and in the advocacy of an economic policy that is willing to incur huge debt, the early Reagan administration is directly addressing solutions to specific Believer circumstances.

While it will be fully explored as a cultural trend in the next chapter of this book, it is worth noting the importance of acts-of-rescue and forgiveness in the events of the Believer era. President Ford's unconditional pardon of ex-President Nixon (1974), the marine rescue of the merchant ship *Mayaguez* from Cambodia (1975), the admission of 140,000 Vietnamese refugees into the United States (1975), the Israeli commando raid to free hijacked passengers at the Entebbe airport (1976), the unconditional pardon of Vietnam-era draft evaders by President Carter (1977), the failed hostage rescue attempt in Iran (1980—surely the final nail in the Carter popularity coffin), the freeing of the hostages on Reagan's inauguration day (1981), and the rescue of American medical students during the Grenada "war" (1983) all illustrate this point. Although the taking of the hostages in Iran brushes the story from the nation's headlines three days later, perhaps the most illustrative example of this phenomenon takes place on November 4, 1979, when the federal government announces an unprecedented $1.5 billion loan guarantee to Chrysler, which has just reported a $460 million loss for the third quarter of the year.

Along these lines, the most relevant act with regard to Believer value formation of the early Reagan years, despite the president's reputation as a tax cutter, may well be his grudging willingness to raise taxes in order to save the Social Security system from bankruptcy (1983).

In the end, Believers seem to have an unnatural expectation, no matter how dire their personal situation may be, of being provided for and protected by forces outside their own direct command. And really, why shouldn't they?

15

THE BELIEVERS
Cultural Expressions of an Era

I used to think that if I died in an evil place, then my soul wouldn't make
it to heaven. Well, fuck. I don't care where it goes as long as it ain't here.
—Frederic Forrest as Chef, *Apocalypse Now* (1979)

Performers were value-formed to appreciate that a strong personality might surmount a challenge from society. Techticians learned that it is not often that society's challenges can be surmounted but that there is still virtue in making oneself useful. Believers are casualties.

Lest this sound too harsh an evaluation, please remember that this is not the Believers' fault, as we are merely exploring the cultural conditions of their value-formation period. As already indicated, Believers do develop appropriate and compelling survival traits—arguably the most charming and worthwhile set of such traits at the disposal of any Value Population. But to see how they get there, one must first consider a value-formation period predicated upon all the ways a human organism and a human society can run out of gas.

MATERIAL RESOURCES

I'm just here for the gasoline.
—Mel Gibson as Mad Max, *The Road Warrior* (1981)

Movies of the Believer value-formation period are saturated with a heavy preoccupation over resource depletion (whether it is oil, money, or food) and pervasive want. Taken to the violent extremes of fantasy (an important concept for good and evil in the Believer era), one encounters plots about resource-related gang warfare in movies such as *Mad Max* (1979), *The Road Warrior* (1981), and *Blade Runner* (1982); desperate acts of personal and political poverty in *Mean Streets* (1973), *The Taking of Pelham One, Two, Three* (1974), and *Dog Day Afternoon* (1975); and even cannibalism in *Soylent Green* (1973) and *The Texas Chain Saw Massacre* (1974). Beyond their thematic linkage, and despite being fantasies, many movies of this era have an almost documentary-style quality that comes across as grainy, dreary, dark, bleak, and anxious—and that certainly augments their fearfulness. Their heroes and survivors, when there are any, are at their very best conditionally victorious and will almost invariably have to fight the same fight another day.

In all, it is a compelling set of fantasies for people in the real world, who have just left a grocery store where beef prices have doubled and who are now sitting in line for an hour to get their car filled with gasoline.

PERSONAL POWER

*At this moment I don't feel shame or fear, but just kind of blah, like when
you're sitting there and all the water's run out of the bathtub.*

—Sissy Spacek as Holly Sargis, *Badlands* (1973)

While the fantasies mentioned above are generally violent in nature, the films that concentrate on character study tend to portray fairly ordinary individuals who are without the willpower to effect positive change. In *Badlands*, the 15-year-old Holly Sargis simply accompanies her 30-year-old boyfriend on a killing spree until ennui overtakes them both. In the era's *noir* movies, such as *Chinatown* (1974) and *Body Heat* (1981), the male protagonists progressively discover they haven't a clue as to what's actually been going on around them, and that almost all of their actions have been performed blindly and ineffectively. It is a vast creative leap downward, but the popular teenage sitcom *Welcome Back Kotter* (1975–1979) captures this miasma of inertia, cluelessness, and slow pace of discovery to perfection.

Some of the more compelling movies of the Believer period, such as *One Flew over the Cuckoo's Nest* (1975), *The Deer Hunter* (1978), and *Apocalypse Now* (1979), do feature brave protagonists who try to take effective action. But at the end of these movies, respectively, Jack Nicholson's Murphy is rendered a lobotomized zombie, Robert DeNiro's Michael Vronsky is surrounded by death and mutilation, and Charlie Sheen's

Capt. Willard, having looked into the heart of darkness, becomes a burned out messenger for a dead madman. In short, it is not exactly a Stephen Covey *(The 7 Habits of Highly Effective People)* era.

THE ABSENCE OF GOD

If it turns out there is a God, I don't think he's evil. I think the worst you can say about him is that basically he's an underachiever.

—Woody Allen as Boris, Love And Death (1975)

It is not surprising that the era as described to this point is challenged when it comes to the issue of God's concern for his flock. Many of the "realistic" films of the era such as *Mean Streets* (1973) and *Midnight Express* (1978), as well as landmark horror films such as *The Exorcist* (1973) and *The Omen* (1976), take great pains to point out that evil is strong, life is often a wicked beating, and neither church nor God exists to provide personal protection. This outlook is even alluded to in the era's comedies, including *Oh, God!* (1977) and *Monty Python's Life of Brian* (1979), where it is made clear that, although God may care for humanity, He's really not inclined to get bogged down in the details of personal salvation or flock-tending.

Ironically, in the cinematic fare of the Believer value-formation period, it is God who is portrayed as the agnostic!

What is especially interesting about this portrayal is that Believers today show a very high statistical involvement in organized worship and a general propensity toward faith in a benign providence. (The issue of providence is discussed a little later in this chapter—and we are talking about a group named the Believers, after all!) So many qualities essential to the Believer experience—community support, the need to repair relationships with fathers, the need to find some sustaining order in the world, the need to be rescued, and the need to participate in love and grace—are encountered in the realm of devotion, it is not all that surprising that Believers would become a Value Population engaged in the search for a meaningful relationship with the Divine. But it is also fairly characterized as a "search"—as in looking for something that's not necessarily or obviously here right now and that was certainly portrayed as remote in their value-formation era.

BANKRUPT INSTITUTIONS

Screw the goddam passengers! What the hell did they expect
for their lousy 35 cents
... to live forever?

—Dick O'Neill as Frank Correll, The Taking of Pelham One, Two, Three (1974)

All of the Value Population eras take their swipes at vested institutions, but in the Believer era one encounters a panicky and near-total sense of ethical and financial collapse. While pictures such as *Magnum Force* (1973), *Three Days of the Condor* (1975), *All the President's Men* (1976), and *And Justice for All* (1979) attempt to realistically capture the nuances and dirty dealings of political and legal power brokers, the heart of the Believer-era matter is laid out in films such as *The Taking of Pelham One, Two, Three* (1974), in which an advisor to the mayor of New York argues that the city simply does not have enough money to ransom a trainload of citizen hostages. This theme is repeated throughout the era, most notably in *Jaws* (1975), in which the Amity city fathers disastrously refuse to close a shark-infested beach because it might depress tourist revenue, and *Capricorn One* (1978), in which government scientists fake a Mars surface landing and then attempt to kill off the reluctant astronauts because of a funding crisis.

What is interesting in the midst of all this is a suddenly very ambiguous consideration of business institutions. On the one hand, greed, manipulation and the oppression of workers are still portrayed as bad during the Believer value-formation period. But there is also an implicit admiration of financial success—of the people and institutions that can create wealth and control it, even if rules are bent in the process. Movies such as *Network* (1976) and *Arthur* (1981) look at this issue ironically and fondly, respectively, but the real thought provokers in this regard are *The Godfather* (1972) and *The Godfather Part II* (1974), in which the inestimable value of an orderly and successful hierarchy makes even murder seem a reasonable expense of doing good business.

MEDIA POLLUTION

You're television incarnate, Diana ... indifferent to suffering, insensitive
to joy.

—William Holden as Max Schumacher, Network (1976)

By the Believer era, mass media has become both omnipresent and vested. In movies, which must be understood as a competitive medium and therefore suspect in its motivations, there is endless sniping at television. While newspaper people are both heroes and villains in the film work of the Believer era, television personnel are almost invariably portrayed as crass, conformist, insensitive, intrusive, manipulative, and inane. In *Annie Hall* (1977), Woody Allen remarks that Los Angeles is clean because "they don't throw their garbage away, they turn it into television shows." In *Taxi Driver* (1976), Robert DeNiro, as the crazed would-be political assassin Travis Bickle, is turned into a media hero for inadvertently saving an unrepentant young prostitute during a deadly confrontation with her pimp.

Believers are the most self-doubting of the contemporary Value Populations and the first Value Population to be born into a mature television culture. These are best illustrated in the brilliant film *Network* (1976), written by Paddy Chayefsky and acted by a flawless cast. It is difficult to render all the film's insight into a single observation, but the following speech by Academy Award-winner Peter Finch, as network news anchor Howard Beele, is well worth keeping in mind:

> You're beginning to believe the illusions we are spinning here, you're beginning to believe that the tube is reality and your own lives are unreal! You do! Why, whatever the tube tells you: you dress like the tube, you raise your children like the tube, you even think like the tube! This is mass madness, you maniacs. In God's name, you people are the real thing. WE are the illusion.

NEW YORK, NEW YORK

I think someone should just take this city and just ... just flush it down the fuckin' toilet.
—Robert DeNiro as Travis Bickle, *Taxi Driver* (1976)

One of the great insights into Believer values may be derived from the era's various cinematic representations of the city of New York. In the real world, NYC reaches the lowest point of its municipal history during the 1970s with soaring personal and property crime rates and a vast array of municipal service problems. In 1975, the city announces it will likely have to declare bankruptcy, and President Ford's initial reaction to a request for aid is basically, as is recorded in a now-famous *New York Daily News* headline, "Drop Dead!" (As a relevant aside, Ford's initial cold decision to forsake a fiscal rescue ranks right up there with Carter's failed Iranian hostage recovery and is probably the event that quashes Ford's bid for a second term.)

What is symbolically devastating in movies such as *Mean Streets* (1973), *The Taking of Pelham One, Two, Three* (1974), *Dog Day Afternoon* (1975), *Taxi Driver* (1976), *The Warriors* (1979), *Escape from New York* (1980), and *Fort Apache the Bronx* (1981) is the abject failure and total renunciation of New York City, America's most important symbol of capitalism, culture, and diversity. A few films, most notably Woody Allen's *Manhattan* (1979) and Dudley Moore's *Arthur* (1981), try to paint a prettier picture, but for most people the Big Apple, and what it stands for, has become rotten to the core.

ROLE ADJUSTMENTS

I Am Woman, Hear Me Roar ...
—Helen Reddy (1972)

It should come as little surprise that the Believer period is further characterized by a radical rebalancing of traditional gender roles in the family, in the work place, and in society at large. Although it is a vast oversimplification of a complex matter, one needs to recognize that the energy and authority traditionally associated with males in our society is at low ebb during the Believer value-formation period. Be this an issue of enlightened personal choice or desperate cultural circumstance (and it is probably both), the world simply moves away from an idealized, some would argue "fantasized," notion of virile male father/soldier/hunter/provider/protector and toward a more inclusive stance regarding the potencies and potentialities of women.

THE LIBERATION OF WOMEN

"Hi, Diana Christensen. A racist lackey of the imperial ruling circles."
"Laureen Hobbs. Badass commie nigger."
—Faye Dunaway and Marlene Warfield, *Network* (1976)

There is no simple observation that encapsulates all the roles that women suddenly start to play in art or in real life during the Believer value-formation period. This is, of course, a large part of the point. To illustrate, consider even a modest list of memorable Believer-era actresses and their Oscar-winning characters, who help define this cultural trend toward women's emancipation:

- Louise Fletcher as Nurse Ratched, *One Flew Over the Cuckoo's Nest* (1975)—an unrepentant emasculator of a ward full of dysfunctional male patients—takes some lumps but ends up lobotomizing her chief tormentor.
- Faye Dunaway as Diana Christensen, *Network* (1976)—a driven media executive, gleefully exploiting anyone and anything that can improve her TV shows' ratings—openly discusses her sexuality as similar to a male's (quick to arouse, quick to consummate, and immediately ready to get back to work).
- Diane Keaton as Annie Hall, *Annie Hall* (1977)—a talented but unsophisticated Midwestern girl eventually outgrows her male mentor and moves on to stardom. (The "masculine" Annie-Hall look starts a major fashion trend of the late 1970s.)
- Sissy Spacek as Loretta Lynn, *Coal Miner's Daughter* (1980)—a talented but unsophisticated country girl eventually outgrows her male mentor and moves on to stardom.
- Sally Field as Norma Rae, *Norma Rae* (1979)—far braver than any of the males she works with in a textile mill, this young single mother risks everything as she agrees to become a union organizer.

This brief list barely touches the dozens of memorable characterizations in which women are variously shown as sexual aggressors, strategy instigators, social experimenters, and staunch defenders of their own self-worth. Even in *10,* a movie that celebrates nothing so much as the female form's effect on the male libido, there is a wonderful moment when Julie Andrews, Mary Poppins herself, gives the finger to the man who's done her wrong. And thanks to Katherine Ross in *The Stepford Wives* (1975), the persona of a traditional suburban housewife takes a memorable knife through the heart.

Some male backlash to all of this does inevitably take place, of course. It is hard to erase an image of a totally buff, virtually naked Arnold Schwarzenegger in *Conan the Barbarian* (1982), commenting that what is "best" in life is "to crush your enemies, see them driven before you, and to hear the lamentation of the women." But it may be safe to assume that more men are acknowledgers, however begrudgingly, of the essential indomitability of the newly liberated woman. As George Wendt playing Norm Peterson observes in an early episode of the classic television sitcom *Cheers* (1982–1983): "Women. You can't live with'm. Pass the beer nuts."

GENTLE MEN

"If a man said that to me I'd break his neck."

"I am a man."

"Well, I mean a much shorter man."

—Woody Allen as Boris Grushenko and Harold Gould as Anton Inbedkov, *Love and Death* (1975)

Traditional male action heroes do exist in the Believer era, particularly and therefore significantly in "fantasy" films. Harrison Ford certainly comes on strong as Han Solo in *Star Wars* (1977) and *The Empire Strikes Back* (1980), as Indiana Jones in *Raiders of the Lost Ark* (1981), and as Rick Deckard in *Blade Runner* (1982)—although he is deathly afraid of snakes in *Raiders of the Lost Ark* and turns out not to be human in *Blade Runner.* The Believer era also yields the "comic book" triumphs of Sylvester Stallone as Rocky (1976), Christopher Reeve as Superman (1978), and, as previously mentioned, Arnold Schwarzenegger as Conan the Barbarian (1982).

For the most part, though, the films of the Believer era that play it a little more closely to everyday reality are noteworthy for the reflective, rather than the active, qualities of their male protagonists. The Believer era is the heyday of films and television programs that star the likes of Woody Allen, Alan Alda, Richard Dreyfuss, Dudley Moore, John Denver, Peter Sellers, and Peter Falk. All of these actors, and most of the characters they play, have virtues aplenty, ranging from empathy to charm to intelligence to sincere artistic temperament to ethical conviction to great wit. But it is hard to ignore a lack of "true grit" or "right stuff " in these figures, who are somehow "safe" and "passive" in ways that more macho heroes are not.

Admittedly, one can point to the characterizations of actors like Jack Nicholson in *One Flew over the Cuckoo's Nest* (1975) and *The Shining* (1980) and Robert DeNiro in *Taxi Driver* (1976) and *Raging Bull* (1980) as being virile enough. But if there is a defining characteristic to these portrayals, it is simply that all of these characters are certifiably crazy or, at the very least, just plain mean—so much for Believer testosterone.

FATHERS AND FAMILIES

"It just seems that you and me have been mad at each other for so long."

"I didn't think we were mad. I just thought we didn't like each other."

—Real-life daughter and father Jane and Henry Fonda as fictional daughter and father Chelsea and Norman

Thayer, *On Golden Pond* (1981)

As has already been noted here, 1980 is an enormously trying year for the United States—filled with downcast conditions and disturbing events. But if one wants to capture the single defining sociological moment that summons up the zeitgeist of the era, it is when, in *The Empire Strikes Back* (1980), Darth Vader, the chief operations officer of universal evil, turns to Luke Skywalker and announces, "I am your father."

Darth Vader represents an extreme in paternal shortcomings, but his character lurks in the nightmares of an inordinate number of children whose values are formed in the Believer era. As may quickly be surmised from a glance at the statistics earlier in this report, there is an historical level of family disruption and disappointment during the Believer value-formation era. Dads become delinquents, dropouts, or at best grumpy old men in a society that challenges vested roles and spurns moral authority, and in which an anxious peace and a weak economy frustrate traditional male strengths.

The artistic representations are sometimes terrifying. In *Badlands* (1973), a father who disapproves of his daughter's date murders her dog; in *Chinatown* (1974), there is paternal rape, incest, and kidnap; in *The Deer Hunter* (1978), there are unprovoked beatings of a devoted daughter; in *The Shining* (1980), a dad, who is having a bad career patch, tries to axe-murder his wife and son. Far too many to list are the movies that somehow involve a father's emotional detachment, divorce, and/or abandonment.

However, not all representations are unsympathetic. In movies such as *Close Encounters of the Third Kind* (1977), *Oh, God!* (1977), and *Altered States* (1980), one gets the message that dads are sometimes summoned on truly urgent missions that are really, really important, no matter how wacked-out those missions may seem to an abandoned family. One wonderful treatment along these lines is William Katt's character Ralph Hinkley in *The Greatest American Hero* (1981–1983), a television show about a divorced father who is enlisted into the aid of the Secret Service when he discovers a costume that provides superpowers (over which, like everything else in his life, he has the most tenuous and intermittent control, as he promptly loses the costume's instruction manual).

Surrogate fathers sometimes do the trick. In *Arthur* (1981), much of the title character's and the film's redemptions are to be found in John Gielgud's Oscar-winning portrayal of Hobson, the avuncular yet firm butler who works to keep Arthur on a moral and responsible path. (There is a great moment when Gielgud, unexpected to viewers, is sitting on the bed and wearing a cowboy hat—perhaps a prescient cultural nod to Ronald Reagan.) Father figures Ben Obi-Wan-Kenobi and Yoda are there to make sure that Luke Skywalker uses "the force" responsibly in *Star Wars* (1977) and *The Empire Strikes Back* (1980). In *On Golden Pond* (1981), Henry Fonda's Norman Thayer, having botched his relationship with his own daughter, discovers he might do yeoman service as a grandfather to her stepchild..

Ultimately, though, it will be particularly interesting to observe how Believers respond to male authority figures, as well as how male Believers may perform in authority roles themselves as they fully enter their social maturity. Meanwhile, it is definitely a case of *caveat employer*—let the employer beware!

THE KIDS ARE TO BLAME

Then one day I hear "Reach for it mister!" I spun around, and there I was
facing a six-year-old kid.
Well, I just laid down my guns and walked away.
Little bastard shot me in the ass!
—Gene Wilder as The Waco Kid, *Blazing Saddles* **(1974)**

Given all that has been observed about the Believer era to this point, it comes as little surprise that the status and welfare of children leave a lot to be desired during this time. Whether one cares to blame parents, society, economic problems, or just a bad crop of eggs (at times all are blamed), kids are sort of beaten off their pedestal during the Believer value-formation period. In a "Me Generation" society virtually flooding with divorce and abortion, children stop becoming the hope of the future and are reclassified as problems, inconveniences, expenses, issues, and, as in The Waco Kid's case, all-around pains-in-the-ass.

This bleak assessment is not universal (thank God!), but it is a powerful and inescapable aspect of the times. It is one hell of a leap from Shirley Temple dancing on the Good Ship Lollipop or Timmy hugging Lassie to the vomit-spewing 13-year-old Linda Blair in *The Exorcist* (1973) or the incarnation of the Antichrist as 8-year-old Harvey Stevens in *The Omen* (1976). A few movies of the period, most notably *Kramer vs. Kramer* (1979) and *Ordinary People* (1980), go so far as to acknowledge that the problems involving children are rarely their fault, but this is by far more exoneration than embrace.

Perhaps the Believer-era scene that resonates most in this regard occurs in *The Godfather Part II* (1974), when Diane Keaton's Kay Corleone tells Al Pacino's Michael Corleone that she had their "evil" fetus aborted. This moment has particular impact, as *The Godfather* sagas, despite their embrace of criminal culture, embrace even more passionately the sanctity of family. In all, it is going to be extremely interesting to observe what percentage of the Believer Value Population simply chooses to opt out of the child-bearing experience and what percent commits themselves to doing a better job of it than they were exposed to in their own childhoods.

REDEMPTION THROUGH RELATIONSHIPS

I wanna be in love with something. Anything. Just the idea. A dog, a cat.
Anything. Just something.

—Jack Lemmon as Harry Stoner, *Save the Tiger* (1973)

Believers sometimes manifest behavior that seems emotionally shellshocked or bruised, but it is an enormous mistake to therefore consider them as heartless. On the contrary, the heart is pretty much where they seem to make their home. Value-formed during a dismal economic and social era that often depreciated their very existence, Believers find themselves validated by the esteem of others—in other words, through friendship and love.

On one level, this valuing of alliances almost harkens back to the clannish Patriots, but what the Believers are expressing is anything but a blind loyalty to the belief system into which one is born. That families can cause a lot of pain is not an insight lost on the Believers. When it comes to whom they believe will actually watch their back, Believers are more inclined to follow their hearts than their heritage.

EMPATHY

Well, boys, it would be hard to call what we've been through fun, but I'm
sure glad we went through it together.

—Harry Morgan as Col. Sherman Potter, bidding farewell to Hawkeye and B.J., *MASH* (1972–1983)

If a single creative work captures the essence the Believer era, it is the television show *MASH,* which extends precisely the length of the Believer period (1972–1983). Nothing comes quite as close as this show to representing how the most hellacious of environments can be endured, and occasionally even vicariously escaped, through the qualities of empathy, humor, and friendship (sometimes with a little boost from fantasy, liquor, and lust). While so much more can be written about *MASH* as a Believer archetype than will be attempted here (for example, in its main and recurring characters almost all of the chief types of Believer value-influencers are present), it is particularly compelling to note that problems in the world of *MASH* are most often personal, but solutions are almost invariably the result of heartfelt ministrations by others.

Throughout the Believer value-formation era, one encounters stories of "misfits" thrown together by circumstance who somehow manage, by emotionally banding together, to achieve if not outright victory at least conditional survival with a little grace. Movies such as *The Bad News Bears* (1976), *The Boys in Company C* (1978), *Convoy* (1978), and *The Warriors* (1979) illustrate this point. So does the television show *Soap* (1977–1981), which brilliantly demonstrates that the only thing that will keep a "modern" family at all functional is a tolerant and flexible empathy, not a reliance on tradition.

LOVE

Every age is the same. It is only love that makes any of them bearable.
—Malcom McDowell as H.G. Wells, *Time After Time* (1979)

The height of empathy is love, and therefore love is the great prize in the Believer value system. While love of course exists long before the Believers, it is really they who give it a pure definition. In the Believer value system, absolutely nothing else matters if, and while, the connection is there.

Although one encounters a bevy of more-or-less "classic" love stories in the Believer era—*The Way We Were* (1973), *Rocky* (1976), *The Electric Horseman* (1979), *Time after Time* (1979), *The Jerk* (1979), *The Main Event* (1979), *Arthur* (1981), *On Golden Pond* (1981)—what really linger are the nontraditional love stories or loves that are only occasionally between traditional couples. Among these are *Harold and Maude* (1972), a 20-year-old male depressive and an 80-year-old female free spirit; *Badlands* (1973), a small-town, 15-year-old high-school girl and a 30-year-old mass murderer; *Manhattan* (1979), a 15-year-old WASP high-school girl and a 30-year-old Jewish intellectual; and *Dog Day Afternoon* (1975), where two 30-year-old male bank robbers are romantic partners attempting to finance a sex-change operation for one of them.

The Believer value-formation era is also characterized by stories of friendships that are virtually love stories—in that a life-and-death context drives relationship development and empathy beyond what anyone might reasonably construe as mere friendship. *Bang the Drum Slowly* (1973), *Blazing Saddles* (1974), *48 Hours* (1982), and *E.T.* (1982) are examples. There is even Art Carney's Oscar-winning performance in *Harry and Tonto* (1974), essentially a love story between an old man and his cat.

Ultimately, in the Believer universe, external differences are rarely impediments to love. Love makes the world go round. Nobody mentioned anything about making it go straight.

THE ART OF TRANSCENDENCE

Boy, if life were only like this.
—Woody Allen as Alvy Singer, *Annie Hall* (1977)

Commentators throughout the ages have observed that great art is created out of suffering. The explanation offered for this is that art has the power to at least temporarily reshape and provide some measure of control over reality. The more difficult the reality, the more art is necessary.

Woven into the fabric of the Believer value-formation period is this awareness about the power of art to help make difficult times more endurable. Major Believer-era films such as *American Graffiti* (1973), *The Godfather, Parts I and II* (1972 and 1974), *Close Encounters of the Third Kind* (1977), *Grease* (1978), *Apocalypse Now* (1979), *E.T.* (1982), and *Blade Runner* (1982) are every bit as important for their amazing breakthroughs in music, set design, costuming, lighting, cinematography, and production values as they are for their plots. The hugely influential movie *Star Wars* (1977) is ultimately just a good guys versus bad guys movie set in space— but man, those special effects! All three Star Wars' Oscars came in "technical" categories.

A great example of what "art" means in the Believer value system is found in John Travolta's star-making film *Saturday Night Fever* (1977). As famed film critic Roger Ebert observes, "Travolta's Tony Manero character inhabits a bleak, sad, and painful world with next to zero prospects for his personal advancement." But all anyone really remembers about the movie is Tony's primping, dancing, and strutting to a BeeGees soundtrack, which is an experience, for the character and for the audience, of no small transcendence.

GIVING PEACE A CHANCE

An eye for an eye only ends up making the whole world blind.
—Ben Kingsley as Mahatma Gandhi, *Gandhi* (1982)

As has already been discussed, the historical peace of the Believer era is a complex blessing. It is not just mitigated by the onerous reality that a reduction in military spending badly hurts the general economy. It is also that a time of peace, at least in the Believer case, seems to correspond with a lack of energy regarding other worthy interests of mankind, like a concern for society's posterity.

Yet for better or worse, whether as a matter of conditioning or conviction, Believers are generally inclined to choose negotiation over a knife fight. It is not that they lack convictions worth fighting for; they just seem to feel that direct aggression is hardly the best way to reduce the world's or their own already generous allotment of pain and chaos.

Powerful antiviolence/antiwar movies of the Believer era like *Deliverance* (1972), *The Deer Hunter* (1978), and *Apocalypse Now* (1979) are pretty adamant about the poison fruits of hostility. But perhaps shows like David Carradine's *Kung Fu* (1972–1973) and Bruce Lee's *Enter the Dragon* (1973) are more balanced in dealing with what is basically a passive-aggressive predicament. If you have any idea what Bruce Lee means when he says, "My style you can call the art of fighting without fighting," then you are well on your way toward understanding Believers.

PROVIDENCE

Use the Force, Luke!
—**Alec Guiness as Ben Obi-Wan Kenobi,** *Star Wars* **(1977)**

Many downtrodden Believers are secure in the belief that there is some small miracle out there with their name on it. This miracle can manifest as a person, a place, a professional breakthrough, or as some universal energy ray that can beam away the baddies in a heartbeat. This may seem naïve to some, but luck has a tendency to change even if it takes a very long time to do so, and Believers can be quite patient about waiting for a good thing.

The payoffs of belief are both profound and strangely subtle. It is Charlie in *Charlie's Angels* (1976–1981) who foots the lifestyle bills for three beautiful women and doesn't even expect a back rub.

It is the hedonistic future of *Logan's Run* (1976), where everything feelgood is free for the asking and, apparently, nobody has to grow the food or clean the toilets. It is Rocky Balboa in *Rocky* (1976), being selected randomly out of the boxing phone book to have a chance in the ring with the champ. It is the heavenly angels in *Heaven Can Wait* (1978), who, when you are accidentally killed, give you a second chance to be a millionaire football star. Also, with the deadly light saber at your very throat, it is Obi-Wan Kenobi in *Star Wars* (1976) with a very timely reminder about the availability of the Force.

The trump card in the Believer value system is an intuitive awareness that to enter a state of grace one has to be open to grace as a possibility (a fact that ironically screens out many of the world's deep thinkers). This premise is explored brilliantly in *Being There* (1979), in which Peter Sellers plays Chance, a simple, passive gardener whose innocent banalities regarding gardening and liking to watch television are misconstrued as deep profundities by a distressed society, including its president, hungry for anyone who might deliver a message of hope. As the audience, we are in on the joke until the very end—until Chance actually does walk across water.

THE BELIEVER IDEAL

"That's quite a lovely Jackson Pollack, isn't it?"

"Yes it is."

"What does it say to you?"

"It restates the negativeness of the universe. The hideous lonely emptiness of existence. Nothingness. The predicament of Man forced to live in a barren Godless eternity like a tiny flame flickering in an immense void with nothing but waste, horror, and degradation forming a useless bleak straitjacket in a black absurd cosmos."

"What are you doing Saturday night?"

"Committing suicide."

"What about Friday night?"

—**Woody Allen as Allan Felix and Diana Davila as "Museum Girl," in** *Play It Again, Sam* **(1972)**

To be truthful, the above-quoted conversation does not fully capture the Believer ideal. What makes it fall a little short is that the come-on is without a happy ending. In the movie, museum girl gives Woody a chilly once-over and walks away.

So much of the rest of this exchange, though, is right on the mark: the museum setting; the empathic appreciation of art; taking a chance on love; the situational domination by the woman; the nerdy but not uninspired wit of the man. Then of course, there is the astoundingly disheartening description of the universe in which all this is taking place.

The great thing about Believers is not simply that they dare to hope, but that they dare to hope for so much against their own previous experience and life's horribly stacked odds—all of this while simultaneously not taking themselves too seriously.

The Believers' true gift is believing that if an essential talent is missing from one's life, a solution will inevitably show up to provide all the necessary instructions, as does Humphrey Bogart's ghost in *Play It Again, Sam.*

In the end, there may just be two less lonely people come Friday night.

16

THE TRANSFORMERS
An Overview

POPULATION OVERVIEW

Age: Born 1984–1995
Size: 17% of the U.S. Population
Spending: $276 Billion Annually (est.)
Themes: The Long Boom/Constant Chaos
Values: Personal Power/Clarity

Summary

While Transformers are still in their adolescence and young adulthood as this is being written, one may safely assume that this Value Population is likely to take a back seat to none when it comes to claiming a share of the world's wealth and power. Whereas Believers, who preceded them, appear to have accepted peace as a path through turmoil, Transformers have received their value conditioning in an era that endorses a far more energetic and assertive approach toward personal survival and selfsatisfaction. Created in a complex time of personal power resurgence amidst chaos, built by the speed and perception-bending qualities of the computer age, and fraught with streetwise intelligence about what separates winners and losers, Transformers, already exquisitely adept and savvy, are likely to survive on their own terms.

The poet called Miss Liberty's torch "the lamp beside the golden door."
Well, that was the entrance to America, and it still is. And now you really
know why we're here tonight. The glistening hope of that lamp is still ours.
Every promise, every opportunity is still golden in this land. And through
that golden door our children can walk into tomorrow with the knowledge
that no one can be denied the promise that is America.

—**Ronald Reagan, Republican National Committee speech (1984)**

TRANSFORMER EVENT MATRIX

Revitalization/Chaos and Contention/Redefinition

Revitalization

After more than a decade of economic difficulty, America's finances take a dramatic turn for the better—by 1984 the United States begins "The Long Boom," a 15-year period of dynamic economic growth.

The United States again becomes the world's premier political power through "symbolic" military victories in Grenada (1983) and Iraq (1991). Even more significant is the victorious conclusion of the 40-year Cold War with the breakup and democratization of the Union of Soviet Socialist Republics (USSR) (1989–1991).

Economic and political stability breed social optimism, and the period sees a sharp rise in U.S. births and a rededication of society to youth and family interests.

Chaos and Contention

Good financial fortune rules the period, but an ugly and pervasive counterpoint of insider stock trading, banking scandals, and financial hucksterism makes the road to riches a tricky one for average citizens.

Sudden geopolitical changes (Japan's economic dominance, the USSR's breakup, Iraq's attempt to annex Kuwait), geological disasters (droughts, earthquakes, floods), and human-made messes (oil and chemical spills, wayward missiles, a space shuttle explosion) corroborate the validity that reality is essentially chaos.

Although many black Americans benefit from the improving economy, a rising tide of dissatisfied poor black youth culturally embrace drugs and gangs as their only route to the status and riches of society.

Redefinition

The 1994–1995 transition period is marked by a time of attempted cultural reorganization that ultimately fails as it expands beyond its "intended" delineations.

The North American Free Trade Agreement (NAFTA) and the European Monetary Institute (1994) redefine national economic borders forever—globalization, for good or bad, is given financial wings.

The Republicans sweep Congress in 1994, and the GOP advocates conservative social values, reduced federal spending, and a free-market economy.

The 1995 bombing of the Oklahoma City federal building, the acquittal of O.J. Simpson, and the arrival of Monica Lewinsky at the White House all hint at a new world without any (ethical) borders.

TRANSFORMER POPULATION VALUES

Power

- *Historical drivers.* From politics to economics to international diplomacy to popular art, the virtue of being more energetic, more resilient, more clever, stronger, and bolder than one's opponent comes back into cultural vogue; the new name of the game is "winners and losers."
- *Value manifestation.* In all fields of endeavor the quest is to be the victor rather than the vanquished, the leader rather than the follower.

Edge

- *Historical drivers.* Inside information is widely presented as the Holy Grail of political and economic success; meanwhile, in popular culture, preparation merged with "street smarts" is praised as central to victory.
- *Value manifestation.* An advantage is an advantage, and the other person is looking for one, too.

Control

- *Historical drivers.* The unexpected reigns in geopolitical (Japan, Soviet Union, NAFTA), geological (droughts, earthquakes, floods), and macro-industrial (oil spills, chemical leaks, space shuttle crash) affairs; "chaos theory" becomes a central concept in the scientific explanation of reality.

- *Value manifestation.* To achieve stability in a world, whose only constant is the unanticipated, is an achievement of heroic proportions.

Challenge and Competition

- *Historical drivers.* America's brilliant showing in the 1984 Los Angeles-based Summer Olympics; the beginning of the Michael Jordan era in the NBA; activities ranging from chess to baseball enjoy huge surges in popularity among youth.
- *Value manifestation.* Tests of will and skill, particularly in contests that directly involve opponents, are far more than tolerated—they are enjoyed.

Loyalty

- *Historical drivers.* Grenada military victory invokes power of allegiance to one's comrades in arms; popular art becomes fixated on bands of strange outcasts and on marginalized contributors banding together to protect the weak and overthrow evil (*Ghostbusters, Revenge of the Nerds, Power Rangers, Beverly Hills Cop,* etc.).
- *Value manifestation.* Alliances are sometimes risky propositions, but the right alliances can increase power beyond all reasonable expectations and their value kept in high regard.

Tradition

- *Historical drivers.* "Family values" orientation of the Reagan administration; "Echo Boom" and the return of children to a place of prominence in social consciousness; recovery of American political and economic institutions.
- *Value manifestation.* Rules, rituals, customs, and associations that endure must have power to do so—and are therefore greatly respected.

Enhanced Perception

- *Historical drivers.* Computer involvement from birth yields a historically unique interactive filter on reality; new paradigms of learning and response are driven by technological capabilities.

- *Value manifestation.* The ability to adapt the speed, accuracy, and versatility of technology to *subjective* purposes will always be perceived as an ace in the hole.

Money

- *Historical drivers.* The economic Long Boom; the broad ascension of Wall Street in the cultural consciousness; the age of the Yuppie.
- *Value manifestation.* Materialism has both good and bad aspects, but in the "power game" there is no better means than money to enhance leverage or to keep score.

Transcendence

- *Historical drivers.* The movement from an era of passive resistance to one in which effort and enterprise are essential to success; in particular, the fall of the USSR lends an "anything can be achieved" aura to the period; popular culture deals extensively with death defiance and immortality.
- *Value manifestation.* The word "can't" is not easily accepted here.

TRANSFORMER MACRO INTERESTS

(Life-phase considerations projected through 2012)

Allowances

Transformers have a particularly astute grasp of money from an early age. Interestingly, however, surveys indicate that rather than receiving allowances, many young Transformers have become more like junior partners in the family economy, receiving money on an as-needed basis for specific goods and services, and contributing an important voice to major purchase decisions such as electronic equipment, cars, and vacations.

Family Friends

The importance of protective alliances is not a notion wasted on young Transformers. But this notion is hardly confined to the relationships they may have with their peers. Transformers also seem to have more meaningful interaction with the friends and colleagues of their parents, with adult neighbors, and with their own friends' parents than did children of preceding Value Populations. Adults simply have the power in society, and Transformers want the security of approaching people for their insights or, if need be, their protection.

Freedom

Inherently wary of the world's dangers, Transformers are still generally eager to try out their skill and mettle in the realms beyond the family "rec room." The real road to success, they quickly intuit, is not a passive path through safety-seeking and closed-off experience. The phenomenon of competitive interactivity on the Web is significantly appealing to this group of youths, as it provides both an outlet for testing aggression and the dual safety of masked identity and an on/off switch.

Income

The anecdotal evidence is mounting regarding not only the Transformers' willingness to pursue paid employment but their absolute eagerness to do so. Quick to the point, the astute Transformers clearly understand that it is one's work that in large part makes or breaks an adult life. Starting early, they realize, has to yield some sort of advantage in ultimately getting the good jobs, and it is the sort of learning experience that comes with added power—a paycheck.

Investments

One may expect Transformers to be a little greedy (as Gordon Gekko observes in the 1987 movie *Wall Street:* "Greed is the essence of the evolutionary spirit."), but they are not likely to be gullible or graceless in the pursuit of wealth building. It is difficult to see this tactical bunch simply flinging their piggy-bank money at high-risk investments, but they already understand that market instruments have potentially much higher yields than bank deposits. Whether it's T-bills, tulips, or town homes, this group is likely to do its homework, accepting advantaged information if they should luck into it, preferring the role of the lizard to that of the fly.

Material Possessions

Early evidence indicates that Transformers are avid shoppers but that their loyalties are very hard to track. Given the roles that power, chaos, and instinctive response play in their value-formation period, one may suspect Transformers are easily rid of anything once it has yielded its finite worth and served its fleeting purpose. The insight worth exploring here is that young Transformers likely see most material goods as symbolic representations of advantage—as personal power tools rather than as "stuff."

Resources

Transformers are sharply aware that some among them have been born into better material circumstances than others. But such awareness is no more than an opening challenge to a Value Population that intuitively understands all that is out there for the taking, tangible and intangible—much of it related to the education and training that can ultimately level all sorts of playing fields. A key, again, is watching this tribe work the Internet and the free-for-all abandon with which it absorbs intellectual property.

Responsibility

With regard to their survival amidst all of the other Value Populations, the real trump card of Transformers may be their generational propensity toward maturity. Early studies are characterizing members of this Value Population as far more involved, sober, steady, and resilient than those who immediately preceded them. Revealingly, teen crime and teen pregnancy rates are now declining sharply, and teen suicide rates are falling for the first time in a decade.

Public Enemies

In some cases, they are still too young to engage society's enemies, but the early signs are intense—think somewhere between Teenage Mutant Ninja Turtles and U.S. Marines. Perhaps more sad and sobering, consider the fact that many of the terrorist bombers training in the Middle East these days are reputed to be young teenage (Transformer-age) girls. Instinctive in aggression, loyal pack hunters, and far more inclined to defend than to yield, enemy and ally alike face much potential danger brewing here.

Talents

Even assuming the universe doles out natural talent in roughly equal measure to all Value Populations, it may nevertheless be true that Transformers have some special advantage when it comes to capitalizing upon whatever gifts may have come their way. The explanation for this is simply that Transformers generally have the right supporting cast of character attributes—patience, perseverance, discipline, control, and a willingness to compete—to nurture their talent into successful manifestation. Today the news is full of artists, athletes, inventors, entrepreneurs and scholars, who are making their marks prior to their 18th birthdays. One suspects there is much more to come.

Relaxation for Transformers

While they're still teenagers and watch their share of television, Transformer leisure tends more toward the dynamic; common threads are self-testing and competition against others in activities ranging from chess and soccer to video games and extreme sports. Social contexts are also important for working out alliances and pecking orders.

17

THE TRANSFORMERS
History Creating Values

We venture far into the realm of
the hypothetical as we attempt to analyze the Value Population we are
calling the Transformers. Here we seek to capture the mature essence of a
population whose youngest members, at this time, are in high school and
have barely started to shave. Some pure conjecture is inescapable as we
speculate about the sort of adults these young people will grow up to be.

Additionally, there is the unavoidable awareness that history tends to
become clearer with the passage of time. An event or trend that still
seems important 30 years after the fact likely is important. In selecting
essential events and trends from the relatively recent history of Transformers, we must rely on practiced intuition rather than confirmed data
(a technique, ironically, that helps to define the performance characteristics of this Value Population).

WINNERS AND LOSERS

As with the demarcation between Techticians and Believers, the difference between Transformers and Believers is greatly a matter of energy.
Having endured something like social and political hibernation through
the post-Vietnam era, the United States suddenly rediscovers its competitive instinct and its collective willpower (perhaps best iconically reflected
in relatively easy U.S. military victories in Grenada in late 1983, and in the
Persian Gulf War's Operation Desert Storm in early 1991). As will be more

fully outlined in a moment, though, nowhere is this resurgence of vitality and optimism better reflected than in the economic upsurge that economic historians have labeled "The Long Boom" (1983–1999).

Also of symbolic importance is that the Transformer period is marked by a return to a strong presidency. While both Ronald Reagan (1980–1988) and Bill Clinton (1992–2000) arouse passionate criticism of their policies and personas, they each have many more admirers than detractors. (Reagan's Gallup Poll approval rating moves as high as 65 percent; Clinton's 73 percent.) Surviving particularly nasty and partisan political battles, both men parlay strong physical and oratorical presences into the perception that the country is, unlike during much of the Believer period, actually being led.

Personal energy, economic potential, and strong leadership are useful indicators of the generally optimistic tone of these times. Yet, one misses an essential part of the picture if he or she fails to acknowledge the era's multilayered complexity. With Transformers, history reaches a watershed moment of nonlinear reality and a permanently fractured mass.

It is in the value-formation period of the Transformers that the proliferation of mass media, through the computerized cacophony of the information age and the emergent multicultural mash of acceptable conduct codes, creates a strong sense of instability in society's values at large. There is hardly anything, anyone, any event, any cause, or any viewpoint that does not solicit some acknowledgment of its particular worthiness amidst an increasingly chaotic and crowded cultural choir. A representative example of the kaleidoscopic energy of the times is found in the emergence of MTV, introduced in 1981 and transformed by movie-like music videos of Michael Jackson and Madonna in 1984, as arguably the most representative and influential broadcast entity of the Transformer value-formation era.

Add to this disharmony of interests and styles the realities of a world acknowledging its limited material resources as the true great prize, and the ground is clearly set for some extremely vigorous contesting of wills.

THE LONG BOOM (1983–1999)

It's the economy, stupid.

—slogan, Clinton-Gore campaign, 1992

It would be almost impossible to understate the role financial matters play in the value-formation period of the Transformers. This is not to imply that modern people haven't always been deeply attached to their wallets, but it is in this era that strategic accumulation and management of money, primarily through market investment and speculation, becomes a daily preoccupation of the common person. With the advent of financial news networks such as FNN (1984), CNBC (1989), Bloomberg (1990), and CNNfn (1995), and an amazing increase in the number of newsletters, periodicals, and newspaper pages devoted to business news—and most particularly, with the ease of access to markets and market information made possible by the proliferation of computers—Wall Street, and all it represents, ascends to the pinnacle of modern cultural concerns.

If one accepts the fact that most Americans suddenly start to feel good about themselves again because they are feeling flush (with potential if not actual profit), one gets the gist of the cultural impact of this period's economy. Emerging from a period of malaise, society becomes aware that a golden rule—*he who has the gold makes the rules*—indeed prevails.

Although there is no way to fully encompass the subject of the economic driven cultural impacts of this period in a few brief paragraphs, three key points regarding value formation should be made:

1. The period is one of enormous economic growth. In 1984, the gross domestic product (GDP) is $3.25 trillion; in 1995, it is $7.25 trillion. See Figure 17.1. The Dow Jones Industrial Average enters the 1984 trading year at 1220.60; it closes 1995 at 5117.10. See Figure 17.2. Coming into 1984, the national unemployment rate is 9.6 percent; by 1995 it has stabilized at around 5.6 percent. Even acknowledging a short but painful economic downturn that occurs in 1990–1991, the financial times can only be characterized as robust.

2. The personal management of wealth proves extremely treacherous. Even as they rise to unparalleled levels, the markets prove amazingly fickle. A torturous learning curve has the majority of trend followers getting beat up by the initial public offering (IPO) market, penny stocks, hot sector shifts, sudden broad market downturns, and bizarrely counter-trend advice from newsletter writers and other financial gurus. Conditioned to believe that any market sell-off is a buying opportunity, and enamored of the power of computerized program trading, the average investor watches in horror as the market sells off $1 trillion of its value over a few week period in October 1989 (including a one-day 23-percent drop on the infamous October 19th). In short, as the markets create some potent winners, they create many, if not more, losers.

FIGURE 17.1

U.S. Gross Domestic Product (GDP)

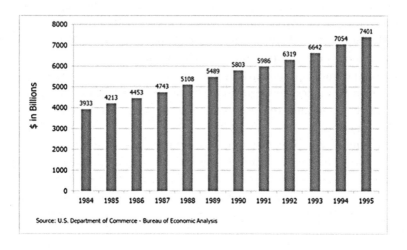

Source: U.S. Department of Commerce - Bureau of Economic Analysis

FIGURE 17.2

Dow Jones Industrial Average

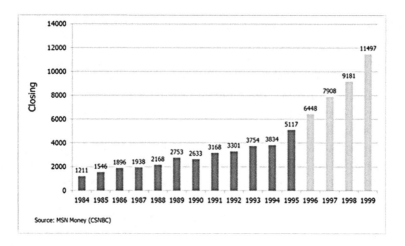

Source: MSN Money (CSNBC)

3. Perhaps most important in terms of value formation, the big financial news stories of the period give legitimate rise to a suspicion that the game is rigged by insiders and can be won only by a brazen disregard of the rules. Insider trading, stock manipulation, junk bond financing, corporate raiding, and rogue speculation are the antiheroic preoccupations of the era. Backed by the deregulatory blessings of Reaganomics, the American savings and loan industry—and the American public—endure a calamitous era between 1986 and 1995 as the FSLIC fails, the Resolution Trust Cor-

poration (RTC) is established, and 1,043 thrift institutions with combined assets of $519 billion simply disappear from the face of the earth.

In short, the Transformer value-formation era is a great period in the history of wealth creation, but equality and ethics hardly seem to tag along.

THE BLACK EXPERIENCE

In much the same way that women find themselves playing a more prominent and definitive role in the Believer value-formation period, blacks underscore the sense of the nation's emerging racial, ethnic, and sexual diversity by advancing to a position of cultural prominence in the Transformer era. This drive toward equality is still resisted by some vested interests, and the results are a mixture of the good, the bad, and the bizarre.

On the positive side, blacks make an ever-increasing contribution to the political and cultural life of the nation and the world. Among the notable events: Colin Powell is the first black man named Commander of the Joint Chiefs of Staff (1989); Clarence Thomas is confirmed as a justice of the Supreme Court (1991); South African Bishop Desmond Tutu wins a Nobel Peace Prize (1984); and in 1986, the United States celebrates the first national Martin Luther King, Jr., day. Perhaps even more significant is the rise of black heroes in popular culture, athletes and artists in particular, typified by the likes of Michael Jackson, Michael Jordan, Oprah Winfrey, Spike Lee, and Whoopi Goldberg, all of whom start their rise to international prominence in the mid-1980s.

Significantly and sadly, though, much of the black experience in the Transformer value-formation period serves as an important counterpoint to the sense of good times and recovery being proclaimed throughout society at large. While statistically there is improvement in the black economic situation (the black unemployment rate dramatically improves from 20.3 percent in 1983 to 12.0 percent in 1995), there is also much social deterioration. An enormous increase in inner-city gang-related black youth crime is recorded in the period from 1985 to 1993, and urban black families experience a correspondingly huge deterioration in quality of life. According to the Bureau of Justice Statistics, in 1985, 11.8 percent of black central-city households are greatly fearful of victimization by crime; by 1991 the figure has grown to 22.7 percent. Much of this crime and fear is linked to drug trafficking, which many black youths contend is their only conceivable route to the status and riches being pursued by the rest of society. It is worth mentioning that another significant contribution of blacks in this era is the fiercely streetwise "hip-hop" culture and rap music, with Run-DMC's *Raising Hell* becoming the first platinum-selling rap album in 1986.

Two massively publicized real-life crime dramas of this era capture the extremes of the period. In the first, black motorist Rodney King is dragged from his vehicle and beaten by four white policemen. Although the act is caught on videotape, the policemen are acquitted by an all-white jury of all but one minor count at their 1992 trial, and the city of Los Angeles subsequently erupts in racial violence that results in the death of 52 people.

In the second, black football hero and media celebrity O.J. Simpson stands trial in 1995 for the murder of his white wife, Nicole, and her white friend, Ron Goldman. Despite massive circumstantial evidence, Simpson is defended brilliantly by a black attorney, Johnny Cochran, in front of a mostly black jury and is found not guilty of the charges after only a few hours of jury deliberation. An AP poll the next day reveals that 59 percent of the white people in the United States believe Simpson to be guilty of the murders, while only 16 percent of blacks feel the same.

But whatever the absolute truths of the respective King and Simpson events, the value-formation lesson seems profound: The poor may expect little justice, and the rich may hope to get away with murder.

CHAOS

Beginning in the mid 1980s, the worlds of academia, business, and even popular culture begin to manifest a broad fascination with *chaos theory*. Basically, this is a way of looking at the world that stipulates that change is a far more natural state than permanence and that reality is far more likely to be diverted from a straight path than to follow one. Central to this thinking is that humanity and nature are wholly vulnerable to the subtlest of external influences (the so-called *butterfly effect*), and in the information age there is no shortage of external influences.

Theory aside, the Transformer value-formation era is remarkable in the number of events that challenge deeply held assumptions about the supposed order of things. While space precludes the full analysis many of the following events rightfully deserve, it is useful to note them and to at least mull over their potential effect on the Value Population born into a period where so much that once seemed solid suddenly seems to be something else. Ultimately, the implication may be the formation of a value system in which success depends far more on tactical skill and opportunism than on rock-hard principle—although things that actually do endure are likely to be admired for that quality alone.

GEOPOLITICAL CHANGES

For more than 50 years, the civilization-threatening antagonism between the United States and the Soviet Union is the essence of world order. Suddenly, under the Soviet administration of Mikhail Gorbachev (1985–1991), the Eastern communist bloc becomes a largely democratic and capitalistic entity, threatening military postures are essentially eradicated, and the Cold War comes to an end. That the Soviet Union, demonized by Ronald Reagan as "the evil empire," can simply cease to be is modern history's most compelling proof that nothing created by humanity is impervious to change.

During the first half of the Transformer value-formation period, the most compelling and enviable economic story belongs not to the United States but to Japan, whose favorable trade imbalance with the United States rises to an annual $50 billion (one third of the entire U.S. trade debt) in 1985. Admired for, among other things, its rigidly structured organizational hierarchy, its cultural integrity, its long-term commitments to personnel and market development, and its tight relationship with government leaders, the Japanese business model becomes the envy of the world. Even with threats of sanction and legislative action by the United States, particularly related to Japanese below-cost dumping of semiconductors and microchips, the Japanese stock market rides a delirious rocket to just under 40,000 yen in 1991 (four times higher than in 1984).

Then, everything in the Japanese economy begins to fall apart. Much is blamed, from a recessionary world economy to political corruption to unconscionable levels of speculation, but most vehemently criticized is the closed, hierarchical, rigid system that was praised for the success in the first place.

Political and economic borders change at a furious pace. The European Common Market, 15 nations strong, institutes its "Single European Market" economy in 1993. In 1994, the North American Free Trade Agreement (NAFTA) goes into effect, creating a virtually tariff-free economic alliance between the United States, Canada, and Mexico.

Geological Curve Balls

During the Transformer value-formation period, Mother Nature in no way sat on the bench being quiet, but consistently provided examples of how the game could be changed at any time.

- The worst spring and summer drought in 50 years renders half of the nation's agricultural counties "disaster areas." (1988)
- Minutes before the start of a World Series game, the Loma Prieta earthquake shakes the San Francisco bay area, resulting in heavy damage and more than 60 deaths. (1989)
- Hurricane Andrew cuts a swath across Florida, leaving $26.5 billion in property damage in its wake. (1992)
- Mississippi River flooding inundates 8 million acres of land. Casualties include 50 dead, 70,000 homeless, and property damage estimated at $12 billion. (1993)
- The devastating early-morning Northridge earthquake in Los Angeles injures more than 9,000 and kills 51. (1994)
- A heat wave in the Northeast and Midwest results in the deaths of 800 people, many of them seniors without access to air conditioning. (1995)

Human-Made Messes

The imperfection of humankind's actions was clearly evident in the myriad disasters that occurred during this value-formation period.

- A chemical leak at a Union Carbide plant in Bhopal, India, kills 2,000 people and injures 150,000 more. (1984)
- The space shuttle Challenger explodes, killing seven crewmembers. (1986)
- A wayward Iraqi missile kills 37 sailors aboard the U.S.S. Stark. (1987)
- A missile mistakenly fired from the U.S.S. Vincennes kills 290 passengers aboard a commercial Iranian jetliner. (1988)
- The oil tanker *Exxon Valdez* runs aground in Alaska's Prince William Sound, spilling 11 million gallons of oil into the fragile ecosystem. (1989)
- A 51-day standoff at the Branch Davidian cult compound in Waco, Texas, ends with a government raid that results in the death of four BATF agents and a fire that kills 80 members of the cult. (1993)
- In an event that partly marks the transition from the Transformer value-formation period to the next value-formation period (one that

is likely to be organized around a wide array of issues related to globalism), a terrorist bomb is exploded outside of a federal office building in Oklahoma City, resulting in 169 deaths. (1995)

Finally, it is necessary to acknowledge that the Transformer era is the period during which AIDS permeates American social consciousness, an awareness formally accomplished in 1986 when U.S. health officials acknowledge 21,000 recorded U.S. AIDS cases and predict a tenfold increase in the year's 11,000 AIDS-related deaths over the ensuing five-year period. Fortunately, the estimate proves a bit high, although American deaths from AIDS do rise sharply, peaking at 50,280 total deaths in 1995. See Figure 17.3. It is hard to better capture a sense of the potential of chaos that is brewing than to consider a microscopic organism that turns the body's immune system against itself and is most often introduced through an act of consensual intimacy.

FIGURE 17.3

U.S. Deaths Due to AIDS

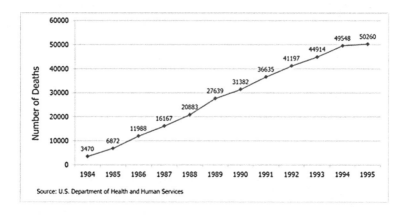

Source: U.S. Department of Health and Human Services

KIDS AND COMPUTERS

Relevant to an analysis of the Transformer value-formation period is an awareness that kids are very much back in vogue. U.S. births increase steadily throughout the 1980s, with a peak period between 1989 and 1993, when more than 4 million American babies are born each year. As will be seen in the subsequent "images" analysis of this Value Population, these children *generally* seem far more welcome and better integrated into society than any children since the Performers. That even "ugly" babies are beautiful is an implication of the Cabbage Patch Kids craze launched in 1986. Ditto for cars, as Chrysler rolls out the family minivan in 1984.

It is reasoned here that the circumstances surrounding this Value Population—the belief in the attainability of material prosperity, the bracing challenge of a chaotic cultural terrain, the affection and guidance of supportive parents—are uniquely arranged to create a population of highly proficient and self-confident adults. But Transformers will also live with an inborn sense that there are many inequities, inconsistencies, and injustices in the world, and so it should not be surprising to find this Value Population collectively possessed of a deliberate edginess they will use to slice through to the heart of any demon (real or perceived) that seeks to intimidate their progress or attempts to either pull their chain or rake their pile. Born into times fraught with both promise and peril, Transformers will likely make their highest priority the attainment of personal power so as to stand among the winners when all is said and done.

Many of the potential tools and tactics of this quest will be discussed in the next chapter, but it is appropriate here to make special mention of Transformers as the first from-birth *e-population*. For what early television was to Performers, the early personal computer is to Transformers.

In January 1983, *Time* magazine selects the computer as its 1982 "Man (Machine) of the Year," noting that a poll of American adults identifies "education of children" as the computer's greatest potential virtue. By 1984, when the Transformers start to arrive, personal computers are in 8 percent of U.S. homes, and a third of all American children have some access to them. By 1995, they are in 37 percent of U.S. homes, and 71 percent of U.S. children have at least some access to them at school. In recent years, computer gaming has become a bigger business than the movie industry, and polls indicate that computers are deemed more essential to this generation than television.

Time will tell what this early computer exposure will ultimately mean for this generation, but it is well worth acknowledging that, unlike 1950s television, the computer is an intensely interactive medium. Members of other event eras may cluck over violent games, pornography, and stolen intellectual property, but to many Transformers, the computer may simply be an extraordinarily powerful tool that trains both thought and perception to a level that an emergent reality, and its still unknown events, will inevitably demand. They will not let you know the truth about this until it is to their advantage to do so. It is the Transformer way.

Chapter

18

THE TRANSFORMERS
Cultural Expressions of an Era

I've distilled everything to one single principle: "win or die."
—Glenn Close as Marquise de Merteuil, *Dangerous Liaisons* (1988)

100 percent pure adrenaline.
—Patrick Swayze as Bodhi, *Point Break* (1991)

LIGHTS, CAMERA, ACTION!

In a review of the thousands of movies and television shows introduced during the Transformer value-formation period, it might be easier to list the movies that *aren't* based on action. If nothing else is gleaned from the cinematic images of this era, we must note that we are dealing with a value-formation period in which life is a thrill ride—an intense adrenaline-rich confrontation between one's will and the wicked twists and turns of truly chaotic circumstances. This is the era of *Beverly Hills Cop* (1984), *The Terminator* (1984), *Aliens* (1986), *Lethal Weapon* (1987), *Die Hard* (1988), *Batman* (1989), *Jurassic Park* (1993), and *Speed* (1994). All very in tune with the hopped-up personality of their time, they spawn multiple sequels, most of these also released during the Transformer value-formation period.

Where analysis of this action-flick phenomenon seems so often wrongheaded is in the judgment brought by critics that this era's art is essentially "mindless and violent." Filtering through their own value systems, critics from other Value Populations fail to accept the historical rightness of the Transformers' moment in time.

After the difficult Believer era, in which energy has been depleted and in which the reactions to confrontation have manifested in considerations of love, peace, and art, it is almost inevitable that a Value Population would come along that puts a much greater premium on action

159

and confrontation than on reflection and passivity.

The cinematic art of the Transformer era is relentlessly devoid of the sort of philosophical inquiry that concerns itself with life's great purpose or meaning. It is about the art of stylish survival, dealing far more in preparedness, power, and proficiency, as opposed to abstract thought. The great objective here is *not* understanding nor even surviving—it is *winning*.

OPPONENTS

I want this guy dead! I want his family dead! I want his house burned to the ground! I want to go up there in the middle of the night and piss on his ashes.

—Robert DeNiro as Al Capone, *The Untouchables* (1987)

"You want to autopsy Lucy?"
"No, no, no, not exactly. I just want to cut off her head and take out her heart."

—Richard Grant and Anthony Hopkins as Dr. Jack Seward and Van Helsing, Bram Stoker's *Dracula* (1992)

"A man like Ringo has got a great big hole, right in the middle of himself. And he can never steal enough, or kill enough, or cause enough pain to fill it up. And so he walks the earth, forever seeking retribution ..."
"For what?"
"For being born."

—Val Kilmer and Kurt Russell as Doc Holliday and Wyatt Earp, *Tombstone* (1993)

Nothing quite captures the intensity or indicates the personal stakes of the Transformer value-formation period like the ferocity of the opponents. In the previous Believer era, the enemy is often faceless and/or institutional, and the dramatic outcome is frequently some form of bureaucratic victimization. With Transformers, the battle between good and evil is fully engaged, and things get very grisly and personal.

On the most literal level, the films of the Transformer cinema rarely shy away from demonstrating that: 1) evil does have a face, and 2) life is painful. Some of the most powerful and frightening villains and monsters ever conceived are revealed in Transformer-era cinema. Psychotic criminals (like Hannibal Lecter in 1991's *The Silence of the Lambs*), perverted lawmen (like Little Bill Daggett in 1992's *Unforgiven*), cannibalistic aliens (like Audrey II in 1986's *Little Shop of Horrors*), killer robots (like the Terminators), immortal ghouls (like the vampires in 1992's *Dracula* and 1994's *Interview with the Vampire*), and cartoon nightmares (like Ursula in 1989's *The Little Mermaid* and Slimer in 1984's *Ghostbusters*) stalk the landscape of the Transformer cinemascape, inflicting heavy damage with the relentlessness of a biblical plague.

Even more than the exaggeration of menace, though, is the palpability of danger derived from deep insight into the complexity of evil— the awareness that it is powerful and compelling and that its face is often the face in the mirror. Much memorable drama of the Transformer era features someone who is essentially good but struggles with the seductiveness of evil. For example, consider Vinnie Terranova in the television series *Wiseguy* (1987–1990), Batman in the first three *Batman* movies (1989, 1992, 1995), Jesus Christ in *The Last Temptation of Christ* (1986), or Detective Sgt. Nick Conklin in *Black Rain* (1989).

As John Corbett's character, Chris Stevens, on TV's *Northern Exposure* (1990–1995) observes:

> There's a dark side to each and every human soul. We wish we were Obi-Wan Kenobi, and for the most part we are, but there's a little Darth Vader in all of us.

Thus, while it is tempting and uplifting to see the struggle of the Transformer Value Population as a heroic fight in a world in which the strength of the enemy and the existence of chaos virtually guarantee there will be some real pain and loss, one really should keep the above Darth Vader thought in mind. For it seems that the young Transformers are being nurtured to believe that the ability to become the enemy may somehow be part of the path to victory—an awareness that is certainly intriguing in the assessment of this Value Population's possible adult fate.

POWER PLAYS

You don't have time to think up there. If you think, you're dead.
—Tom Cruise as Lt. Pete "Maverick" Mitchell, *Top Gun* (1986)

A rifle is only a tool. It is a hard heart that kills. If your killer instincts are not clean and strong you will hesitate at the moment of truth. You will become dead marines.
—R. Lee Ermey as Gunnery Sgt. Hartman, *Full Metal Jacket* (1987)

Fear causes hesitation, and hesitation will cause your worst fears to come true.
—Patrick Swayze as Bodhi, *Point Break* (1991)

Transformers appreciate how a good plan, inside information, or a shrewd tactic may give an advantage, but they're really much more instinctive than strategic by nature. Famed film critic Roger Ebert has written extensively about a movie phenomenon he calls "the talking killer," in which all someone has to do to eliminate an enemy is to pull the trigger, but instead they start a conversation which invariably gives the target a chance to turn the tables or effect an escape. Nobody appreciates the point of this observation like a Transformer.

Movie after movie in the Transformer era, including those mentioned above, illustrate that the best thing one can have going for oneself in a confrontation is an unhesitating killer instinct. This instinct is born of equal parts fearlessness, trained skill, and a very self-serving and circumstantial regard for rules. Great images of Transformer-era cinema include Kevin Costner as G-man Elliot Ness, deliberately throwing gangster Frank Nitti off a building in *The Untouchables* (1987); Tom Cruise as ace pilot Maverick, flying his F-16 in a forbidden maneuver, inverted over a Russian MIG, in *Top Gun* (1986); Mel Gibson as Detective Martin Riggs, handcuffing himself to a citizen threatening suicide and forcing the citizen to jump from the ledge in *Lethal Weapon* (1987); Clint Eastwood as gunslinger Bill Munny, walking into the sheriff's office and stoically executing the lawman who has wrongfully killed a friend in *Unforgiven* (1992); and Arnold Schwarzenegger as secret agent Harry Renquist, commandeering a harrier jet he barely knows how to fly in order to save his wife and daughter in *True Lies* (1994).

Despite the obvious crazed individualism of the above acts, other films of the period also strongly portray the value of having one's back covered by a protective brotherhood and/or sisterhood in this era, with important defensive alliances ranging from street gangs in *Colors* (1988) to mafiosi in *Goodfellas* (1990) to a circle of staunch women friends in *Fried Green Tomatoes* (1991). Particular homage is paid to marines— *Heartbreak Ridge* (1986), *Full Metal Jacket* (1987), *A Few Good Men* (1992), *Scent of a Woman* (1992), among others—as a group that successfully, and most often honorably, institutionalizes the fierce "trained-instinct" ethos of this era; or as expressed in *Heartbreak Ridge* by Clint Eastwood playing Gunnery Sgt. Thomas Highway: "Improvise. Adapt. Overcome."

HEROISM AND TRANSCENDENCE

If you put your mind to it, you can accomplish anything.

—Michael J. Fox as Marty McFly, *Back to the Future* (1985)

You're five-foot nothin', a hundred and nothin', and you have nearly a speck of athletic ability. And you hang in there with the best college football team in the land for two years. And you're getting a degree from the University of Notre Dame. In this life, you don't have to prove nothin' to nobody but yourself.
—**Charles Dutton as Fortune, Rudy (1993)**

I'm a god. I'm not "the" God... I don't think.
—**Bill Murray as Phil Connors, Groundhog Day (1993)**

A great insight into the Transformer era is revealed in the following list of movies and TV shows: *All of Me* (1984), *The Terminator* (1984), *Back to the Future* (1985), *The Purple Rose of Cairo* (1985), *Highlander* (1986), *The Princess Bride* (1987), *Beetlejuice* (1988), *Quantum Leap* (1989), *Always* (1989), *Field of Dreams* (1989), *Bill & Ted's Excellent Adventure* (1990), *Flatliners* (1990), *Ghost* (1990), *Defending Your Life* (1991), *Buffy the Vampire Slayer* (1992), *Death Becomes Her* (1992), *Dracula* (1992), *Demolition Man* (1993), *Groundhog Day* (1993), *Last Action Hero* (1993), *Interview with the Vampire* (1994), and *Fearless* (1994).

In every one of the aforementioned films, there is *at least* one major character who is not bound by time, has returned from the dead, or is effectively immortal. This diverse list collectively reveals the intensity of the Transformer life quest that, at least symbolically, is not even bound by the laws of nature. Although the Performer Value Population sees itself as stars in plays about themselves, in a similar fashion it may be said that Transformers are dealing with a perception of the universe in which they have become heroes in their own myths.

Not strictly a movie phenomenon, a version of this superhuman capacity to transcend the most absolute of human limitations permeates the youth culture of the Transformer period in television shows, toys, and movies as well. Cultural phenomena such as Teenage Mutant Ninja Turtles and He-Man and the Masters of the Universe, are the earliest iterations of the will-to-transcendence in the Transformer value makeup. That "average" human beings can accomplish the impossible through the focusing of attention and will is pure myth, but it is a myth Transformers have been cutting their teeth on since birth.

What is most interesting about this Transformer concept of heroic capacity is that its ramifications are ultimately so pervasive and democratic. One can aspire to heroism not only in the make-believe realms of traditional myth *(Ladyhawke; The Princess Bride)* or in the supra-realistic domains of modern action-hero myth *(The Terminator; Die Hard)* but in the everyday sphere of the common person. The impact of such important and popular movies as *Dances with Wolves* (1990), *Rudy* (1993), and *Forrest Gump* (1994) is that their profoundly non-super title characters each manage to develop a hero's fortitude, bravery, skill, and opportunistic instincts, each ultimately claiming a remarkable life's victory in the difficult "real" world.

How far this mythic ethos may stretch into or mitigate the Transformer value system is yet to be known, but the far-reaching possibilities can be seen by statements made by a number of Transformer-era protagonists. For example, in *A Bronx Tale* (1993), Robert DeNiro as Lorenzo Anello, a Bronx bus driver, tries to dissuade his son from the glamour of organized crime: "You want to see a real hero? Look at a guy who gets up in the morning and goes off to work and supports his family. That's heroism."

KEEPING SCORE: MONEY, JUSTICE, AND LOVE

There may be a mythic quality to the value system of Transformers, but there is also a strong connection to the affairs of the real world. Transformers seem particularly drawn to activities in which strong wills are pitted against one another. Among the thematic concerns that dominate the cinema of the Transformer period are money, justice, and love.

Money

> *"Guess what I'm going to do?"*
>
> *"What?"*
>
> *"I'm going to come back from the dead."*
>
> *"Aaahhh. And what makes you think you can do that?"*
>
> *"Because I'm rich."*

—Lily Tomlin and Steve Martin as Edwina Cutwater and Roger Cobb, *All of Me* (1984)

> *The point is there's a gulf in this country; an ever-widening abyss between the people who have stuff and the people who don't have shit. It is like this big hole in the ground, as big as the fucking Grand Canyon, and what's coming out is an eruption of rage, and the rage creates violence, and the violence is real, Mack.*

—Steve Martin as Davis, *Grand Canyon* (1991)

> *That watch costs more than your car. I made $970,000 last year. How much do you make? You see pal, that's who I am, and you're nothing.*
>
> *Nice guy, I don't give a shit.*
>
> *Good father, fuck you! Go home and play with your kids!*

You wanna work here, close!
—Alec Baldwin as Blake, Glengarry Glen Ross (1992)

One is tempted to conclude that the message of Transformer-era drama with regard to wealth is that money is essentially corrupting, and that people who renounce its influence over their lives are better off. In part, this message is communicated via a relentless dissection of the irritating, self-absorbed habits of materialistic Yuppies in movies such as *Lost in America* (1985), *The Money Pit* (1986), and *Big* (1988), and on television series such as *L.A. Law* (1986–1994), *Beverly Hills 90210* (1990–2000), and *Seinfeld* (1990–1998). Even more damning are movies such as *Wall Street* (1987), *Pretty Woman* (1990), *Other People's Money* (1991), and *Glengarry Glenn Ross* (1992) that portray the financial elite as morally ruined monsters with cruel snaky styles and insatiable mercenary appetites.

What cannot be mitigated by the easy moralism of such an outlook, however, is the breadth and passion brought to the consideration of wealth in the Transformer era and the fact that the relationship to wealth is far more a love-hate relationship than it is just a hate relationship. That capitalism is a great enabler of pain and injustice is part of the equation. But so is a grudging acknowledgment in this competitive era that, as Michael Douglas' character Gordon Gekko proclaims in *Wall Street* (1987), "Greed is the essence of the evolutionary spirit."

It is rightfully noted that the Transformer cinema celebrates heroes whose primary appeal is their brash, streetwise financial savvy. Rodney Dangerfield's Thornton Melon in *Back to School* (1986), Paul Newman's Eddie Felson in *The Color of Money* (1986), and Kevin Bacon's Jack Casey in *Quicksilver* (1986) are examples. Also to be acknowledged are sympathetic characters such as baseball phenom "Nuke" LaLoosh in *Bull Durham* (1988) and the eponymous hero of *Forrest Gump* (1994) whose natures are the epitome of naïveté, but whose lives are in part enviable and remarkable because they are rich.

Ultimately, there's little getting away from the fact that, in art and real life, the Transformer era is an intense, competitive, financially obsessed period in which power is pegged to the heft of one's wallet. The feeling harkens back to the Patriot era in which it was valid to criticize or poke fun at the rich, but it sure would have been fun to be among them. A telling moment occurs in the film *Speed* (1994), when Keanu Reeves' character, Detective Jack Traven, confronts Dennis Hopper as psychopath Howard Payne, who has wired a hostage to a bomb in order to make his escape with millions of extorted dollars.

Says Traven: "You're crazy! You're fuckin' crazy!"

Responds Payne: "No! Poor people are crazy, Jack. I'm eccentric."

Justice

*You're not gonna learn what it means to be a cop by eating hot dogs and
picking your teeth and asking stupid questions. We live this job, it is
something we are, not something we do! Every time a cop walks up to a car
and has to give a speeding ticket, he knows he may have to kill someone or
be killed himself.*

*That's not something you step into by strapping on a rubber gun and
riding around all day. You get to go back to your million-dollar beach
house and your bimbos and your blowjobs, and you get 17 takes to get it
right. We get one take. It lasts our whole lives. We mess it up and we're
dead.*

—James Woods as Det. Lt. John Moss, The Hard Way (1991)

*Lawyers are like nuclear warheads. I have them because the other guy has
them, but the first time you use them it fucks everything up.*

—Danny DeVito as Larry "the Liquidator" Garfield, Other People's Money (1991)

"I didn't kill my wife."
"I don't care."

—Harrison Ford and Tommy Lee Jones as Dr. Richard Kimble and Deputy Marshall Samuel Gerard,

The Fugitive (1993)

An enormous amount of the dramatic art of the Transformer era is
devoted to a consideration of legality. But this is not primarily a philosophical consideration of justice as it is an abstract ethical principle. For
Transformers, the legal system is something like a mix between a chess
match and a socially sanctioned street brawl in which adversaries give it
their best shot until somebody resigns or goes to prison.

This is not an entirely cynical outlook. One should keep in mind that
the Transformer worldview embraces an awareness of horrible villains
operating against a backdrop of chaos. The movies and TV shows of the
Transformer era relentlessly hammer home the point that the enforcement of law by valiant policemen and dedicated court officers are society's best armor against evil.

By the same token, however, there is also the awareness that life is far
too complex to fit comfortably into any one set of rules or behaviors.
Social issues are as often gray as they are black and white. (The TV show
L.A. Law, which ran from 1986 through 1994, is given a lot of credit for
being among the first series to explore such thorny issues as the obligations of doctors to treat AIDS patients, the rights of the terminally ill to
select death, and the social accountability of the mentally ill.) Similarly,
the legal system authorizes its agents to exert significant power in the

affairs of society, and Transformers are deeply aware that this or any power may lead to wrongful misapplication or outright corruption.

Transformers seem to appreciate both the fierce tactical contests and the personal tests of will. Whether one sees the legal system for the issues or for the people involved, it is not really about the law—it is about the pursuit of advantage and the production of adrenaline. One may reasonably hypothesize that adult Transformers will be attracted to law, as it is a uniquely appropriate arena for their emerging values and talents, and the pay can be pretty good too.

Love

"David, may I please have some ANSWERS?"
"Delaware, all of the above, 90 degrees."
—Cybil Shepherd and Bruce Willis as Maddie Hayes and David Addison, *Moonlighting* (1985–1989)

Love don't make things nice. It ruins everything. It breaks your heart. It makes things a mess. We aren't here to make things perfect. The snowflakes are perfect. The stars are perfect. Not us. Not us! We are here to ruin ourselves and to break our hearts and love the wrong people and die.
—Nicholas Cage as Ronny Camereri, *Moonstruck* (1987)

"I just gotta know, are we going to love each other?"
"I'd like to. But he's out there right now, and I've gotta go to work."
—Kim Bassinger and Michael Keaton as Vicki Vale and Batman, *Batman* (1989)

The Transformer era has a split personality when it comes to affairs of the heart. The extremes are represented by the quote from *Moonstruck* cited above, which demonstrates the intense Transformer capacity for surrendering to the full power of passion. The quote from *Batman* is indicative of the other extreme—basically that love may be a distraction from more important business.

In either case, love is dangerous. It is not just emotionally risky, but more important to a Transformer, it places power over oneself in the hands of another. Some of the most famous movies of the Transformer era—*Jagged Edge* (1985), *Fatal Attraction* (1987), and *Basic Instinct* (1992), to name just a few— explore the living horror that desire may become to those who indiscriminately surrender to the wrong lover (an urgent insight in the era of AIDS).

Even in the less-homicidal love stories of the era, there is a sense of romance being measured against personal power requirements. Quite revealingly, all of the following popular movies and TV shows feature couples whose central form of relating to one another is competitive banter, a verbal sparring that simultaneously seeks to establish, albeit affectionately, both personal dominance and a safe emotional distance in a relationship: *Moonlighting* (1985–1989), *Roxanne* (1987), *Witches of Eastwick* (1987), *Bull Durham* (1988), *Roseanne* (1988–1997), *When Harry Met Sally* (1989), *Northern Exposure* (1990–1995), *Pretty Woman* (1990), *The Cutting Edge* (1992), *My Cousin Vinny* (1992), *Lois & Clark* (1993–1997), *Maverick* (1994), *Clueless* (1995), and *Mad about You* (1992–1999). The implicit message is that there is something equally dangerous and dull about unqualified adoration.

If there is anything approaching an ultimate insight regarding love in the art of the Transformer era, it may be found in such "odd couple" love stories as 1988's *Rain Man* (brothers), 1990's *Pretty Woman* (corporate raider/prostitute), and 1991's *Thelma & Louise* (female best friends). The lesson in all of these is that there is a point at which one must accept certain powerlessness over other people who, even if they love you, will pretty much do what is in their nature to do. No wonder many victory-driven Transformers, like Batman, would rather take their chances contending against pure evil.

KID STUFF

"Hey—you ever get into fights when you were a kid?"
"Huh—plenty."
"Yeah, but it wasn't like the problem I have, right?"
"Why? Fighting fighting. Same same."
"Yeah, but you knew karate."
"Someone always know more."
"You mean there were times when you were scared to fight?"
"Always scare. Miyagi hate fighting."
"Yeah, but you like karate."
"So?"
"So, karate's fighting. You train to fight."
"That's what you think?"
"No."
"Then why train?"
"So I won't have to fight?"
"Miyagi have hope for you."
—Ralph Macchio and Pat Morita as Daniel LaRusso and Mr. Miyagi, *The Karate Kid* (1984)

"Do you know what it means to have contempt for your opponent?"
"No."

"It means to hate them. You have to hate them Josh, they hate you."

"But I don't hate them."

"Well you'd better start."

—**Ben Kingsley and Max Pomeranc as Bruce Pandolfini and Josh Waitzkin, *Searching for Bobby Fischer* (1993)**

Sometimes a baby's gotta do what a baby's gotta do.

—**Elizabeth Daily as the voice of Tommy Pickles, *Rugrats* (1991–1994)**

The single most important child-specific value-formation focus in the Transformer era is this: the best strategy for successful existence is to quickly develop power and gain control over one's own circumstances. It is important to note that this has not always been a requirement of childhood, which at one time was culturally accepted as a grace period for innocence afforded by protective adults.

As has been made clear in the discussion of the Believer era, childhood culturally took it on the chin in the 1970s. But by the mid-1980s, we find Transformers to be well-informed and street-savvy kids who, even if in perfectly well-adjusted family circumstances, have an almost natal awareness that they are going to have to contend for their piece of the action.

This is a very broad area for discussion and illustration, and full justice to this (speculative) insight will not be accomplished here. It is worthwhile, however, to look at some of the major manifestations and implications of this power-seeking phenomenon as revealed in the movies and TV shows of the Transformer value-formation period. They give a good indication as to why this Value Population will be something special to come up against in their maturity.

SKILL ACQUISITION

Tough guys don't do math. Tough guys fry chicken for a living.

—**Edward James Olmos as Jaime Escalante, *Stand and Deliver* (1987)**

I've got better things to do tonight than die.

—**Neilson Ross as the voice of Springer, *Transformers: The Movie* (1986)**

Transformer kids seem to appreciate that desire is only half the battle in the quest for power. The far more difficult part is life-skill development that, on the most traditional level, is composed of apprenticeship and discipline. *The Karate Kid* (1984), *Back to School* (1986), *The Color of Money* (1986), *Teenage Mutant Ninja Turtles* (1987–1995), *Dirty Dancing*

(1987), *Stand and Deliver* (1987), *Bull Durham* (1988), *Bill & Ted's Excellent Adventure* (1989), *Dead Poet's Society* (1989), *The Freshman* (1990), *Rising Sun* (1993), and *Mr. Holland's Opus* (1995) are just some of the Transformer-era stories in which young seekers find skilled and passionate teachers and, with the practice of proper techniques, achieve significant personal victory.

Because skilled and passionate teachers aren't always available, Transformer-era youths manage to use play as a pragmatic power development tool. The youth culture of the Transformer era, including its movies and television shows, are filled with games and toys that involve latent powers, strategy lessons, and tactical role-playing. Robots and action figures dominate the youth shows of the era, invoking tactics of mind and muscle in the midst of mythic confrontation. For example, *Transformers,* a critically acclaimed Japanese-made cartoon series that ran in the United States from 1984 to 1987, was made into a full-length movie in 1986, and was subsequently spun off into an action figure toy line so hugely successful that its manufacturer, Hasbro, reports that it is still "one of the top ranking toys in the world today" (2004). The ultimate tactical board game, chess, is very much in vogue, and the computer as a gaming device allows aggression and response simulation unparalleled in human history. For example, as early as 1984, in *The Last Starfighter,* a bored youth in a trailer park manages to adapt a video gaming skill to saving an interstellar civilization, and by 1995, in *Hackers,* 11-year-old technology savants are realistically bringing the global economy to its knees.

NEW TRADITIONALISM

This is my house. I have to defend it.
—**Macaulay Culkin as Kevin McAllister, *Home Alone* (1990)**

Heroes get remembered, but legends never die. Follow your heart, kid, and you'll never go wrong.
—**Art LaFleur as "The Babe," *The Sandlot* (1993)**

"... and then Mommy kissed Daddy, and the angel told the stork, and the stork flew down from heaven, and put the diamond in the cabbage patch, and the diamond turned into a baby!"
"Our parents are having a baby too."
"They had sex."
—**Micah Hata, Jimmy Workman, and Christina Ricci as Young Girl, Pugsley, and Wednesday, *Addams Family Values* (1993)**

Not only is the future-oriented power of technology exploited in the youth material of the Transformer era, but there is also a respect for the strength of much that can only be characterized as traditional. Families, social institutions, and even the game of baseball are reclaimed as worthy in this Value Population.

Of course, these foundational and sustaining essences are mostly modified by the edginess and street sophistication of the times. Cliff Huxtable, Homer Simpson, Al Bundy, and Gomez Addams are hardly traditional dads in a 1950s sense (okay, maybe Bill Cosby's Huxtable is almost there, but the fact that the Huxtables are a black family *does* make a cultural difference today versus in the 1950s), but at least they are present, fundamentally loving, and loyal. Their children are portrayed as similarly devoted and eccentric. They know, among many other things that 1950s kids didn't know, how the mortgage gets paid and where babies really come from.

As has already been indicated, social institutions and functions are far more back in vogue in this period than the previous one. While certainly not always presented as paragons of skill or virtue, countless teachers, policemen, lawyers and soldiers in the Transformer era cinema are presented as admirable and kid-considerate. While politicians and priests are hardly popular, there seems to be far more earnest consideration of their difficult social situations and less propensity to simply slam their shortcomings.

One of the most powerful tributes to tradition in the Transformer era, one with deep roots in the realm of childhood, is an obvious thematic fascination with baseball. Little of the game's cultural significance—as a field of battle, as a test of will, as an expression of attachment, as a rite of passage, as a stage for heroes and villains, as a place of innocence lost and found, as an important commercial enterprise, as a significant global export, or as a national secular religion—is left unexplored in films that include *The Natural* (1984), *Bull Durham* (1988), *Eight Men Out* (1988), *Major League I and II* (1989; 1994), *A League of Their Own* (1992), *Mr. Baseball* (1992), *The Sandlot* (1993), *Rookie of the Year* (1993), and *Angels in the Outfield* (1994). Capturing the least cynical, most hopeful tone is *Field of Dreams* (1989), which, in the following passage spoken by James Earl Jones as author Terence Mann, presents the power of the game as an enduring American myth:

> The one constant through all the years, Ray, has been baseball. America has rolled by like an army of steamrollers. It has been erased like a blackboard, rebuilt, and erased again. But baseball has marked the time. This field, this game, is a part of our past,

Ray. It reminds us of all that once was good, and that could be again. Oh, people will come, Ray. People will most definitely come.

KID POWER

"You think about this: when you get old, these kids—when I get old—they're going to be running the country."
"Yeah."
"Now this is the thought that wakes me up in the middle of the night. That when I get older, these kids are going to take care of me."
"I wouldn't count on it."
—**Paul Gleason and John Kapelos as Richard Vernon and Carl, *The Breakfast Club* (1985)**

I say we just grow up, be adults, and die.
—**Winona Ryder as Veronica Sawyer, *Heathers* (1989)**

My parents keep asking how school was. It's like saying "how was that drive-by shooting?" You don't care how it "was." You're lucky to get out alive.
—**Claire Danes as Angela Chase, *My So-Called Life* (1994)**

Despite some acknowledgment of worthy teachers and traditions, the presentation of youth themes in the Transformer era hardly dwells on the subsidiary role children play in an adult world. There is a consistent and palpable sense of both irony and superiority in the mouths of babes in this era. Youthful protagonists act very much as if they are simply waiting their turn to be in charge—and then all bets are off.

Not everything is as grim as the quotes cited above would indicate, although the edgy character of the outlook is sincere. But the thought that kids can succeed where adults fail is also a part of such gentler entertainment as *Back to the Future* (1985), *The Goonies* (1985), *Pee Wee's Big Adventure* (1985), *Home Alone* (1990), and *Last Action Hero* (1993). Particularly insightful is the movie *Big* (1988), in which a 13-year-old, *transformed* by a wish into an adult, quickly works his way from a data-entry position to vice president of new products at a toy company, thanks to behavior that is variously judged as refreshingly honest, brilliantly creative, and ultimately "adult."

The other important power aspect of the kids of this Value Population is that they are disposed toward recognizing, in self-defense as much as anything else, each other's most powerful capabilities and qualities.

Screening one another constantly for empathy, they enter into significantly loyal friendships and alliances. Some of the most engaging of these are formed by ultimately triumphant "outcasts," as happens in such movies as *The Goonies* (1985), *Real Genius* (1985), *The Breakfast Club* (1985), *Stand by Me* (1986), and *Revenge of the Nerds I, II, III, and IV* (1984, 1987, 1992, and 1994).

If they are Transformers, even the nerds know time is on their side if they just watch each other's backs.

THE TRANSFORMER IDEAL

Pain can be controlled; you just disconnect it.

—Michael Biehn as Kyle Reese, *The Terminator* (1984)

They're poor, they're the unwanted, yet they're fighting for our society and our freedom. It's weird isn't it? They're the bottoms of the barrel and they know it. Maybe that's why they call themselves grunts, cause a grunt can take it, can take anything. They're the best I've ever seen, Grandma, the heart and soul.

—Charlie Sheen as Chris Taylor, *Platoon* (1986)

You think I'm a loser? Because I have a stinking job that I hate, a family that doesn't respect me, a whole city that curses the day I was born? Well, that may mean loser to you, but let me tell you something. Every day when I wake up in the morning, I know it is not going to get any better until I go back to sleep. So I get up. I have my watered-down Tang and my still-frozen Pop Tart. I get in my car with no gas, no upholstery, and six more payments. I fight honking traffic just for the privilege of putting cheap shoes onto the cloven hooves of people like you. I'll never play football like I wanted to. I'll never know the touch of a beautiful woman. And I'll never know the joy of driving through the city without a bag over my head. But I'm not a loser. Because, despite it all, me and every other guy who'll never be what they wanted to be, is out there, being what we don't want to be, forty hours a week for life. And the fact that I didn't put a gun in my mouth years ago—that little fact makes me a winner, baby!

—Ed O'Neill as Al Bundy, *Married ... with Children* (1987–1997)

Transformers, as can already be gleaned from this analysis, are more likely to celebrate the traditional mythic qualities of heroic victory than any other Value Population. This is the era of the superman: the fearless

Mel Gibson, the indestructible Arnold Schwarzenegger, the indomitable Bruce Willis—all daring anything and risking everything to beat the bad guys and to keep the world, or at least their own loved ones, safe and free. Throw in some of the tangible prizes of victory—money, love, nice stuff—and you have the Transformer fairy tale *par excellence.*

The catch, though, is that Transformers are likely to be complex and far more intense than they are idealistic, really tending not to believe in fairy tales. Any appreciation of victory they have will likely be derived from an awesome respect for, and often a direct knowledge of, defeat. Transformers are learning that self-mastery is hard and that one often encounters oneself as the harshest challenge on the path to virtuosity and virtue.

So it is that the greatest of Transformer ideals appears to be the transformative power of perseverance—whatever the odds, whatever the setbacks, whatever the opponents, whatever the risks, whatever the stakes. Simply keeping one's will going when body, spirit, and common sense are trying to call it quits is at the heart of whatever may really pass for success in the Transformer worldview.

Here at the close of this analysis, we reiterate that Transformers are only kids as this is being written. But they give every early indication of having the power to truly transform the world.

19

THE OWLS
An Overview

POPULATION OVERVIEW

Age: Born 1996-2007
Size: 13% of the U.S. population
Spending: $88 billion annually (est.)
Themes: The Internet Age/Globalism
Values: Personal Experience/Insight/Heroism

Summary

At the time of this writing, Owls range in age from three to fourteen, so the caveat that much of the following is speculative is well noted. Nevertheless, if the principles of culture-based generational value formation continue to hold true, as they have with previous Value Populations, it is now reasonable to make some educated guesses as to what the Owls will manifest as their defining values in their collective adolescence and maturity. If, from this point on, the authors don't always dwell on the theoretical assumptions of this material, let this acknowledgment of the hypothetical nature of this work at least be recorded here at the outset.

It is further well-noted, in particular as we approach the value essence of the Owls, that the authors themselves have benefited from more than a half-decade of reflection and experience with the original Value Population material. Perhaps no greater revelation has come than that regarding the early years of any Value Population's collective cultural passage, a time when the values of the preceding Value Populations are emphasized. These pre-existing values, it is now evident, are taught to and internalized by the new Value Population for macro-cultural continuity and survival, and must be appreciated before they can be solved, rejected, augmented, or changed to the new Value Population's singular generational advantage.

This last insight is resonant because it is at the heart of knowing the Owls. For, as will be argued at length in the coming chapters, no Value Population has ever been faced with greater issues of generational synthesis than the Owls. This is a Value Population that must simultaneously come to terms with the tribalism of the Patriots, the individualism of the Performers, the pragmatism of the Techticians, the faith of the Believers, and the competitiveness of the Transformers. All of these qualities are encountered in a particularly complex and convoluted—one may arguably add hostile—period of global history, a time of unprecedented technology-driven, intellectual and emotional din.

Thus, it should in no way be surprising if the key value trait of the Owls proves to be an urge to distill and synthesize competitive value concepts, to hunt for broad worldviews that are blessed with 'absolute' integrity and meaning. Birthed in an era of boundless political posturing, of endless and often dubious information, of fierce ideology proliferation and pontificating doubletalk, Owls are reasonably characterized as seekers of "clarity," pinning their survival to a seeker's proprietary development of worldliness and wonder. Their collective path will certainly be no easy one, as temptation and predation and dissembling and resource scarcity will lurk around every bend, but they are likely to possess talents formed by their cultural apprenticeship—important owl-like talents, such as skill for hunting (truth) and a nascent ability to both see and fly in the dark.

It depends on what the meaning of the word 'is' is.
Bill Clinton, grand jury testimony, Monica Lewinsky affair (1998)

I just want you to know that, when we are talking about war, we are
really talking about peace.
George W. Bush, HUD speech (2002)

OWL EVENT MATRIX

Expansion / Ideological Conflict / Vulnerability

Expansion

To understand the Owls is to first appreciate how expansive and full of potential everything seems to become in the second half of the 1990s. Bill Clinton's second presidential term coincides with an enormous up-tick in America's financial fortunes, reflected in a "blow off" stock market phase, a national budgetary surplus, relatively full employment, and a humming technology-based economy. No less an authority than the Harvard Business Review proclaims "the triumph of capitalism" (January 1997); and Fed Chairman Alan Greenspan most memorably character-izes financial market behavior as "irrational exuberance" (December 1996), an admonition that only briefly stops the markets from exuber-antly going much higher.

In this period, the 'common man' forges a personal connection to just about everything in the universe via the Internet and its global con-nectivity, simultaneously relishing the iconic abundance of such cultural come-ons as virtual shopping, prospering real estate investments, gas-guzzling and gadget-packed SUVs, super-sized hamburgers, successful missions to Mars, the cinematic opulence of the Titanic, and a new mir-acle potency drug called Viagra. Expansiveness and optimism are cer-tainly the order of the day in the American culture as the Owls takes flight.

Ideological Confrontation

One may point to the impeachment of Bill Clinton, or the rancorous Bush/Gore presidential race of 2000 and its bitter legal aftermath, or the hue and cry over the questionable economic policy initiatives (in-creased debt/lower taxes) of the early Bush administration as historical fulcrums in the Owl value-formation period. It would be hard not to argue, however, that the quintessential iconic act of the mid-Owl period is the destruction of the World Trade Center twin towers on September 11, 2001. More than an unexpected and unconscionable act of terrorist aggression, this event encapsulates the historical moment when every-thing in contemporary life becomes at risk and, maybe even more im-portantly, seeing is no longer sufficient for believing. Mired in a shadowy network of explanations, the bombing of the Trade Center very quickly becomes a matter of broad and contentious interpretation, and truly establishes an era in which left/right belief-based ideological allegiances, and no small amount of self-interest, take precedence over any real initiative for establishing objective truths in the realm of national and international affairs.

After the 9/11 bombing, matters of war, politics, the economy, national security, religion, immigration, and human rights, to name but a few policy areas of many, enter into a time of rancorous and historically unprecedented partisan discord. Certainly, this is facilitated by a brand new world of electronic communication that gives a voice (often lacking civility, in part because of anonymity) in the public debate to everyone, be they inflamed or insightful or insincere or flat-out insane. Lucid insights and even "facts," such as there may be, have little chance against the new media vehicles for the unfiltered and frequently hostile sharing of everything.

In this portion of Owl history, adversarial perspective really does encroach upon reality, and "truth" becomes a matter not of objectively collected data but of the collectivization and control of point of view.

Vulnerability

In 2003, the United States launches a military campaign against terrorist forces based in Iraq. While this action will be more closely examined elsewhere in the Owl material, there is no denying that the leaders of the U.S. portray this act as necessary to curtail a global terrorist threat, and that the "war on terror" will be preemptive in a way which will enhance the security of American citizens and allow overt military involvement to be efficient and relatively short-term. In fact, the war proves neither efficient (original budget estimates of $50 to $60 billion are at least a trillion dollars short of the actual costs) nor effective in curtailing a terrorist threat (a National Intelligence Estimate report by the combined U.S. intelligence community in the Fall of 2006 indicates the war has actually caused a bigger threat); and American military casualties increase every year throughout the Owl value-formation period.

Whatever difficult ramifications the war on terror has in American culture, however, it is perhaps true that even broader-based pain is experienced by the American public in the realm of its once-flush financial affairs. Warnings of "unsustainable expansion," particularly with regard to debt-based financing, prove terribly accurate in this period. American home values plummet, job losses mount, and in December of 2007 the U.S. officially enters into recession.

Symbolically, even the Harry Potter series of books, likely the era's greatest youth-oriented cultural icon, comes to an end in 2007. In the final book Harry's personal owl Hedwig is partnered with the good wizards in battle and is murdered by evil wizards when he accidentally intercepts a "killing curse." While things work out okay for Harry in the end, rarely does the death of a popular character enter into children's literature as unapologetically as it does here.

So forgive the Owls if they tend to view all benefits as fleeting, all information as suspect, and all propositions as risky...who is to tell them otherwise?

OWL POPULATION VALUES

Truth

- *Historical Drivers.* Throughout their lives, Owls will be preoccupied with the question "Is this true?" Owls will have spent their entire lives sorting through a global culture of half-truths and self-promoting propaganda, thus their BS detectors will always be on.
- *Value Manifestation.* Attempt to con an Owl at your own risk. If your subterfuge fails, don't ever expect to be taken at your word again. And, to be appropriately honest about it, it's rather likely this well-trained Value Population will be excellent at a little strategic deception themselves, knowing that there is nothing like a lie to catch a liar.

Ethics & Integrity

- *Historical Drivers.* Issues of morality flood public discourse in the Owl period, in areas ranging from the justifications for war, to the behavioral expectations of leadership, to the rights of personal freedom, to the obligations of the rich to the poor, to the necessity of environmental stewardship, to the spiritual costs of euthanasia and abortion, etc. Having strongly expressed opinions in these matters becomes a rabid cultural fixation.
- *Value Manifestation.* Owls may intuitively appreciate that ethics are not just a matter of morality but also a matter of consistency. Integrity may depend less on ultimately subjective concepts of good vs. bad and more on resolving the issue: "Do you really believe what you say you believe in and always act accordingly?" Owls will watch closely before they befriend any behavioral doctrine or agenda.

Connection

- *Historical Drivers.* Living in the shadow of five other Value Populations and cast into a sea of cultural turmoil fed by a data stream that just won't quit, Owls could be forgiven for simply drowning in dissension and details. But like the Performers, who grew up in the shadow of world war and the possibility of nuclear annihilation and decided to celebrate rather than cower, one already senses in the Owls a desire to create lifelines.

- *Value Manifestation.* Whether one speaks of connections to causes, other people or, perhaps most intriguingly, concepts, the Owl modus likely depends upon assembling widely disparate elements into brand new big pictures of meaning and understanding. Given access to everything, the real miracle of their lives will be sifting through the sands of particularity to come up with conceptual castles that are broadly hospitable to places, people and ideas satisfactorily stabled together.

Disruption

- *Historical Drivers.* Every era has its images of chaos. Thus, the crumbling towers of the World Trade Center, the savage destructiveness of Hurricane Katrina, and the pictures of bombed-out Baghdad all have parallels throughout history. What makes it different for the Owls is the broadcast immediacy and intimacy with which these events now enter into our lives and the facility with which we can discuss these events on the Internet.

- *Value Manifestation.* The suggestion here, however radical or counter-intuitive, is that the Owls will be unprecedentedly experienced with, and open to, acts of disruption. In a society that presently tends toward locking itself into destructive dogmatic conflicts and the vaguest of data-based certainties, the idea that the world can change radically and unexpectedly may actually be appealing to the Owls, something they can, in fact, use to a long-term "better world" advantage. It's probably a good thing there won't be many Patriots left around.

•Challenge/Adventure/Risk

- *Historical Drivers.* One sees it throughout the culture of the Owl value-formation period: a massive (and brave) predisposition towards questing through uncertain terrain towards equally uncertain, if hopeful, goals. The War on Terror may be the best broad-scale evidence of this condition, but rising cultural involvement with everything from unregulated foreign economies, to stock market investing, to deficit financing, to poker playing and sports gambling, to televised "reality" competitions (think Survivor and the many winner-take-all shows it has spawned), to "epic" film series such as *Star Wars* and *The Lord of the Rings*, to the vast proliferation of on-line multi-player "war" games shows a public both physically and psychically predisposed towards going a long way out on a limb, with hope and courage perhaps but no certainty of benign results or rescue.

- *Value Manifestation.* By the same token that modern communication brings everything so much closer, it also opens up the universe to so much more potential discovery. In a virtual, information-rich, technology-loaded age, close and far blur in their physical and psychic definitions, and answers, turning points and results may lie anywhere. The Owls will doubtless be investigators, speculators and voyagers in many realms.

Optimism & Humor

- *Historical Driver.* As has already been discussed, the Owls are born in an era in which point of view takes precedence over objective reality. However harsh life gets, and it certainly shades towards grim by 2007, the Owls are not far from the hope and abundance of their early value-formation period. The historical glass is half-full.
- *Value Manifestation.* The Owl universe is one in which you get to choose the way you feel about important issues. Thus, it's simply nobler and better for mental health to generally see things through a light filter than a dark one. Plus, the whole business of user-generated truth lends itself, in the face of life's inevitable comeuppances, to being flat out funny.

Space

- *Historical Drivers.* It almost seems trite to point to a program so desperately fighting for its budget, but space exploration actually makes a great deal of news during the Owl period. The Hubble Telescope, the International Space Station, and several successful Mars landings (particularly the Rovers launched in 2003) all make front page news throughout the Owl period. Of course, this is largely symbolic, as the real issue for most of us on Earth is a shrinking of our natural domain and the encroachment of so much data and moment-to-moment crises on our consciousness.

- *Value Manifestation.* Literally and figuratively, one can expect the Owls to put a premium on personal space and freedom. Whether one speaks of a bold voyage into uncharted domains of the (spiritual) wilderness (the book/movie *Into the Wild* is a remarkable icon in this regard), an unscheduled mid-day indulgence at a salon or mall, or simply the remove suggested in various forms of meditation (or napping), the Owls will frequently be inclined to get as far away as they can from the complex and pressing problems of a crowded world in the hopes of obtaining renewed energy and perspective.

Creative Intelligence

- *Historical Drivers.* In 2001, the futurist Raymond Kurzweil writes an important essay titled, "The Law of Accelerating Returns." Basically this piece, building upon Moore's Law of exponentially growing transistor capacity, describes a contemporary technological world that is growing so rapidly in its ability to process information that it is reasonable to soon expect "a paradigm shift that will make technological change so rapid and profound it represents a rupture in the fabric of human history." Whether history actually ruptures or not, this acceleration towards a globe-changing knowledge "singularity" will most certainly happen on Owl time.
- *Value Manifestation.* It may be the Techticians who create the apparatus for information capture and transfer, but it will be the Owls who will have to figure out how to use it for the greater good. Be surprised at nothing the Owls pursue, from molecular biology to ballet, in a knowledge context they have much important work to do. (By the way, contrary to much 'common wisdom,' several serious journal articles during the Owl period make a good case for the fact that children are actually getting smarter.)

"Magic"

- *Historical Drivers.* The Owl popular culture, as evidenced in such wildly popular book/movie series such as *Harry Potter* and *X-Men* as well as in its flirtation with performance magicians such as David Blaine and Chris Angel, demonstrates a strong fascination with the power of heightened human perception. The Owl era is a time when both technology and a sense of human evolution begin to suggest changes in mankind's relationship to reality, hinting at the availability of latent and previously undiscovered gifts that magnify man's power over both his physical and conceptual environments. Interestingly, a slew of

Owl-era scientists embark on serious considerations of God, and lines between physics and metaphysics begin to blur.

- *Value Manifestation.* Applied at any other time in Value Population history, the word "magic" would clearly suggest a detachment from the "real" world and perhaps an ethos of weak-minded orientation towards wishing for what one cannot manifest in "real" life. For the Owls, however, magic is a much sturdier concept. Essentially for the Owls, magic deals with extraordinary capabilities that mankind is (may be?) in the process of discovering or acquiring, through faith practice or biology or technology or luck or the hidden design of history. The value suggested here is openness to the discovery of truly extraordinary solutions for the most vexing of human problems— an openness that involves spirit, heart and mind alike, as well as a few well-timed abracadabras.

OWL MACRO INTERESTS

(Life-phase considerations projected through 2022)

The ever-increasing speed and uncertainty that characterize contemporary life make prognostications of the Owls' future interests seem somewhere between arbitrary and crazy. Expanding technology, exponential data growth, hair-trigger global politics, resource shortages, climate change and the like make linear projections of the Owl future the iffiest of propositions. Add to this the reasonable proposition that the Owls will be inclusive rather than exclusive by temperament, and one is forgiven for not immediately sighting Owl interests circa 2030 or so.

Having made this necessary qualification, however, it is fair game within the parameters of this study to project future interests in terms of current cultural preoccupations and trends. One may fairly conclude that there will be little of exact cultural duplication down the road. But there will almost certainly be echoes.

Being Lost

For other Value Populations, the term "adventure travel" might suffice. For the Owls, though, born into a world of endless information and social inter-connectedness, not to mention mass produced global positioning devices, the real life prize is likely to be getting completely off the grid, even if just for a while. Situational uncertainty will be attractive not only for the sake of adventure and adrenalin but also for its impact on perspective—a shaking up of reality to see how matters might randomly realign themselves, hopefully for some greater good.

Consider the Tom Hanks film *Castaway* (2000) and the immensely popular and conceptually Byzantine television series *Lost* (debuted in 2004) as useful icons. If they ever are to understand anything, the Owls likely will believe, they will occasionally need to be a little out at sea.

Creative Endeavors

Those who follow trends in American education are well aware that contemporary curricula reflect an obsession with test scores and objective performance in basic academic subjects, paired with a simultaneous diminishment in attention to the arts. The Owls, who are being educated in the midst of this era of practical quantification, have also been saddled with a "less creative" judgment as a result of such passive activities as television-watching and Internet-surfing. On the face of it, one might reasonably conclude that the result of such 'training' is going to be a generation of dull pragmatists and logicians, with the Owl "creatives" coldly diagnosed and dismissed in youth as irresponsible outcasts and/or victims of Attention Deficit Disorder.

And yet, the traditional penchant of a new Value Population to defy the mores and expectations of its predecessors, plus the Owl quest for new viewpoints and meaning in an era of vast cultural expansion and ambiguity, plus the potential edginess of technology application that is unsuspected/undiscovered by the currently reigning Value Populations, plus the increasing historical necessity for truly creative solutions to complex global-level problems, all suggest that abstract, high concept, artistic, original thinking may not be dead as the dodo quite yet.

Art, music, drama, film, dance, creative writing, spiritual introspection and the like should do just fine as Owl-era personal proclivities—by historical necessity and choice.

Do-Overs

One may point to the adolescence of any generation as a time of relative tolerance regarding rules. Consider the "do-over," a vested tradition in childhood games when vague instructions, close calls, and unintended accidents force a choice between fighting and friendship. Some may use the device to cheat a bit, but ultimately it is a rule at the heart of peaceful civilization.

The suspicion here is that the Owls will be particularly inclined to activities in which the do-over is a reasonable expectation. From video games in which death is always a temporary affair, to (second) family lives that are saturated with stepparents and half-siblings, to an era of public personalities crawling in and out of rehabilitation, to an educational system increasingly disposed towards performance 'mulligans,' to even the easy erasure of computer text, Owls are being raised in an era in which nobody seems to be held completely to a set of objective rules and standards, and everyone gets a second chance.

Reality may have some nasty surprises for the Owls down this road, but meanwhile let's have a do-over.

Ethnic Culture

Globalization and the resultant proliferation of diverse ethnic influences in everyday life are critically important in defining the Owl value-formation era and will be handled at some depth in the next chapter. While there is still some significant political resistance to the encroachment of "outsider" influences in domestic affairs, it is nevertheless an historical certainty that the racial/ethnic/belief profile of 'traditional America' is not long for this world. Beyond the statistical proof of change (in 2005, the U.S. Census Bureau estimated that 45 percent of American children under the age of five belonged to minority groups), there is endless evidence of a new multicultural world in the Owl lifetime.

Suffice it to note that the music and foods and languages and customs of the world are present and always will be in the Owl experience. Simply put, Owls, whatever their native ethnicity, are highly unlikely to live a life without the FIFA World Cup, salsa music and udon noodles.

Gambling

It's worth noting that casino gambling, sports betting, and poker have a heyday of growth in the value-formation period of the Owls. According to the American Gaming Association, commercial casino revenue grows to a peak of $34 billion in 2007, and in the same year revenue from all gaming tops $92 billion, both figures representing nearly a 50 percent rise from the start of the decade. Global revenue from online sports betting and poker, much of it illegal, is now reliably estimated in excess of $20 billion annually, from a base of zero at the start of the Owl period.

While perhaps not entirely classifiable as "gambling," one may certainly see some resonance in online stock trading, particularly the high-speed, high-risk phenomenon of "day trading." According to Dun & Bradstreet, the number of online trading accounts grew from less than a million to over 35 million in the first seven years of the "Internet Age." Monthly trading volume in the Owl era exceeds that of the pre-Internet age by an approximate multiple of ten.

While general economic conditions in any era will certainly have a deciding impact on economic activity, there's little denying that taking a chance has a strong resonance in the value matrix of the Owls. This is a group that is intrepid, highly values optimism, has a propensity to believe in luck, and has the audacity to personally accept the mental challenge of figuring out opponents and attempting to beat the odds. Sure, traditional investing and money management have their places too, but a decade of calamitous headlines and compromised expertise has given the Owls every reason to believe that reliance upon our vested financial institutions offer neither ethical nor economic advantage. In matters of fortune, Owls will take their own chances.

Nature

It is a bit of sociological irony that the high concept/broad thinking Owls have been value-formed in an era dominated by the data-intense/pragmatic Techticians. For all their real differences, however, both Value Populations have a rich respect for nature as a repository of wisdom and spiritual refreshment. To both groups, the natural world and its animal kingdom constitute the universe's one truly perfect system, whether measured by science or appreciated as divine art.

It is easy to predict that the Owl era will continue to be one of encroachment upon animal habitats and the natural resources of the world in general. But Owls, the guess is here, will not be inclined to let the precious wilderness go, or the climate to change for that matter, without a stalwart defense. Growing scarcity is likely to make the heart grow much fonder.

Reality Programming

The era that spawned the likes of *Survivor* (2000–) and *American Idol* (2002–) and *Big Brother* (2000–) to name just a few of television's most popular "reality" series, is probably not going to come to a quick close if the Owls have any say. This may outrage or disappoint more fastidious realists, who can't comment often enough that much of the content in these ratings-conscious shows, as well as their competitive outcomes, is scripted and manipulated beyond any semblance of fairness or impartiality. What needs to be noted here, however, is that reality television programming quite faithfully mirrors the general reality of the Owls' overall cultural formation period, offering a way to test one's wits against lies, bullying, fighting, plotting, unfair advantages, rigged outcomes, multicultural casts—the whole "real world" shebang.

Perhaps someday when they achieve maturity, Owls will explain that anyone who takes reality at face value is a bit of a dope. Observe the true stacking of the deck and develop a strategy for dissembling, however, and maybe you'll be the last person on the island. Or maybe you'll just get lucky, and Ty Pennington of *Extreme Makeover: Home Edition* (2003-?) will show up and build you a new house.

To the Owls, reality programming might be best thought of as a set of actual real-life training lessons. And enthusiastic enrollment in this preparedness academy may continue for a long, long time.

Spirituality

Looking out in this regard, it is first important to stress the distinction between religion and spirituality. Owls are likely in the long-term to be a Value Population indisposed to most institutional epiphanies, traditions and regulations, accepting little at "faith value" because "that's the way it's always been known and done." Modern culture has granted the Owls an early insider's perspective regarding the manipulative tendencies and failures of authority, and reasonable doubt is bound to be a tool in the Owl value bag.

By the same token, Owls are also bound to be quite unprejudiced when it comes to human potential. If the Owl life can be boiled down to a simple principle of understanding (it probably can't, by the way), it's that the goal of life is to achieve optimum perspective over the broadest possible field of human endeavors. The existence of philosophers, sages and spiritual leaders who have apparently stretched the bounds of consciousness in their varied deep reflections and spiritual practices, is a juicy bit of knowledge for people trying to establish a clear view of what everything is really all about.

Seekers by nature, the Owls are likely to travel deeply within as well as without.

Splurges

Owls are likely to have a complex relationship with the material side of life. Born in a Value Period that is initially marked by great relative affluence and ample consumption, there is a portion of the Owl character that will probably always feel entitled to a fair share of stuff. Besides, and this is also key to Owl character, having and being able to do stuff is fun.

At the same time, though, Owls may be a little less inclined than some to marry responsibility and effort, especially the dull and dry stuff that seems mostly like duty, to practical finance. It's not going to be a matter of laziness or lack of intelligence or even a willingness to sacrifice; it's just that Owls are probably going to be so interested in an unencumbered exploration of the universe that they will tend to regard material goods of only relative importance and the daily grind that leads to a regular paycheck as counter-productive to their spiritual growth.

Ultimately, though, Owls are likely to be broad-minded and voracious with regard to whatever their attention is focused upon, including capital goods. In many ways, the Owl intent is to ingest the universe. Amazon, WalMart, and all-you-can-eat buffets may yet be in for a long and healthy run—a few big bites at a time.

Wonder Drugs

Consider energy boosters, sexual potency pills, fat blockers, medical marijuana, sedatives, anti-depressants, muscle relaxants, steroids, and protease inhibitors, just for a start. In the Owl era, all of these became very media friendly, very easy to get and, when prescribed by a doctor, very legal. Identified by *Fortune Magazine* as the globe's most profitable enterprise on an ROI basis, annual global pharmaceutical sales double from $300 billion to $600 billion in just the eight years between 1998 and 2006.

Of course, this doesn't begin to touch the trade in illegal drugs (a global market that may today be as much as two thirds of the legal market in dollar value) or, since we're talking psychological elixirs and biological fortifications, the burgeoning dietary supplement industry. So you're growing up Owl-ish and you don't feel quite right in body or soul? There's a pill for that.

Relaxation for Owls

This is not likely to be a problem, as escape and fascination are central to the Owl nature. Getting them to accept the urgency of a narrowly focused crisis is going to be a much bigger issue. Owls will be very comfortable around spaceships (real and metaphorical) but perhaps not so much around fire extinguishers.

20

THE OWLS
History Creating Values

Assessing the Owl historical value-formation era is not for the faint of heart.

Here, we confront so much recorded data as we pry open the truly vast information troves of the Internet age! Likewise, we fall upon so many recorded opinions (Internet ditto) and yet so little of the essential perspective granted by time (2007 was yesterday)! How does one even dare approach a meaningful recapitulation of such an over-described and under-ripened period of history?

Oddly, it is by the nature of that very question one shall come to know the Owls.

"IT IS WHAT IT IS"

Where I come from, we believe all sorts of things that aren't true. We call it history.
From the musical *Wicked* (2003), lyrics by Stephen Swartz

If the Owl era may be permitted an identifying historical catch phrase, it would be hard to top "It is what it is." While the origins of this phrase are uncertain, its use reaches a cultural peak in 2004 when George W. Bush utters these words on the evening of his successful reelection after being told that the voter exit polls don't look good for him. The same year and throughout much of the decade, the phrase is endlessly employed in sports, business, and political reporting as an explanation of what goes wrong or right or just randomly happens.

The sub-text of this Zen-like pronouncement is, of course, that explanation is not going to be a particularly helpful source of clarification. In the communications maelstrom that is the Owl era, the phrase "It is what it is" does not convey just the impracticality or even the inconvenience of entirely accurate explanations. It goes so far as to hint at their worthlessness and maybe even their impossibility.

Something happens to both information and knowledge during the Owl era that arguably scrambles the nature of human comprehension. Emergent phenomena that will be discussed in this chapter—the Internet, globalization, multiculturalism, economic dislocation and, most importantly, the ascendance of ideology as the final arbiter of truth—contribute to a data-flood of virtually biblical proportions, a confluence of raging swollen idea streams that drown meaning in a sea of competitive perceptions. During the Owl era, the world becomes a Wonderland game of connect-the-dots in which not only are the dots not numbered in order, there are an infinite amount of them to be connected.

In every Value Population analysis prior to the Owls, it has been meaningful to dwell upon headline events and to mine their cultural import. And certainly Owl value formation must visit the likes of: the tech-driven stock market blow-off top of the late 1990s; the impeachment of Bill Clinton (1999); the rancorous Bush/Gore election (2000); the horror of 9/11 (2001) and its sharp political aftermath; the war in Afghanistan and Iraq (2003–); the rancorous Bush/Kerry election (2004); Hurricane Katrina (2005); the housing boom (2005 price peak) and bust (2006–); and so forth. In no other era, however, does the straightforward study of "real news" appear to yield so little in terms of "real" understanding, as forefront events are so frequently lost in the various interpretive moods and personal distractions of the crowd.

Unlike the Transformers, who are value-formed in an era which at least has some collective appreciation of what is important and what constitutes victory and loss, the Owls are participating in a formation event governed by a set of hopelessly indeterminate rules and goals. In a world in which anyone can hold a lens up to any event and parse its significance, it is not enough to rely upon what one sees—what matters is who is holding the lens.

In truth, one may expect the lifetime challenge of the Owls to be a perennial encounter with "It is what it is," and to have to actually make some sort of honest and useful determination of what "it" actually is. This search for understanding will likely partake of scholarship, and travel, and concentration, and research, and cogent analysis, and meditation, and faith, and intuition, and esoteric philosophies, and magic and any number of activities that may be classified as perceptual enhancements. What it very likely does not include is taking anything at all, not even momentous historical events, at face value.

THE INTERNET

When I took office, only high energy physicists had ever heard of what is called the Worldwide Web. Now even my cat has its own page.

Bill Clinton, announcement of Next Generation Internet initiative (1996)

As the Transformers are identified as the first Value Population to grow up from birth with the power of personal computing, so must the Owls be defined by their lifelong affiliation with the vast transactional capabilities of the Internet, first made commercially available to the world by Netscape (Mozilla, 1994) and Microsoft (Internet Explorer, 1995). This limited space is hardly adequate to the task of defining all the ways the Worldwide Web and wireless communications technology may impact Owl value formation, but it is clear that it would be impossible to under-report their significance. This is the era in which well-respected scientists, philosophers, academics, inventors, and social historians, identify the Internet as a tool and a sign of civilization's evolution, a harbinger of a not-so-distant global future populated by techno-humans interlinked in seamless collective consciousness.

Far-fetched stuff? Not if one can navigate (and work a 4G cell phone) like a baby Owl.

While considerable amounts of data can be produced to quantify the Internet phenomenon, perhaps the most interesting data point is referenced in the 1996 Bill Clinton quote above. For the phenomenon that has changed and continues to change almost every facet of life on our planet is, quite remarkably, less than two decades old in its original mass public inception. In that eye blink of (Owl period) history, here are some of the essential things that have already been forever changed:

TRUTH

Create a virtually endless stream of data and marry it to an unlimited forum for unexpurgated personal opinion, and "fact" becomes a pretty tenuous commodity. It's not just that search engines (particularly Google, launched in 1998) have opened up the information floodgates that funnel the flow of the world's 234 million websites to their 1.75 billion users; it's the general lack of content filtering that boggles the pre-

Web mind. Consider as an example the often angry and profane dialogues spawned on the Internet's 125 million self-promotional blogs (a concept launched some years earlier, "blog" is still hip enough to be Merriam Webster's "word of the year" in 2004), no subject bona fides except an Internet connection required. Or note that Wikipedia (launched in 2001), now the world's most consulted research site, is based on the random submissions and edits of anyone who cares to claim expertise. You're online, and you're basically anonymous, and you're telling the absolute truth? To an Owl, that's already a major hoot.

COMMUNICATION

At just about the same time Bill Clinton is giving his 1996 future-of-the-Internet speech (remember how avant-garde the term "Information Superhighway" sounded at the time?), Microsoft releases the very first iteration of its Outlook e-mail program. By the end of the Owl value-formation period, the Worldwide Web is processing in excess of 200 billion e-mails every day (about 80 percent of which are spam). Just as e-mails largely put the Fax machine into mothballs, so are ever faster and bolder technologies (text message-friendly 3G network devices arrive in 2001), applications (e.g. Skype in 2003), and message formats (e.g. Twitter in 2006) challenging e-mail's electronic supremacy today. Nevertheless, it is the e-mail that deserves credit for establishing the reign of the easy, efficient, virtually instant, ubiquitous, and often-intrusive communication—and for pushing such quaint qualities of formal correspondence as polite restraint, grammar, and reflecting before one speaks into the dustbin of history. Restraint? Manners? You need some time to think and process? LOL!

RELATIONSHIPS

While long-distance relationships and cross-town trysts certainly enter the picture before the Owl period, nothing has the effect of reducing the world's human geography like the Internet. From the earliest advent of the Web, the romantic (and often pornographic) matching up of 'randomly' located humans becomes one of its most avidly pursued features. Starting from a zero base in the mid 1990s, online dating grows to a 500-million-dollar industry by 2007, embraced by 20 million people at any given time and at least partly responsible for more than 100,000 marriages each year (*Online Dating Magazine*). Romance is not, of course, the only relationship endeavor influenced by the Internet, as one can hardly find a hotter trend in modern culture than social networking. Historically, the first social network site, Six Degrees, appears in 1997. The "big year" though is 2003, when MySpace, LinkedIn and Facebook all have their launches. It would also be remiss not to mention the 16 million mostly young individuals involved in the global MMOG (massive multiplayer online game) phenomenon, highlighted by World of Warcraft's 10 million "active subscribers" acquired in only three years, from its 2004 release to the end of the Owl period. See Figure 20.1. What these and many other examples represent, of course, is the freewill associating of individuals from around the corner and/or around the globe based on likeminded interests and affiliations rather than geographical proximity. Who are your neighbors in such a world? Where is your prince? Who is your enemy? It's a good thing that Owls have wings—well, at least metaphorically.

FIGURE 20.1

Total Massive Multiplayer Online Game (MMOG) Active Subscriptions

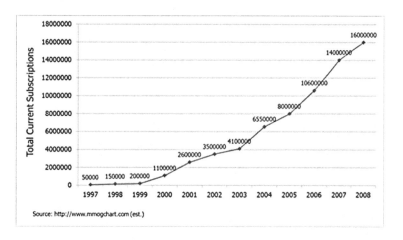

Source: http://www.mmogchart.com (est.)

COMMERCE

In a later chapter, we'll get into the long-range effect that the Internet may have on Owls as employees and colleagues (and how it's not going to be easy to persuade them to form a straight line). Meanwhile, though, it's certainly worth noting the cumulative economic and cultural impact of such online enterprises as Amazon and eBay (both launched online in late 1995) as well as the online operations of such traditional retailers as WalMart and Target. From non-existence, U.S. e-commerce revenues rise to well over $100 billion annually by the end of the Owl value-formation period. One particularly noteworthy enterprise is Craigslist (online in 1996), which effectively supplants newspaper classified-advertising and which firmly establishes the principle "There isn't anything you can't get in a person-to-person transaction online." The Owls are the first Value Population to live in a world of unrestricted fingertip consumption in a universal marketplace—and in Owl-time the implications are quite likely to change just about everything we know about the consumer economy.

In total, all of this is truly consciousness-changing. And to manage their fate with any degree of success, the Owls will have to value foresight and wisdom indeed.

GLOBALIZATION & MULTICULTURALISM

It has been said that arguing against globalization is like arguing against the laws of gravity.

Kofi Annan, Secretary General of the United Nations, recipient of the 2001 Nobel Peace Prize

It has already been noted, and it will be dealt with again further on in this chapter, that a chief characteristic of the Owl value-formation period is the broad surrender of objectivity to aggressively partisan ideological debate. This has to be mentioned at the outset of a discussion of globalization and multiculturalism, because these areas are particularly subject to passionate position-taking. Whatever the descriptive truth of the Owl-era mash-up of global politics, multinational finance, international migration, cross-exposure to cultural customs, and racial and ethnic intermingling, it must not be forgotten that in the minds and hearts of a good portion of mankind, these are issues that pass through considerably thick filters of "good" and "bad" related to one's own heritage and self-interests—you know, values.

Having made this observation, though, and even acknowledging that Owl children being value formed are surely influenced by the debate on such globalization topics as immigration, it has to be objectively noted that the world in the Owl era has become more than figuratively a much, much smaller and intertwined place. Certainly the Internet, as discussed in the previous section, has had a major impact. Reaching out electronically and engaging with someone (or their economy or their culture) on the other side of the globe becomes a common and affordable occurrence of everyday life—hardly a general state of affairs prior to the Owl era.

Even beyond the global melding of everything from commodity trading to restaurant menus, modern electronic communication tools deserve some of the credit for actually moving people around the planet.

International migration peaks during the Owl period (a remarkable 850,000 legal and illegal foreign nationals enter the U.S. annually in the relatively flush economic years 2000–2005) as émigrés find out about jobs and living opportunities through online social networks and then, after migrating, stay so much more easily connected to the folks back home. Similarly, even in a time of travel fears related to terrorism, electronic communications form the informational and security backbone of global tourism as overseas flights from the United States rise from 19 to 30 million in the years between 1996 and 2007, and foreign air travel to the U.S. recaptures the 2000 peak of 25 million travelers per year by the end of 2007.

Still, as already indicated, many people can see matters of globalization and multiculturalism only in terms of stark major events and in very personal emotional terms. The creation of the World Trade Organization (1995), the Kyoto Protocol (1997), the bombing of the World Trade Center (2001), and the war in the Middle East (2003–?) are of course crucial events in global history and will be touched upon further on in the section on ideology. The emphasis here, though, is how young Owls are going to be formed by the experience of globalization and multiculturalism on a granular personal level and in the United States. Frankly, this seems a matter of turning what was once described as a melting pot into an electric blender.

Statistically, the U.S. Census Bureau projects that, by the year 2042 (revised from 2050), white Americans of European descent will no longer comprise a majority of the U.S. population. This will be true of the American school population approximately ten years earlier. In 2050, when Owls will be in their 40s and early 50s, they will be immersed in a society whose ethnic/racial origins are 45 percent European white, 30 percent Hispanic, 15 percent black, and 10 percent Asian American, not counting the increasing number of birth permutations among all racial and ethnic groups.

Not surprisingly, the Owl popular culture is a blended 'foreshadowing' period featuring the likes of: Latin pop music (bilingual Latin stars such as Ricky Martin, Enrique Iglesias and Shakira are among those who launch the "Latin Invasion" in the late 90s that produces U.S. record sales in excess of $600 million by 2000); international soccer (the most frequently entered news search term on Google in 2002 is "World Cup;" second is "Iraq"); Japanese media franchises (Nintendo's Pokémon hits the scene in 1996 and quickly becomes the second most lucrative video game-based media franchise in the world); and the rise of young golfing phenom Tiger Woods (of Caucasian, black, American Indian, and Asian descent, Woods describes himself as a "Cablinasian," and he becomes arguably the world's most popular athlete, raking in endorsements at the unprecedented level of $100 million per year by 2007). In 2006, when the youngest Owls are old enough to be actively engaged in culture selection, Disney releases the eminently multicultural and multiracial High School Musical, which, in twelve showings on the Disney Channel that year, is seen by 37 million unique viewers, produces the best selling musical recording of the year, and yields two very popular sequels.

All of this barely captures, of course, the entirety of global and multicultural influences in the process of Owl value formation—no more than it is possible to toss an easy conceptual loop around the impact of the Internet. What can be indicated here, however, is that the Owl value-formation period uniquely calls for a value response to the cultural presence and potential of the whole world in all its diversity, right here, right now. While it no doubt pains many to believe it, the Owl cultural value dial is likely already set to frappé.

THE ECONOMIC DECLINE OF AMERICA'S MIDDLE CLASS

There are no easy choices. Easy choices are long gone.

Alan Greenspan, Chairman of the Federal Reserve

Economic decline is every bit as touchy as multiculturalism, but it must be addressed when describing the Owl value-formation period. Even though a definitive U.S. Recession doesn't begin until December of 2007, this, along with the presidency of Barack Obama, forms in our estimation the likely dividing point between the Owl value-formation period and the period that comes next. Still, we must postulate here that the Recession is the economic exclamation point rather than the sentence, and that the phenomenon of middle and lower class economic decline is actually entrenched in the history of the Owl value-formation period.

While a complete description of the economic ebbs and flows of the Owl period might take several volumes plus a whole lot of courage, it's not impossible to capture some major threads. Driving the plot are a tech boom and bust, a housing boom and bust, and a palpable amount of intrigue with regard to the activities of certain major financial institutions, large corporations, and various agents and agencies of government. Vast wealth creation in the stock market (from the end of 1995 through 2000, the DJIA rises 6,000+ points, more than doubling in value; in the same time frame the tech-heavy NASDAQ gains a breathtaking 600 percent); the go-go impact of major corporate mergers (in just the year 1998, Citicorp/Travelers, MCI/WorldCom, Deutsche Bank/Bankers Trust, and Exxon/Mobil all tie the knot); the NASDAQ 'dot-com' crash (a $5 trillion decline in market value between 2000–2002); a string of unprecedented Federal Reserve interest rate cuts (13 straight cuts between 2001–2003 reduce the short-term fed funds rate from 6.5 percent to 1 percent, fueling the housing boom); enormous government deficits (cutting tax rates while funding a war doubles the national debt from $5 trillion to $10 trillion in the Owl era); and the subprime mortgage crisis (home values plummet and U.S. housing defaults reach an all-time high in the first quarter of 2007) are all big up and down factors that must figure into a comprehensive economic history of the times.

Much as with globalization, however, even these terrifically impactful economic/financial headlines may not tell the entire value-formation story. Certainly, we can garner the fact that the period is one of tremendous swings and that, despite ending on a down note, the Owl value-formation milieu does contain some very high highs, including the experience of a robust consumer economy as a contemporary rather than an historical phenomenon. Owls, who have already been characterized here as possessing an optimistic bias, are likely to have a latent value of entitlement, or at least a periodic expectation of fulfillment, when it comes to material goods and personal wealth.

The darker side of the story, however, is not merely one of the dramatic eradication of wealth signaled in an unprecedented stock market decline, or even in a drastic deflation in real estate values. With regard to the United States in particular, the Owl period may well be seen in retrospect as the time when the tide of history itself moved rather permanently against the American middle and lower classes. Contemporary scholars offer three possible reasons for this claim:

GLOBALIZATION

This has not proven to be an economic benefactor to the average working American. Rather, "free trade" benefits have mostly accrued to multinational corporations and their stockholders. Formerly significant U.S. industries that have moved a major portion of their employment overseas during the Owl period include: consumer electronics, auto parts and furniture, with the number of full-time manufacturing jobs in the U.S. declining from 17.5 million to 13.4 million between 1998–2008 (U.S. Department of Labor). Many higher paying "information" jobs have also fled, as the concept of "service outsourcing" to nations such as

India and Russia has taken hold since 2000. Perhaps most illustrative is the fact that U.S. median household income has been on a consistent downward trend throughout the 2000s.

DEBT

It is reasonably argued that a great portion of U.S. consumption is financed not by income but by debt. In the Owl value-formation period, the total of U.S. private and public debt more than doubles from $4 trillion to $9 trillion. In this same period, the U.S. savings rate plummets to the lowest of all economically developed nations, while debt financing—much of it based on suddenly deflating home equity—soars. See Figure 20.2. Economists point out that debt is the ultimate form of optimism, the putting of one's money where one's mouth is regarding a better economic tomorrow. By the end of the Owl period, however, the cause for such optimism, and the means to repay the debt, seem increasingly elusive.

FIGURE 20.2

Household Savings Rates for Selected Countries

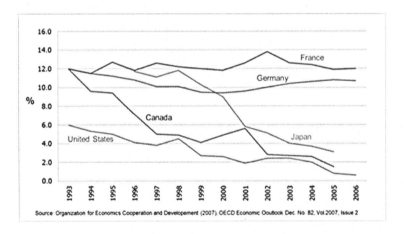

Source: Organization for Economics Cooperation and Development (2007), OECD Economic Outlook Dec. No. 82, Vol.2007, Issue 2

VULNERABILITY OF THE U.S. DOLLAR

Both globalization and debt figure into the third factor in this shaky scenario. This subject truly does need more space than will be allotted here, but the bottom line is that the reason the U.S. can amass so much public debt is largely because the dollar is the world's reserve currency. It's an oversimplification, but this means that any nation that wants to engage in foreign trade, particularly with regard to commodities like oil, must do so in dollars. As long as this is the case, the U.S. is in an attractive position to issue debt instruments such as treasury bonds that are denominated in dollars. While the rise of China is likely to be one of the major trends to be studied in the next value-formation period, there is lots of evidence of Chinese money-muscle flexing in the Owl period. And it's not just China, as the U.S. also uses the Owl period to build up a hefty negative trade imbalance with Japan and Europe. In the Owl period, a large shadow passes over the perpetual reign of the dollar as the world's strong currency, a fruition that would severely hamper the U.S. ability to take on even more debt—a sobering thought whatever one's economic class. It needs to be emphasized that it is not the authors' intent to draw hard and fast conclusions about where the American economy is headed in the long run. Certainly, there are other ways to cast this information, and even more certainly there are historical unknowns. What is important here is an understanding of how the milieu described may impact the value formation of the Owl Value Population, particularly the social classes that have a right to feel ever more distanced from the implicit material promises in the American Dream.

It is perhaps useful here to invoke the Transformers, who will share much history with the Owls. For Transformers, the prospect of economic trial is likely to breed a winner vs. loser outlook, with Transformer values oriented towards engaging whatever is before them with an eye to seizing power and gaining a share of the booty. The Owls, on the other hand, may simply approach the close-in game as a hopelessly sticky affair, relying on a broad outlook, "wings," and a hunter's luck to find them something somewhere worth tracking and consuming, no matter how distant.

If Transformers are built for fight, Owls are built for flight—but don't let the latter convey anything but an elevated and extensive search for a profitable place and perspective.

A COLLISION OF IDEOLOGIES

We are Unitarian Jihad, and our motto is: "Sincerity is not enough." We have heard from enough sincere people to last a lifetime already. Just because you believe it's true doesn't make it true. Just because your motives are pure doesn't mean you are not doing harm. Get a dog, or comfort someone in a nursing home, or just feed the birds in the park. Play basketball. Lighten up. The world is not out to get you, except in the sense that the world is out to get everyone.

Jon Carroll, columnist, *San Francisco Chronicle*; excerpted from the column "Unitarian Jihad," cited as the #1

"media story" shared in the blog posts of 2005 (blogpulse.com)

What is likely the single most important cultural factor in the value-formation period of the Owls is also the hardest to fairly or adequately describe. In an era in which technology and globalization create a de facto high-speed and omnipresent connection to all human ideation and events, and in which diminishing planetary resources create ever-greater human needs and competing material priorities, it is not surprising to find universal clarity and consensus, and even civility, among civilization's victims. What one apparently does get in such a situation, and what marks the Owl value-formation period above all other factors, is a virtually endless stream of partisan and often fundamentalist agendas, a dysfunctional rainbow of arch, blustery and sharp-elbowed ideologies painting enormously complex realities in primary hues of self-serving meaning—objective truth (whatever that means anymore) be damned.

The key here is that historical events and concerns that are so clearly essential to the timeline of the Owl period are not clear at all when it comes to ascribing their meaning. Nobody would deny the importance of events like the bombing of the World Trade Center or the invasion of Iraq, or of broad public policy concerns such as The Patriot Act or the response to Hurricane Katrina, or of essential social issues such as healthcare, abortion, gun rights, stem cell research, mercy killing, and same sex marriage. In the cultural period of Owl formation, though, the key issue one confronts regarding any of these is not the fact of the situation but the political orientation of the fact source, as if that patently simplistic determination is in itself enough to beggar the need for any further advisement or commentary. (For excellent insight into the importance of ideological "framing" in contemporary political discourse, we recommend the work of George Lakoff, Professor of Cognitive Linguistics at the University of California at Berkeley.)

What suffers at the granular level of this oversimplification is a regard for truth. If the ideology is supreme, then empirical truth that challenges the ideology cannot be admitted and may even be forcibly dismissed. Significantly, the Owl period is flooded with instances of reality-bending and ethical compromise that are presented as accidents, circumstantial necessities, or as the unvarnished issue of right-thinking, rather than the fruits of partisan strategy, self-absorption, or wanting something to be true (or, more cynically, undiscovered). Some cultural events and artifacts that are relevant here include:

- Fox News hits the airwaves in the fall of 1996 and soon evolves into America's most popular cable news network. Fox creates a whole new concept of what it means to be a national news agency, becoming the chief icon of a media era (trailblazed by AM radio personality Rush Limbaugh) in which aggressive ideological commentary increasingly trumps dispassionate fact reporting. While a mountain of evidence exists to the contrary, Fox adopts the slogan "Fair & Balanced" and refuses to admit to any ideological bias. The ascendant right wing media spends much of the late 1990s vilifying (it's not too strong a term) U.S. president Bill Clinton. Dissatisfaction with the sitting president is not just a matter of political ideology, but one of personal character. Clinton wins admiration from a majority of the American public by largely managing to stay above the name-calling, but it all goes sour for him (and right-wing pundits rejoice) when the Monica Lewinsky sex scandal breaks. More than the clear impropriety of sexual relations with a White House intern, the public trust is shaken when Clinton attempts to obfuscate the truth of the affair in Grand Jury testimony. "It depends on what the meaning of 'is' is," definitely captures the Owl-era zeitgeist.

- It's not just Bill Clinton, though, as the political era of the Owls is in many ways dominated by the questionable ethics of elected officials. One name that surfaces in the late 1990s and that will forever be associated with the Owl era is Jack Abramoff, a congressional lobbyist on behalf of Indian gaming interests. Abramoff's work, for which he is eventually convicted and jailed, includes generous gifts and campaign donations to a posse of elected officials who support the interests of Abramoff's clients. One especially important individual caught up in the scandal is Tom DeLay, Republican Majority Leader of the U.S. House of Representatives, who famously opens the 2005 session of Congress by spearheading a self-protecting change to the House ethics rules. DeLay later resigns and is eventually criminally convicted of money laundering in connection to campaign financing. In 2006, a poll by the Pew Research Center reports that 81 percent of all Americans believe that the bribing of members of Congress by lobbyists is "common practice."

- But it's not just political heroes who wilt. In all of sports there's hardly a more honored record than most home runs in a baseball season, which stands at "61" for 37 years. Between 1998 and 2001, however, that seemingly unassailable total is topped six times, and it soon becomes clear that part of the reason is the new generation's use of banned performance-enhancing substances. Perhaps the nadir of baseball's so-called "steroid era" comes when star slugger Rafael Palmeiro testifies to a 2005 session of Congress: "I have never used steroids. Period. I don't know how to say it any more clearly than that. Never." He tests positive for steroids five months later.

- Assuredly, the period is also marked by a sexual abuse and cover-up scandal in the Roman Catholic Church. An 2002 expose in the Boston Globe centers around the activities of Archbishop Bernard Law and ultimately leads to his resignation, a national "outing" of hebephilic priests, and literally thousands of accusations of covered-up sexual predation. While this grave and disturbing development hardly needs elucidation on moral grounds, the tone of Owl times is well captured in a statement by William Donohue, president of the American Catholic League: "The far right will tell you the reason we have this problem goes back to Vatican II. We made too many reforms. They blame everything on the reforms. The far left says the problem we have today is we didn't make enough reforms. ... Both sides greet the bad news about the Catholic Church, particularly regarding matters sexual, as good news because they feel vindicated."

- A "sky is falling" mentality grips America's political and business communities as the calendar marches toward a fateful millennial turning to the year 2000. The "Y2K" problem, stemming from how the digits of the year are recorded on computers, leads to enormous garment rending from economists, corporate spokespersons, consultants, and enormously concerned politicians on both sides of the political spectrum. This quote by New York's Democratic Senator Daniel Patrick Moynihan is representative: "I have no proof that the sun is about to rise on the apocalyptic millennium of which Chapter 20 of the Book of Revelation speaks. Yet, it is becoming apparent to all of us that a once seemingly innocuous computer glitch relating to how computers recognize dates could wreak worldwide havoc." An estimated half-trillion dollars are spent to address the issue, a lot of that with the companies of the pundits who predict the problem. The event is ultimately a colossal fizzle and its "truth" is captured by Stanley Bing, writing in *Fortune* in February of 2000: "It is clear by now that the nations, companies, and individuals that did nothing because they were too stupid to prepare for the Y2K global disaster fared exactly as well as AT&T, which reportedly spent more than $500 million on the problem."

- Without any consent from the musicians whose copyrighted work is made available for free via its Internet service, Napster makes a full frontal attack on the notion of intellectual property when it launches a wildly popular, free music file-sharing system in 1999. Proponents of the service, including a number of musicians, hail it as a portentous advance in technology and the democratization of art.

Many though, including the U.S. justice system that shuts the service down in 2001, tend more to the opinion of Hilary Rosen, CEO of the Recording Industry Association of America, who comments, "Napster is essentially using the music to make money for themselves, and that's the part that's both morally and legally wrong."

- It requires no great detective work to discover corporations and financial institutions that severely test the public trust during the Owl period, with names such as WorldCom, Merrill Lynch, AIG, Nortel, Tyco International, Xerox, Global Crossing, Halliburton and Lehman Brothers among a lengthy list of companies, accounting firms, banks, and brokerages that are tainted by scandals relating to "disinformation" in the Owl years. Especially poignant perhaps is the fate of Arthur Andersen, one of the world's leading accounting firms, forced to surrender its CPA credentials in 2002 after being found criminally guilty of fraud in the audit of Houston-based Enron Corporation. "Think straight, talk straight" was the oft-quoted motto of company founder Arthur Andersen. But such a notion seems little more than a quaint historical artifact in the ethically murky and opportunistic financial climate of the Owl period.

- After the 9/11 attack on the World Trade Center, George W. Bush tells the world that, in the matter of Osama Bin Laden, he wants justice, and that means the hunt and capture of the terrorist al-Qaeda leader "dead or alive," a phrase he uses on more than one occasion. Asked less than two years later about progress in the search for the terrorist leader, the president comments: "I don't know where bin Laden is. I have no idea and really don't care. It is not important, and it is not our priority." It is hardly the only occasion where the president and/or Congress send a perplexing message about the strategies and objectives in the War on Terror. Particularly noteworthy is the heavily lobbied Patriot Act (passed in 2001, somewhat modified in 2005), ratified by both houses of Congress and supported by both political parties, a curiously named law that suspends many important civil liberties in the name of preserving freedom.

- Many other examples of ideology-influenced "truth" can be extracted from the American War on Terror, both at home and abroad. The existence of WMD, the early declaration of victory, and the role of oil in the objectives of the military campaign are all debatable issues that are offered as solid fact by partisans. One of the more curious developments has to be the congressional election of 2006 in which the Democrats recapture the House largely on the basis of a promised curtailment of military involvement in Iraq and then vote almost immediately to finance a troop surge.

- Many other little and not-so-little issues participate in the skewed-truth tenor of the times. Mad cow disease, avian flu, electronic voting machines and defense contractors are just a few of the issues seen through partisan lenses and an eye to someone's profits. Even a subject that might seem as reasonably non-partisan as the benefits of good nutrition is put through the ideological wringer of various interest groups. "Obesity" becomes the villain on a lot of political and social agendas, for example, but the results of a $415 million, eight-year-long study of 49,000 Americans that is published in the *Journal of the American Medical Association* in 2006 concludes that a low-fat diet has no discernible long-term health benefits with regard to major disease. The findings of a completely different study just a year earlier, conducted by the National Cancer Institute and the Centers for Disease Control and Prevention and that are also published in the *Journal of the AMA*, are that extreme obesity is a health risk, but that greater life expectancy is statistically correlated to actually being moderately overweight. It is a fair summation to report that many groups, whose existences are predicated upon a fat fatwah, find these entirely credible findings not to be to their advantage and simply dismiss them as "unbelievable."

It is perhaps only fitting that the essence of all of the preceding is best distilled by a comedian. In the very first segment of his Comedy Network television show launched in the fall of 2005, Stephen Colbert introduces the word "truthiness," a term that captures the contemporary predisposition towards elevating the feeling one has in one's gut—i.e. a strong personal preference—over any empirical data or expert knowledge in determining what is true. The word quickly passes into wide media circulation and embraces the era's zeitgeist so perfectly that it earns "word of the year" citations from the American Dialect Society (2005) and the *Merriam-Webster Dictionary* (2006).

So, are there really no truths left to which the Owls may collectively abide? A consideration of Owl popular culture in the next chapter attempts to answer that question. For the record, though, it is what it is.

21

THE OWLS
Cultural Expressions of an Era

"The Matrix is everywhere. It is all around us. Even now, in this very room. You can
see it when you look out your window or when you turn on your television. You can
feel it when you go to work... when you go to church... when you pay your taxes. It is
the world that has been pulled over your eyes to blind you from the truth."
"What truth"?
"That you are a slave, Neo. Like everyone else you were born into bondage. Into a
prison that you cannot taste or see or touch. A prison for your mind."
Laurence Fishburne as Morpheus and Keanu Reeves as Neo, *The Matrix* (1999)

One of the questions arising from these Value Population analyses is why the authors place such an emphasis on an era's culture, especially cinema. The answer, as briefly as possible, is that the actual events of a value-formation period merely constitute what is transpiring on the surface of collective consciousness. In culture, one encounters what creative and relatively uninhibited minds think about what is going on in the depths—an activity that encompasses prognostication as well as description, and that centers itself about the dramatic representation of current events' consequences and meaning. This preamble is relevant to all of the Value Population cultural discussions but nowhere more so than with the Owls. Immediately preceded by a Value Population, the Transformers, in which competitiveness and winning are at the center of the value zeitgeist, the Owls are seemingly destined to ask a collective generational question: "What exactly is it that you intend to win?" For the Owls, material possession and managerial position just may not seem like entirely satisfactory answers.

What may be the hardest thing for other Value Populations to buy into about the Owls is that they seem poised to question some fairly established cultural precepts in which they may find themselves entrapped rather than liberated. In bedrock social areas such as politics, religion, economics, employment, family, civics, consumerism and so on, there is every indication that nothing will be accepted as valid merely because it is historically vested. In a world marked by nothing so much as the clash of competitive outlooks, the urgency for the Owls is more than likely not going to be defense of someone else's dogma but a search for personal conceptual liberation.

At least, that is what is suggested by Owl-era value-formation culture as far as we can see right now.

THE QUEST

The real truth is, I probably don't want to be too happy or content.
Because, then what? I actually like the quest, the search. That's the fun.
The more lost you are, the more you have to look forward to. What do you
know? I'm having a great time and I don't even know it.
—Calista Flockhart as Ally McBeal, *Ally McBeal* (1997–2002)

If Transformers are the masters of the close-in confrontation, then Owls are certainly the lords of the broad viewpoint. Fulfillment in the first case comes from engagement. In the latter case, one must seek perspective.

No dramatic form is more influential in the cinema of the Owl value-formation period than that of the personal quest. Whether in the guise of classic fantasy tales such as *The Lord of the Rings* (2001–2002–2003) and *Star Wars* (1999–2002–2005), or expressionistic fables such as *Fight Club* (1999) and *Kill Bill* (2003–2004), or modernistic tales of self-discovery such as *The Truman Show* (1998) and *Cast Away* (2000), or children's stories such as *Finding Nemo* (2003) and *The Polar Express* (2004), the Owl period abounds with central figures who are willing to go, literally, as far as it might take to find an essential truth about themselves and the world they inhabit. In literature, Robert Fagles' translation of Homer's *Odyssey* is a *Time Magazine* Book of the Year in 1996, and the following year the same honor is bestowed upon *Into the Wild* author John Krakauer's *Into Thin Air*, the tale of a calamitous expedition to the top of Mt. Everest.

The epiphanies in these woks and their brethren are appropriately far ranging, dealing with issues of good versus evil, God's intention for mankind, fate versus free will, personal ethics and obligation, the roles of faith and good works, the nature of heroism, the essence of perception, the meaning of existence, and a host of other heavy stuff. Helping to define these matters and give them even further gravitas is the fact that some of these quests come to very bad ends. Yet there is something in the nascent Owl worldview that suggests an Owl's need to discover truth and, however great the unknown and its consequences, an eagerness to embrace the journey.

Even in what are ostensibly children stories, the Owl value mandate is made clear: "The thing about trains...it doesn't matter where they're going," says Tom Hanks as The Conductor to a young boy in *The Polar Express* (2004). "What matters is deciding to get on." Or as Mike Myers as the eponymous animated ogre in *Shrek 2* (2004) tells his traveling companion Donkey voiced by Eddie Murphy, "The kingdom of Far Far Away donkey, that's where we're going...far, far away."

THE SKY MAY ACTUALLY BE FALLING

Los Angeles, New York, and Washington D.C. have been left in ruins.
Joe Fowler as the Reporter, *Independence Day* (1996)

Throughout the rest of this chapter, a case will be made regarding unique Owl survival mechanisms and even the generally brave and hopeful nature of Owl value-formation culture. It would be a disservice to that analysis, however, to not first point out that Owls will almost certainly come to appreciate that, for the children of 9/11, these are hardly perfect times and that ours is not a perfect world. Faced with unprecedented global peril, in fact, what may even bring the most eventual honor to the value matrix of the Owls is a generational disposition towards looking past the most terrible of calamities and preserving a sense that there is always an opportunity if one can make it to tomorrow.

Even so, it would be an important oversight to look past the sheer scope of devastation in Owl-era culture. Representative blockbuster movies such as *Independence Day* (1996), *Mars Attacks!* (1996), *Titanic* (1997), *The Fifth Element* (1997), *Deep Impact* (1998), *Armageddon* (1998), *Fight Club* (1999), *Gladiator* (2000), *Perfect Storm* (2000), *The Core (2003)*, *The Last Samurai* (2003), *The Day After Tomorrow* (2004), *Million Dollar Baby* (2004), *War of the Worlds* (2005), *V for Vendetta* (2006), *300* (2006), and *I Am Legend* (2007), not to mention just about every popular video game of the era, all offer up mammoth depictions of destruction ranging from the demise of central character(s) to the wasting of considerable portions of the earth itself. In all, it is abundantly clear that Owl-era culture portrays a world in which the vulnerabilities are enormous and not everything is likely to end up okay.

Of course, much of this "entertainment" caters to a Transformer sensibility that is prepared to encounter life as a blood sport in a world filled with chaos. It is in their overriding propensity to treat even the end of the world philosophically, however, where the preceding movies become quite Owlish. In movie after movie of the Owl era, even the worst ends are explored for their inherent philosophical value and their contribution to human evolution—and time after time, the lesson drawn is that the experience and acceptance of loss is the prelude to wisdom.

"Mankind survived the last ice age," representatively observes Dennis Quaid as climatologist Jack Hall in *The Day After Tomorrow* as the world experiences a meteorological disaster that kills roughly half the population of the U.S. and displaces the rest. "We're certainly capable of surviving this one. All depends on whether or not we're able to learn from our mistakes."

Or maybe the key admonition is contained in *Chicken Little* (2005), an updated Disney version of the timeless "sky is falling" fable. In the Owl-era version we learn that the much-derided Chicken Little is telling the truth, as what is actually falling are the pieces of an invading alien spacecraft. The truth that may be required to save mankind, it is quite apparent to the young Owls, is hardly predetermined by the congenitally close-minded.

CORRUPT AUTHORITY

The future of the planet is in the hands of a bunch of retards I wouldn't
trust with a potato gun.
Bruce Willis as Harry Stamper, *Armageddon* (1998)

We have previously chronicled the Believer problem with establishment authority, pointing out the value-formation ramifications of widespread father abandonment and a general sense of uncaring in the culture with regard to male authority figures. A negative portrayal of authority returns with a vengeance in the Owl period, although this time the charge of "uncaring" is joined by incompetent, manipulative and cruel. And for what it is worth, women are now also allowed in on the act.

One hardly needs the representations of "art" to show how ethically fallen are the mighty during the Owl value-formation period, as has already been illustrated in the previous Owl chapters. Although it is reviled as slanted polemic by the voices on the political right, Michael Moore's documentary *Fahrenheit 9/11* (2004) captures the tone of the times in its portrayal of the Bush Administration's actions during the most politically potent crisis of the Owl period. The president's reading of a children's book as the airplanes hit the Trade Center towers, and his golf course admonition to "watch this drive" as he discusses global terrorism, become powerful iconic leadership images of the age.

Artistically powerful in the leadership context is one of the great villains in the *Harry Potter* series, Doris Umbridge, who propels much of the action in *Harry Potter and the Order of the Phoenix* (2007). The quintessential evil ideologue, Umbridge deposes the kindly Dumbledore as head of Hogwart's School of Witchcraft and Wizardry, and proceeds to corrupt the students' preparation as wizards by giving them crappy books and forbidding them to practice their craft. Thematically invoking the era's "patriot act" headlines, Umbridge creates an Inquisitorial Squad to enforce her politically motivated edicts, and in a famous scene burns the sentence "I will not lie" into Harry Potter's arm when he refuses to retract an honest account of a politically charged personal experience.

While not always dealt with in such heavy overtones, throughout the culture of the Owl value formation there is a sense that much of leadership is, if not evil, at best irrelevant to what is urgent—and true—in life. Coaching his friend Pedro, who is running in a school election, John Hezder as the laconic Napoleon Dynamite (2004) advises, "Just tell them their wildest dreams will come true if they vote for you." Or as a very minor character in *X-Men: The Last Stand* (2006) puts it when the president demands to be acknowledged during a crisis: "Oh Mr. President, shut up."

Taken at face value, it appears that the Owls will be a generation that unabashedly questions traditional authority—that is if they pay any attention to it at all.

STRAIGHT TALK

"Can you really trust another human being?"
"Yeah, I think so."
"No. The answer is you cannot."
Robert DeNiro as Jack Byrnes and Ben Stiller as Greg Focker in *Meet the Parents* (2000)

Perhaps the real issue regarding the failure of authority in the Owl cultural era is the fact that it is almost impossible for anyone with a social agenda to consistently tell the truth. Small wonder there is simply no greater imperative in the Owl scheme of things than unbridled honesty. Perusing the cultural evidence one easily comes to the conclusion that it is forgivable to an Owl to sometimes accept a mistake but never to just endure bullshit. ("Falsehood" would have been the more gentile word selection, but it doesn't quite capture the appropriate spirit.)

So it is that the Owl-era culture is rich in the presentation of the most amazingly unvarnished pronouncements of personal truth. These unfiltered assessments, such as the quote from *The Matrix* regarding the mind's prison that heads this chapter, are variably profane, crude, funny, judgmental, strident and profound. Certainly, they may be challenged as absolute truths, but they are formidable as the products of intelligences, saying and describing exactly what they mean. Consider…

…in *Little Miss Sunshine* (2006), Paul Dano is Dwayne, a teenager who reaches the point at which he can longer bear the shortcomings of his family and asks to be left at the side of the road: "No, you're not my family! I don't wanna be your family! I hate you fucking people! Divorce? Bankrupt? Suicide? You're fucking losers, you're losers! No, please just leave me here, Mom. Please, please, please. Please… just leave me here."

…in *Good Will Hunting* (1997), Ben Affleck is Chuckie Sullivan, a working class Bostonian who confronts his mathematical genius friend Matt Damon who, as Will Hunting, has just remarked how friends will always be neighbors and grow old together: "Look, you're my best friend so don't take this the wrong way, but in twenty years if you're still livin' here, comin' over to my house, watchin' the Patriots games, workin' construction, I'll fuckin' kill ya. That's not a threat, that's a fact, I'll fuckin' kill ya…Cuz tomorrow I'm gonna wake up and I'll be fifty, and I'll still be doin' this shit. And that's all right. That's fine. I mean, you're sittin' on a winnin' lottery ticket. And you're too much of a pussy to cash it in, and that's bullshit. 'Cause I'd do fuckin' anything to have what you got. So would any of these fuckin' guys. It'd be an insult to us if you're still here in twenty years. Hangin' around here is a fuckin' waste of your time."

…in *Talladega Nights: The Ballad of Ricky Bobby* (2006), the very high-spirited children of a famous race car driver confront their grandfather, who expects them to behave more decorously and respectfully. "Greatest generation my ass," spits out one of the kids. "Tom Brokaw is a punk."

As in other areas of Owl culture, art is not entirely necessary to make the point about how difficult it is to express truth and, therefore, how precious it is. The Owl era is comedian/commentator John Stewart memorably telling the media's talking heads during an appearance on the CNN show *Crossfire* (2004), "What you do is not honest…What you do is partisan hackery." In the same year, it is humor columnist Dave Barry observing in his end-of-the-year review, titled "No Thanks for the Memories": "The federal budget deficit continued to worsen, despite the concerted effort of virtually every elected official in Washington— Republican or Democrat—to spend more money."

"Everybody lies," intones High Laurie in his Emmy winning portrayal of the cantankerous, straight-spoken Dr. Gregory House on the television program *House M.D.* (2004–2012). It is a difficult starting point for human interaction—but if anyone will deal with the situation successfully by tirelessly piercing the veil, it will likely be the lied-to-since-birth Owls.

IT DOESN'T COMPUTE

"You are making a mistake. My logic is undeniable."

"You have so got to die."

Fiona Hogan as the voice of the supercomputer V.I.K.I and Will Smith as Detective Del Spooner

in *I, Robot* (2004)

As if the broad truth-seeking expanse of the Owl worldview isn't already hard enough to circumscribe, one must also consider the apparent Owl discomfort with logic and linear processes. It's not an entirely unexpected state of affairs, as it has already been shown that Owls tend to feel that most data is corrupted by the subjectivity of its source, and that even the cleverest of data constructs is hardly likely to enhance truthfulness. And so we are confronted with quite an important turn of cultural events in the Owl value-formation era, as the Age of Information is essentially t-boned by an Age of Meaning.

It's not that the Owl era culture advocates lazy thinking, as Owls are actually inclined to delve very deeply into any subject they find compelling and may manifest real genius in such matters. It's just that the Owls have every right to be unimpressed by massive compilations of data forced into structured rubrics that 1) don't "feel" meaningful and 2) don't actually improve the general condition of human interaction and enterprise. In the business world, interestingly, there is quite a sudden Owl-era fascination with the principle of "emotional intelligence," a concept introduced by Daniel Goleman in the *Harvard Business Review* (1998), touting qualities of self-awareness and empathy, as opposed to technical skill and rational intelligence, as the determinant factors in leadership success.

In movies, the condemnation, sometimes quite comical, of lives built on hierarchical structure and precise logic is everywhere. The 'global crisis' movies such as *Independence Day* (1996) and *Armageddon* (1998) and *The Core* (2003) and *The Day After Tomorrow* (2004) all advance the premise that human destiny orbits around the wildly unpredictable. Other films, such as *Good Will Hunting* (1997) and *A Beautiful Mind* (2001) and *Into the Wild* (2007), make eloquent points about essential knowledge hardly ever being derived in a structured academic context.

In the movie *Matrix Reloaded* (2003), Merovingian, a powerful computer program that advances the principle of causality rather than choice in human affairs, comments: "What is the reason? Soon the why and the reason are gone and all that matters is the feeling. This is the nature of the universe. We struggle against it, we fight to deny it; but it is of course a lie. Beneath our poised appearance we are completely out of control."

Or maybe the Owl outlook is just as simple as this comment from Paul Bettany as the academic Charles Hermon in *A Beautiful Mind*: "Mathematics is never going to lead you to a higher truth, and you know why? Because it's boring."

HOPE

"I know. It's all wrong. By rights we shouldn't even be here. But we are. It's like in the great stories, Mr. Frodo. The ones that really mattered. Full of darkness and danger, they were. And sometimes you didn't want to know the end. Because how could the end be happy? How could the world go back to the way it was when so much bad had happened? But in the end, it's only a passing thing, this shadow. Even darkness must pass. A new day will come. And when the sun shines it will shine out the clearer. Those were the stories that stayed with you. That meant something, even if you were too small to understand why. But I think, Mr. Frodo, I do understand. I know now. Folk in those stories had lots of chances of turning back, only they didn't. They kept going. Because they were holding on to something."

"What are we holding onto, Sam?"

"That there's some good in this world, Mr. Frodo... and it's worth fighting for."

Sean Astin as Sam Gamgee and Elijah Wood as Frodo Baggins,

The Lord of the Rings: The Two Towers (2003)

At this point in the analysis, it almost seems that the Owls are in need of some kind of rehabilitation. We've learned that logic is a dead end, everyone tells lies, authority is corrupt, the world is full of destruction, and worthwhile goals are, as Shrek puts it, "far, far away." What hope is there for such a generation?

Well, strangely, it turns out that hope may be the very best thing Owls have going for themselves.

Not to put too fine a point on the argument, but if one is not bound by the dogmatic viewpoints and the prejudices of others, then the rules of conceptual engagement with the world are entirely of one's own choice. So much in the cinema and literature of the Owl period, not to mention the era's current events, is a matter of the classic confrontation between the forces of good and evil. What's fascinating is how often the former are freely embraced and championed, even when the odds are long and after heavy dues have been extracted.

In *Remember the Titans* (2000), Denzel Washington is Coach Herman Boone, an African-American football coach faced with the task of bringing together a racially divided Virginia community of the 1970s.

"This is where they fought the battle of Gettysburg," Boone tells his players as they head to their first training camp. "Fifty thousand men died right here on this field, fighting the same fight that we are still fighting among ourselves today. This green field right here, painted red, bubblin' with the blood of young boys. Smoke and hot lead pouring right through their bodies. Listen to their souls, men. I killed my brother with malice in my heart. Hatred destroyed my family. You listen, and you take a lesson from the dead. If we don't come together right now on this hallowed ground, we too will be destroyed, just like they were. I don't care if you like each other of not, but you will respect each other. And maybe...I don't know, maybe we'll learn to play this game like men."

Or consider remarks by Hugh Grant as the British Prime Minister in *Love Actually* (2003): "Whenever I get gloomy with the state of the world, I think about the arrivals gate at Heathrow Airport. General opinion is starting to make out that we live in a world of hatred and greed, but I don't see that. It seems to me that love is everywhere. Often, it's not particularly dignified or newsworthy, but it's always there—fathers and sons, mothers and daughters, husbands and wives, boyfriends, girlfriends, old friends. When the planes hit the Twin Towers, as far as I know, none of the phone calls from the people on board were messages of hate or revenge— they were all messages of love. If you look for it, I've got a sneaking suspicion...love actually is all around."

Of course, there are also characters in the culture of the Owls who reject hope. In both *Fight Club* (1998) and *V for Vendetta* (2006), for example, hope is actually portrayed as weakness, something delusional, an obstacle to clarity and freedom. Yet, even the characters who voice these sentiments have a hope for the spiritual liberation that lies beyond worldly hope. And if you can understand that apparent contradiction, perhaps there's some hope that you will understand the Owls.

INTEGRITY

Inside each and every one of us is one true authentic swing...Somethin' we was born with... Somethin' that's ours and ours alone... Somethin' that can't be taught to ya or learned... Somethin' that got to be remembered...

Will Smith as Bagger Vance, *The Legend of Bagger Vance* (2000)

Belief is a quality that is as important to the Owls as it is to The Believers. Unlike their Value Population predecessors, however, Owl belief manifests as more than passive faith that everything will 'somehow' work out well over the long term. Far more dynamic and expansive in nature, Owl-era seekers believe in the potential of an individual to be in tune with the universe—to seek and embrace a quality of personal and universal authenticity that may best be labeled as one's "integrity."

In literally dozens of popular Owl-era movies as dramatically and stylistically divergent as *Fight Club* (1998), *The Perfect Storm* (2000), *Spider-Man* (2002–2004–2007), *Kill Bill* (2003–2004), *The Incredibles* (2004), and *High School Musical* (2006), plots turn on protagonists believing in and being true to their inner selves.

In the highly acclaimed martial arts fantasy *Crouching Tiger, Hidden Dragon* (2000), Michelle Yeoh is Yu Shu Lien, a great warrior. Her sincere advice to the callow young noblewoman who strives to defeat her: "Whatever path you decide to take in this life...be true to yourself."

In the philosophically rich, cult science fiction favorite *Serenity* (2006), derived from the cult favorite television series *Firefly* (2002), the spiritual adviser to the renegade crew of the Serenity is Shepherd Book, played by Ron Glass. The crux of his counsel to the highly complex crew: "I don't care what you believe in, just believe in it."

Even in a contemporary comedy such as *The Devil Wears Prada* (2006), Adrian Grenier as the sous chef Nate delivers the ultimate put-down to his girlfriend, who has apparently changed her personal style and values for a glamorous job: "I wouldn't care if you were out there pole-dancing all night, as long as you did it with a little integrity!"

It's noteworthy that, unlike the Transformers, winning and losing is not ultimately what is at stake here. Victory and loss in the Owl value-formation period may very well be in the realm of the material world, but true triumphs take place in the realm of the spirit. One of the era's most lauded films, Clint Eastwood's *Million Dollar Baby*, makes this point when, on her deathbed, Hilary Swank as the paralyzed fighter Maggie Fitzgerald asks for her manager's assistance in committing suicide: "I can't be like this, Frankie. Not after what I've done. I've seen the world. People chanted my name. ...You think I ever dreamed that'd happen? I was born two pounds, one-and-a-half ounces. Daddy used to tell me I'd fight my way into this world, and I'd fight my way out. That's all I wanna do, Frankie. I just don't wanna fight you to do it. I got what I needed. I got it all."

SOCIAL CONTRACTS

Whatever life holds in store for me, I will never forget these words: "With great power comes great responsibility."

Toby MacGuire as Peter Parker, *Spider-Man* (2002)

Each and every Owl may engage in a unique quest to discover a personal and powerful "integrity" in this lifetime. Stressing such a matter, however, is not to imply a lack of concern with one's fellow man. Certainly, Owls appreciate both the necessity and the benefits of relationships and community, although as argued throughout the Owls chapters, in the Internet age this is far more dependent upon determining common 'universal' creed than it is upon local geography.

It's worth mentioning that as with every other Value Population, likely since the beginning of time, the Owl-era culture presents love as a cornerstone of meaningful human interaction. A truly remarkable variety of traditional and untraditional love stories populate the Owl culture, with such popular films as *Perfect Storm* (2000), *Cast Away* (2000), *The Family Man* (2000), *Gladiator* (2000), and *The Notebook* (2004) going so far as to present love as the ultimate transcendent human condition, even capable of trumping time and material reality. While so much more could be said about the power of love in the Owl worldview, its value stature is neatly captured by a memorable lyrical injunction from the culturally iconic Broadway show/movie *Rent* (1996 show, 2005 movie): "Measure your life in love."

Even so, Owls are decidedly the sort of Value Population that will eschew the notion that one social concept—even one as powerful as love—fits all situations. Germaine to the Owl worldview is a sense that one's life presents a never-ending series of forks in the road, and that one is constantly forced to make directional choices. In the Owl culture, true fulfillment is often presented as a free will turn onto a principled path marked by empathy—a caring respect for people we may not even particularly like, much less love—even if it is a less direct route to our own self-interest.

This premise is at the center of the enormously popular film *Jerry Maguire* (1996), in which a sports agent played by Tom Cruise rejects the duplicity and manipulativeness of the sports agent profession. Although he has profited greatly as an agent, Cruise/Maguire circulates a report titled "The Things We Think and Do Not Say: The Future of Our Business" and loses his job because of it. The moral victory eventually translates into a real victory and much self-awareness, but it's a long road.

The dramatic dynamic engendered by issues of "common interest" versus "self-interest" also memorably drives the action of the highly lauded television series *Boston Legal* (2004-2008). Representing the profit interest is the comically narcissistic attorney Denny Crane, portrayed by William Shatner, who comments in one episode, "I'm so far up the ass of big business, I view the world as one giant colon." On the opposite side of the moral spectrum is gracefully eloquent attorney Alan Shore, played by James Spader, who one time characteristically comments, "You know what I miss about our country, Denny? Not the loss of our civil rights so much as our compassion, our soul."

In *Spider-Man 2* (2004) Peter Parker's Aunt May, played by Rosemary Harris, counsels her super-powered nephew to always act selflessly in the interests of the greater good. "I believe there's a hero in all of us," says Aunt May, "that keeps us honest, gives us strength, makes us noble, and finally allows us to die with pride, even though sometimes we have to be steady and give up the thing we want the most. Even our dreams." This theme of sacrificing one's own interests for a greater good is echoed in many other 'hero' movies, including *Saving Private Ryan* (1998), *Pearl Harbor* (2001), *Batman Begins* (2005), *Man on Fire* (2004), *Superman Returns* (2006) and *Ghost Rider* (2007).

Ultimately, the key here is an appreciation that the Owl value system will tend to embrace a social contract that is entered into freely and has ethical merit. In *Harry Potter and the Chamber of Secrets* (2002), Richard Harris as Professor Albus Dumbledore tells Daniel Radcliffe as Harry Potter, "It is not our abilities that show us what we truly are. It is our choices." Choosing to embrace the family of man through true love or genuine empathy is generally regarded in Owl culture as a choice well made.

MAGIC, MUTATION & ANIMAL MAGNETISM

Why is it divine or human? Can't human be divine?
Tom Hanks as Robert Langdon, *The DaVinci Code* (2006)

And then there is *Harry Potter*, the landmark series of seven books written by British author J.K. Rowling, published between 1997–2007, about the education of a young wizard and his cohorts.

To be sure, in many ways the *Harry Potter* series of books and films is a Transformer 'entertainment' phenomenon, as good takes on evil in a death struggle for control of the world. Beyond the power struggle, however, or even the morality play that is central to an appreciation of the Owls, lies something even more profound. It's the youth-friendly opening of the gate between the world of "muggles" (non-wizard humans) and the world of magic, invoking the premise that a condition of extraordinary power and consciousness is somehow natural to humankind.

All that has been written in the Owl material up to this point has stressed qualities and situations that, while occasionally extreme, are subject to human consideration and resolution. The Owl era, though, is also culturally cognizant of what certainly feels like a metamorphosis in consciousness, driven by the need to process all the currents of a global communications age, as discussed in the preceding chapters. Owl-era culture for very good reasons confronts an evolutionary question, namely, "Must mankind become something more than human in order to survive?"

It is ultimately this question that most directly led to the naming of this Value Population as Owls. In Harry Potter, owls are essentially quasi-magical messengers that are the instruments of communication among wizards in the 'real' and magical worlds. Also in the *Harry Potter* books, students at the Hogwart's School of Wizardry are in constant preparation for a comprehensive fifth-year examination called the O.W.L., an acronym for Ordinary Wizarding Levels that include such subjects as divination, charms, care of magical creatures, and defense against the dark arts.

In ancient mythology, it may be briefly mentioned, the owl is the sacred animal totem of Pallas Athena, the goddess of wisdom. Athena's greatest gifts, according to classical scholars, are the ability to recognize patterns in human affairs and to quickly grasp the inter-relatedness of diverse concepts. Characterized as intellectually edgy, forthright and blunt, the born-in-armor Athena is aptly characterized as a warrior in the battle for divine understanding, a description that may also come to one day suit the value 'mythology' of the Owls.

It should be stressed that the Owl-era magic/mutation cultural phenomenon is hardly limited to *Harry Potter*. A partial list of the movies (many of them series) that explore the phenomenon of cross-species (including alien and robotic) alliances and human 'augmentation' includes: *Mighty Morphin' Power Rangers: The Movie* (1995); *Toy Story* (1995, 1999, 2000); *Men In Black* (1997, 2002); *Lord of the Rings* (2001, 2002, 2003); *Shrek* (2001, 2004, 2007), *A.I. Artificial Intelligence* (2001); *Spider-Man* (2002, 2004, 2007); *Minority Report* (2002); *Hulk* (2003); *Terminator 3: The Rise of the Machines* (2003); *I, Robot* (2004); *The Incredibles* (2004); *Batman Begins* (2005), *Night at the Museum* (2006), and *Transformers* (2007). In many of these and other movies such as *The Chronicles of Narnia: The Lion, The Witch and the Wardrobe* (2005), *March of the Penguins* (2005) and *The Golden Compass* (2007), there is also a special invocation of the wisdom and powers of the animal kingdom in service to and/or as moral objectives for mankind.

Deserving of special mention here is the *X-Men series* (2000, 2003, 2006), literally plotted around a political struggle between an emerging mutant population with super-human powers and a threatened establishment society. A dead-on parable for the political currents of the time, the series gets much of its dramatic heft from a schism among the mutants themselves. At the center of the debate are Patrick Stewart's Dr. Charles Xavier, who is in favor of mutant assimilation into the establishment culture ("mankind is not evil, just misinformed"), and Ian McKellen's Magneto, who is in favor of mutant displacement of the human race ("we are the future…they no longer matter").

Both men would agree to the following, however, the first lines spoken in the three movies. (Patrick Stewart is narrating.) It is a statement that really gets to the heart of the matter as we observe the coming to value maturity of the Owls: "Mutation: it is the key to our evolution. It has enabled us to evolve from a single-celled organism into the dominant species on the planet. This process is slow, and normally takes thousands and thousands of years. But every few hundred millennia, evolution leaps forward."

In a special part of their consciousness, Owls may not only believe they can leap but that, like Harry Potter's owl, they can fly.

COMEDY

What's he like?

God? Lonely. But funny.

Linda Fiorentino as Bethany and Alan Rickman as Metatron, *Dogma* (1999)

For all the earnestness, ardor, and occasional magic that the Owls are likely to bring to their search for meaning in the world, they are not going to be above having a good laugh at their own expense. Throughout the Owl value-formation era, cultural efforts that strive to understand and define the world are simultaneously cognizant that the task is often a fool's quest. Assimilating all there is for the Owls to assimilate is reminiscent of the observation about putting ten pounds of feathers in a five-pound bag, with all the the attendant prospects for mirth and mayhem.

In retrospect, the Owl value-formation era may actually come to seem like something of a comedic golden age. In a world in which passionate opinions and self-serving agendas often masquerade as truth and every human eccentricity has its day in some media forum, comedic characterization from satire to slapstick is a natural. Comic stalwarts such as Will Ferrell, Vince Vaughn, Ben Stiller, Owen Wilson, Jack Black, Adam Sandler, Jim Carrey, Mike Meyers, Jackie Chan, Chris Rock, Chris Tucker, Martin Lawrence, Kathy Griffin, Sarah Silverman, the legion of performers in live comedy clubs and on the Comedy Central channel, and the creators of such television shows as *South Park* (1997–) and *The*

Family Guy (1998–) are as iconic of the Owl-era culture as any politician or pundit.

What Owl-era humorists primarily lend to our understanding of Owl values is that the search for enlightenment is so easily derailed by the everyday foibles of man. An attempt has been made in these chapters to point out all of the brave and noble things the Owl Value Population may someday be if it should rise to the challenge of its cultural conditioning. The Owl-era humorists offer a balance by dramatizing the likely stumbling blocks of (Owl) character that can cause a seeker's path to meander in energy-sapping yet chuckle-inducing circles, including:

- Argumentativeness: Suspect of the truths of others, the Owls will always have another view of the matter, which they won't hesitate to express.
- "Cartman, that's the dumbest thing you've ever said...this week.." – Matt Stone as Kyle in *South Park* (1997–)
- Directness to the Point of Rudeness: Owls will rarely be linguistically delicate in telling it like it is. This will not necessarily win popularity contests.
- "When the shootin' started, he was way too cool. And normally when there's shootin' white people aren't that cool, man. They either run around in circles, or screaming out 'Aaaaagh'!" –Chris Tucker as James Carter in *Rush Hour 2* (2001)
- Resistance to Absolutes: Owls will look for certainties, but certainties are so hard to identify. Rules seem so often subjective and outcomes so indeterminate.
- "At the stroke of midnight, my father (Satan) will be completely deteriorated and all your souls will be mine. Soon you will see things more horrible than you can even imagine. Well...maybe not that horrible...but still pretty bad." – Rhys Ifans as Adrian in *Little Nicky* (2000)
- Delayed Adulthood: The flip side of open-mindedness is an unguarded naiveté. Owls may find it very hard to develop a role within a conforming 'adult' social niche.
- "You think I like avoiding my wife and kids to hang out with nineteen year old girls everyday?" –Vince Vaughn as Bernard "Beanie" Campbell in *Old School* (2003)
- Proneness to Depression: The Owl quest for meaning is a lengthy journey, and there are so many things that can go wrong between here and there.
- "Give up, just quit, because in this life, you can't win. Yeah, you can try, but in the end you're just gonna lose, big time, because the world is run by the Man. The Man, oh, you don't know the Man.

He's everywhere. In the White House...down the hall...Ms. Mullins, she's the Man. And the Man ruined the ozone, he's burning down the Amazon, and he kidnapped Shamu and put her in a chlorine tank! And there used to be a way to stick it to the Man. It was called rock 'n roll, but guess what, oh no, the Man ruined that too, with a little thing called MTV! So don't waste your time trying to make anything cool or pure or awesome 'cause the Man is just gonna call you a fat, washed-up loser and crush your soul. So do yourselves a favor and just GIVE UP!" – Jack Black as Dewey Finn in *The School of Rock* (2003)

- Potential Inclination to Substance Abuse: "Big Pharma" + illegal drugs = a pill for everything, including expanded consciousness. The Owls are likely to experiment.

- "So I'm rappelling down Mount Vesuvius when suddenly I slip, and I start to fall. Just falling, ahh ahh, I'll never forget the terror. When suddenly I realize 'Holy shit, Hansel, haven't you been smoking peyote for six straight days, and couldn't some of this maybe be in your head?' And it was. I was totally fine. I've never even been to Mount Vesuvius." –Owen Wilson as Hansel in *Zoolander* (2001)

- Bad Auditory Processing—A.D.D.: Submerged deeply in their own swollen stream of consciousness, the Owls may seem to not be listening.

- "Well my friend Sweet Jay took me to that video arcade in town, right, and they don't speak English there, so Jay got into a fight and he's all, 'Hey quit hasslin' me cuz' I don't speak French' or whatever! And then the guy said something in Paris-talk, and I'm like, 'Just back off!' And they're all, 'Get out!' And we're like, 'Make me!' It was cool." –Seth Green as Scott Evil in *Austin Powers: International Man of Mystery* (1997)

- Feelings of Being An Outsider: Owls are explorers, within and without. Sometimes one is just not going to feel part of the local reality.

- "I've sent in my application to the *Real World*. So I'm hoping to hear back from that. I'm putting A LOT of my eggs into that basket, the MTV basket. I'm also thinking about getting a gun, and dealing crack. Being a crack dealer. Not like a mean crack dealer, but like...like a nice one. Kinda friendly like, "Hey, what's up, guys? Want some crack?" I'm just waiting on those two things to flesh themselves out." – Will Ferrell as Ricky Bobby, *Talladega Nights: The Ballad of Ricky Bobby* (2006)

- Capable of Self-Sabotage: Owls may take risks that go well beyond what a prudent person might do in a given situation. Add an inclination to honesty, and talon-in-mouth may easily result.

- "I guess that's how life is, isn't it? Some people are drenched, freezing to death, on a stupid boat, with a stupid hat, while others are in a comfy news studio, suckin' up all the glory. Oh, well. No big deal."
  – Jim Carrey as Bruce Nolan in *Bruce Almighty* (2003)
- Smart but Underachieving: Owls may well arrive at meaningful insights and develop unique talents but are perhaps not so inclined to do the mundane work of putting them to practical use.
- (Below, a wannabe crime-fighting group discusses adding a member.)

  "Well, there's The Sphinx, of course."

  "The what?"

  "The Sphinx."

  "I know this guy. Big crime-fighter from down South. Big-league hitter down there."

  "What's his power?"

  "Well, he's terribly mysterious."

  "That's it? That's his power? He's mysterious?"

  "Well, TERRIBLY mysterious."

  – Hank Azaria as The Blue Raja, Ben Stiller as Mr. Furious, William H. Macy as The Shoveller, *Mystery Men* (1999)

One may certainly cheer for the Owls to rise above these obstacles to success, as well they might. But don't cry for them. They are certain to get the human comedy at least as well as any Value Population that has preceded them.

THE TYRANNY OF STUFF

You sold your soul to the devil when you put on your first pair of Jimmy Choo's. I saw it.

Emily Blunt as Emily, *The Devil Wears Prada* (2006)

It has already been observed that the Owls are likely to have a complex relationship with life's material realities. Like any other Value Population, the Owls will certainly understand that, when it comes to the world's supply of goods and services, having is better than not having. The likelihood of a relatively testing economic future may drive this point home even more strongly, and the answer to the question posed by one of the era's most popular television shows, *Who Wants to Be a Millionaire?* (1999–2009), is bound to remain "everyone."

To be fair, there is even a current in the Owl culture that goes so far as to celebrate the joy of unbridled consumption. Powerful Owl icons in this regard include television series such as *Sex and the City* (1998–2004) and *Entourage* (2004–2011), entirely unapologetic and extremely popular appreciations of the earthy rewards of sybaritic living. Even in works that are less relentlessly celebratory of "the good life," such as *The Devil Wears Prada* (2006) and Elizabeth Gilbert's hugely successful memoir *Eat, Pray Love* (2006), there is a sincere acknowledgment that fine material things may have exquisite value beyond their price, qualities capable of elevating the human spirit.

For all of the preceding, however, the culture of the Owl value-formation period does not cast a particularly fond eye on consumerism. The detractors argue that we tend to become enslaved by goods not only financially but in ways that are injurious to our very souls. This is, of course, not a new notion in the realm of human affairs, but it is well worth remarking just how often mindless acquisition is called out in the popular American culture of the Owl value-formation period.

"We're not only wired to want what we can't have," observes Calista Flockhart as the title character in *Ally McBeal* (1997-2002), "but we're also wired to want what we really don't want."

"That's what it's all about, isn't it?" rhetorically asks Jim Carrey as The Grinch in *How the Grinch Stole Christmas* (2000). "Gifts, gifts, gifts, gifts, gifts. This whole Christmas season is stupid. The avarice never ends."

"When you're living in America at the end of the Millennium," goes a snarky song lyric in the musical *Rent* (2005), "what you are is what you own."

The subject of consumerism is dealt with with humor in films such as *Josie and the Pussycats* (2001), in which we learn that rock music is a front for subliminal advertising to teenagers, in *Thank You for Smoking* (2005), in which we get an insider's view of the lobbying and public relations machinations of big tobacco, alcohol and firearms, and in *Fun with Dick and Jane* (2005), in which a suburban couple embraces a life of crime to finance the capital requirements of their threatened middle class lifestyle. While occasionally dark, all of these are mild compared to some of the dramatic takes on the subject. Arguably, the single most impactful film of the Owl era is *Fight Club* (1999), which vents an enormous amount of frustration at consumerism and, ultimately, the global economic system.

"We are consumers," summarizes Brad Pitt as Tyler Durden in one point in the film. "We're the bi-products of a lifestyle obsession. Murder, crime, poverty, these things don't concern me. What concerns me are celebrity magazines, television with 500 channels, some guy's name on my underwear. Rogaine, Viagra, Olestra…It's all going down, man."

Certainly, it would be presumptuous to conclude that the Owls are on the verge of rejecting the consumer economy that is the cornerstone of American capitalism. Perhaps the struggle to determine ultimate Owl values in this area is best contained in a host of like-minded songs that include Jennifer Lopez' *Jenny from the Block* (2002), Faith Hill's *Mississippi Girl* (2005), Gwen Stefani's *Orange County Girl* (2007), and Fergie's *Glamorous* (2007) in which conspicuously famous and rich women get even more famous and rich by singing about their ongoing attachment to their humble roots. Quite frankly, the Owls may not be buying it.

CONFRONTING CULTURAL COMPLEXITY

"What's got your wand in a knot?"
"He's from Durmstrang! You're fraternizing with the enemy!"
"The enemy? Who was it wanting his autograph? Besides the whole point
of the tournament is international magical cooperation. To make friends!"
"I think he's got a bit more than friendship on his mind. He's using you."
"How dare you! Besides, I can take care of myself!"

Emma Watson as Hermione Granger and Rupert Grint as Ron Weasley,

Harry Potter and the Goblet of Fire (2005)

By the end of the Owl value-formation period, American society divides along ideological lines. One major group, largely conservative in orientation, adopts a perspective that honors a 'traditional' history of American hegemony in which the major stakeholders are white Christian males, their families and their faith groups. A second group, far more liberal, acknowledges the rising tide of mutating gender roles, sexual orientations, racial compositions, and exotic ethnicities in a world that has gone intractably global, behaviorally diverse, and multicultural in its evolutionary path.

The aim here is not to predict a political victory for one side or the other. It is merely to acknowledge that Owls are value formed in an era during which many of the bedrock precepts of an insular American social structure are challenged with a passion and in an amount that is unprecedented in American experience. As has already been argued in earlier chapters, it is likely that Owls will prove to be integrators rather than rejecters of exogenous concepts, although it will admittedly be a bumpy ride.

Three diverse topic areas that are hugely represented in the culture of the Owl value-formation era, and deserve at least some brief consideration here, are: next-generation feminism; gay culture; and international perspective.

Next-Generation Feminism

*I'm a bitch, I'm a lover / I'm a child, I'm a mother /I'm a sinner, I'm a
saint /I do not feel ashamed.*

Meredith Brooks, *Bitch* (1997)

It is probably safe to assume that this is the last Value Population in which feminism is even much of a talking point. So much of the women's movement in earlier cultural eras directs itself towards an appreciation of the collective rights of women in a male-dominated world. In the Owl era, several decades down the feminist road, the notion of a collectivized female consciousness actually begins to fade, as the hard-earned opportunity for a woman to be a fully self-realized individual on her own terms transcends any mere identification with gender.

This hardly means an end to women who are devoted wives and moms, or invaluable executive assistants, or hopeless romantics, or sexual libertines, or just plain girly-girls, for these are choices that can unapologetically be made—and all these types still figure prominently in Owl-era culture. It's just that these traditional roles are now augmented by myriads of others, especially in the professional sphere, as well as very complex character variations on the earlier archetypes. The richness of feminine perspective and possibilities likely reaches an apex in the three year run of *Lilith Fair* (1997–1999), an ambitious and wildly popular touring music festival featuring solely the work of such essential female artists as Sarah McLachlan, Erykah Badu, Sheryl Crow, and Bonnie Raitt, among many others.

Cinematically, the point of women having made it to full cultural citizenship is viscerally driven home via all the films in which women are just flat out warriors. Characters such as Sarah Michelle Gellar as the title character in *Buffy the Vampire Slayer* (1997–2003), Halle Berry as the mutant Storm who eventually comes to lead the X-Men (2000, 2003, 2006), Angelina Jolie as the explorer/adventurer Lara Croft in the *Lara Craft: Tomb Raider* movies (2001, 2003), Uma Thurman as deadly martial artist The Bride in *Kill Bill* (2003, 2004), Kate Beckinsale as the vampire warrior Selene in the *Underworld* films (2003, 2006), and Hilary female as fighter Maggie Fitzgerald in *Million Dollar Baby* (2004) certainly drive home the point that a contemporary woman has the potential to be anything she damn well puts her mind and heart to. It's meant as farce, but it's quite iconic that Alanis Morissette in the movie *Dogma* (1999) actually plays God.

Bottom line and one by one, lady Owls ought to be a hoot.

Gay Culture

I always thought of Dumbledore as gay.

Harry Potter author J.K. Rowling to fans at New York's Carnegie Hall, 10/19/07

Sexual politics, particularly issues relating to the civil rights of homo-
sexuals, is a very big deal in the Owl era. Sadly, as with so many key topics of the times, this is an area that invokes the primacy of emotional
conflict, between inflexible partisan/belief agendas and the tolerant
acceptance of the diversity of human character. Having acknowledged
this, however, it is hard to deny that the Owl era ushers in a much greater cultural appreciation and acceptance of those whose sexual orientation is either totally or partially same-sex.

As with feminist issues, the portrayal of gay culture in the Owl era
morphs into something far more than a monochromatic identification
of what "all gays are like." Simply in terms of occupation, the Owl era
gives us complex gay or bisexual portrayals of such people as teachers
(Kevin Kline as Howard Brackett in *In & Out*, 1997), hit men (James
Gandolfini as Winston Baldry in *The Mexican*, 2001), district attorneys
(Elisabeth Rohm as Serena Southerlyn on *Law & Order*, 2001–2005),
accountants (Christine Taylor as Kate Veatch in *Dodgeball*, 2004), cow-
boys (Heath Ledger and Jake Gyllenhaal as Ennis Del Mar and Jack
Twist in *Brokeback Mountain*, 2005), race car drivers (Sacha Baron Cohen
as Jean Girard in *Talledega Nights: The Ballad of Ricky Bobby*, 2006), and
wizards (Richard Harris and Michael Gambone as Prof. Dumbledore in
the *Harry Potter* series), among others. In published interviews regarding
such diverse and eccentric characters as candy maker Willie Wonka
(*Charlie and the Chocolate Factory*, 2005), barber/executioner Sweeny
Todd (*Sweeney Todd: The Demon Barber of Fleet Street*, 2007), and particularly pirate Capt. Jack Sparrow (*Pirates of the Caribbean*, 2003, 2006, 2007)
played by Johnny Depp, who admits relishing the sexual ambiguity of
the roles, famously admitting to having told one Disney executive who
voiced concerns over the portrayal of Capt. Sparrow: "Didn't you know
that all my characters are gay?"

Even with regard to the more 'standard' portrayals of gay men as either hysterically feminine or dryly witty, there is an element of genuine
appreciation and even affection that enters the cultural equation. Nathan
Lane and Robin Williams create a landmark moment in American culture
with their portrayal of a gay couple in *The Bird Cage* (1996), giving a rich
and engagingly raucous human quality to the cliché of taboo same-sex
coupling. Not long afterwards comes the cultural celebration of
metrosexuality (straight yuppie guys getting into grooming and taste),
highlighted by the television show *Queer Eye for the Straight Guy* (2003–

2007) whose gay male cast offer 'straights' such inestimably useful lifestyle advice as: "Here's a tip for you. When buying a velour tracksuit, stop."

Sometimes 'gay' issues are presented with tremendous nuance, as in *Boys Don't Cry* (1999), a gritty drama that wins Hilary Swank an Oscar for her role as a girl disguised as an amorous boy; or *Chasing Amy* (1997) in which Ben Affleck falls hard for a woman he later learns is a lesbian; and particularly as in the television series *Queer as Folk* (2000–2005), a true landmark in the exploration of gay lifestyles and relationships. Sometimes there is little nuance at all, as with the Big Gay Al (he runs a sanctuary for gay animals) and Mr. Garrison (an elementary school teacher in *South Park* (1997–) who is perhaps cartoon land's first sex change recipient). Sometimes there is just the odd, as with the baby-oriented television show *Teletubbies* (1997–2001), whose Tinky Winky character is singled out for censure by conservative cleric Jerry Falwell for carrying a purse and being costumed in some of the symbols (purple suit, triangular antenna) of the Gay Pride movement.

What it comes down to, really, is that gay existence is neither a foreign nor a fixed matter in the Owl culture. Maybe the single most important Owl-era gay cultural achievement is the television series *Will & Grace* (1998–2006), in which we witness that not only are "straights" interacting with gays in everyday life, but they may be each others' dearest and most dependable of friends. Ultimately, it's not that the Owls won't appreciate that the world is rife with differences in sexual orientation, but they may ultimately come to the generational conclusion that the most important human organ is the heart.

International Perspective

> *In less than an hour, aircraft from here will join others from around the world. And you will be launching the largest aerial battle in the history of mankind. "Mankind." That word should have new meaning for all of us today. We can't be consumed by our petty differences anymore.*
>
> **Bill Pullman as President Thomas J. Whitmore,**
>
> **Independence Day (1996)**

In the real world of the Owl era, people are very much at each other's throats. As discussed earlier, this is in part a matter of the technology-driven globalization phenomenon that places alien beliefs and cultural agendas more proximate to one another than they have ever been in history. Humans defend territory as an instinctive matter of survival, and in the interlinked Internet era of the Owls it suddenly appears that everybody is figuratively and literally trampling upon everyone else's turf.

While empathic or peaceful solutions to culture clash do not rise too often in the din of the Owl value-formation period, the Owl creative culture at least suggests another path, even if it's a largely theoretical one. Whether driven by the necessity of globe-threatening external events (*Independence Day*, 1996; *The Day After Tomorrow*, 2004), or the vagaries of friendship and friendly competition (*Bend it Like Beckham*, 2002; *Harry Potter and The Goblet of Fire*, 2005) or the irresistible call of love (*My Big Fat Greek Wedding*, 2002; *Love Actually*, 2003; *Spanglish*, 2004), Owl culture at least makes room for an ideal in which people of differing cultures can be brought together in shared feelings and common cause. Even when things end badly, as they do in the multinational drama *Babel* (2006) or the Best Picture Oscar-winning multiethnic drama *Crash* (2005), there is no getting around the Owl-era cultural thesis that one's humanity deserves to come before one's nationality or ethnicity.

Honestly, it is way too early to tell if the Owls will come to embrace their (foreign) fellow man. Whatever practical and philosophical conditions exist to encourage such a path, there is a lot of history to suggest that a tolerance for differences is not mankind's strongest suit. And yet there is a special glimmer in Owl consciousness that may get them to that higher ground, as evidenced in this monologue from the culturally spot-on *Harold & Kumar Go to White Castle* (2004), delivered by Kal Penn as Kumar Patel to his friend Harold Lee, played by John Cho, when the latter is on the verge of giving up on a stoner quest to find a particular fast food hamburger: "Our parents came to this country, escaping persecution, poverty, and hunger. Hunger, Harold. They were very, very hungry. They wanted to live in a land that treated them as equals, a land filled with hamburger stands. And not just one type of hamburger, okay? Hundreds of types with different sizes, toppings, and condiments. That land was America. America, Harold! America! Now, this is about achieving what our parents set out for. This is about the pursuit of happiness. This night...is about the American dream."

THE OWL IDEAL

The most beautiful thing in the world is, of course, the world itself.

Tom Hanks as Chuck Noland, *Cast Away* (2000)

You are wrong if you think the joy of life comes principally from the joy of human relationships. God's place is all around us; it is in everything we can experience. People just need to change the way they look at things.

Emile Hirsch as Chris McCandless, *Into the Wild* (2007)

By the power of truth, I, while living, have conquered the universe.

Hugo Weaving as V, *V for Vendetta* (2006)

And so we have moved the baby Owls far out on the branch of predicted values. Admittedly, we could have it all wrong. Perhaps they will be close-minded stay-at-homes with no more adventurousness and curiosity than a clutch of acorns.

What seems more likely, however, is the emergence of a Value Population that is geared towards seeking sense in all the variety of mankind and all the immensity of the universe. This is, we recognize, more than a bit abstract. But a failure in understanding the Owls is far more likely to come from ascribing limits to their perceptual capabilities and ambitions than in value-linking them to the conceptual immensity of the times into which they have been born.

History has, of course, a way of roughly taking on seekers and idealists. Yet if we are to believe the cultural representations of their value-formation period, Owls are going to be equipped to stare into the immensity without flinching. As Russell Crowe playing the general/gladiator Maximus in the film *Gladiator* (2000) observes: "Death smiles at us all; all we can do is smile back."

Yet, it would be wrong to leave off with the conclusion that Owls are merely going to be fatalists. They are simply not going to be inclined towards easy truths and self-delusion. Ultimately, life for the Owls will be mostly an opportunity to find out about life, hopefully with at least some potential for doing some good along the way.

In the film *Pearl Harbor* (2001), Ben Affleck plays Capt. Rafe McCawley, an American Navy pilot who, prior to the entrance of the U.S. into World War II, travels to England to help the RAF fend off the Nazi air invasion. Caught cheating on the pilot's eye exam, he is asked by a nurse why he is so anxious to die. His answer makes a pretty serviceable Owl motto: "Not anxious to die, just anxious to matter."

22

LOOKING FORWARD
"Who's" Next?

The Owl value-formation period seems to be coming to an end when, in December of 2007, the economy finally takes a deep sigh and the U.S. officially enters a two-year recession. To further acerbate the economic situation, on October 1, 2008, the U.S. stock market starts a weeklong decline in which the Dow Jones Industrial Average falls 1,874 points or 18.1 percent.

At the same time, natural disasters are taking their toll on the world and the country. The acute devastation of individual natural disasters across the world pushed 2008 to the number three spot in the most expensive disaster years on record, according to a report by Munich Re Group.

In the United States, the 2008 hurricane season is the third most costly on record, behind only the 2004 and 2005 seasons, with over $47.5 billion in damage. The most damaging event was Hurricane Ike, which struck Galveston, Texas, in September and caused some $30 billion in damages along the Gulf Coast. Hurricane Gustav caused $10 billion in damages in the Caribbean and Gulf of Mexico.

The tornado season in the United States is also severe in 2008, with about 1,700 tornadoes causing several billion dollars in damage.

In December, 2008, ice storms in the northeast left 1.7 million customers without power for days. Almost a week after the storm, more than 100,000 customers were still without power, affecting the holiday shopping season and crippling the business and transportation of many cities for days.

Unfortunately, even with the government spending more than $1.7 trillion in 2008 and early 2009 to bail out failing companies such as Bear Stearns ($30 billion), Fannie Mae/Freddie Mac ($400 billion), American International Group ($180 billion), the auto industry ($25 billion), the troubled Asset Relief Program (TARP) ($700 billion), Citigroup ($280 billion) and Bank of America ($142 billion), the U.S. unemployment rate begins to quickly rise at the beginning of 2008 until it hits its second biggest high in over 60 years at 10 percent in October of 2009.

All of this discord has finally driven society to hit a point where it is no longer willing to sit back and ride the tide of fear and worry about the future, and when an unknown but charismatic black presidential candidate, Barack Obama, asks the country if they think that together we can change the status quo, the country resoundingly screams and votes, yes we can!

However, the Washington battleship proves to be a tough vessel to turn as even with a democratic president and a democratically controlled congress, little change seems to emerge.

Ironically, at the start of 2011, while many Americans are feeling broke, having lost a major portion of their life savings in the decline of their home equity and their stock market portfolios, and often being unemployed even with huge stimulus packages being spent, many Fortune 500 corporations report record profits and many billionaires see their net worths hit new highs.

This gulf between the haves and have-nots seems to be steadily growing, leaving more and more people across the country feeling dissolute and confused. In an effort to take back what is theirs and no longer rely on the government or Wall Street to take care of them, two movements emerge. The political Tea Party movement begins with a libertarian agenda during the 2008 presidential election and continues to grow through the formation of Obamacare. This movement advocates strict adherence to the United States Constitution, reducing U.S. government spending and taxes, and reduction of the U.S. national debt and federal budget deficit. On September 17, 2011, in Zuccotti Park, located in New York City's Wall Street financial district, a liberal nonviolent street protest named Occupy Wall Street (OWS) begins with the slogan, "We are the 99%," and aims to address the growing income inequality and wealth distribution in the U.S. between the wealthiest 1 percent and the rest of the population.

Clearly, it is not the purpose here to delve too deeply into the various natural disasters or financial unrest that has occurred at the beginning of this value-formation period, but rather to recognize and acknowledge the incessant global apocalypses, economic dissolution and overall dystopia that are becoming prevalent during this time. Under the influence of everything from financial catastrophes, to political violence, to seemingly contact natural disasters, this new Value Population seems poised to learn that being conservative, guarded, and likely even pessimistic about the present, the future and what someone else might do for you might be valuable lessons to learn and hold onto.

Despite the unsettling implications of these difficult events, the task of assessing the value set of the individuals being value formed in this era is not necessarily grim. One is well reminded to consider the Performers, a Value Population formed in the constant shadow of a nuclear-tipped Cold War, who ended up as perhaps the most affirmative and life-embracing of all the Value Populations.

With that in mind, this new cohort group may conceivably prop itself up on a platform of action that actually turns the tides—to seek to find his or her own niche in which to guide and direct others. Perhaps out of locked-down emotions might emerge a propensity for this group to be politically focused, well-organized, and leaning toward individual leadership to get things done.

When we look at our various Value Populations, we can track a cycle between those that have emotional processors (Performers, Believers, and Owls) and those with Analytic Processors (Patriots, Techticians, and Transformers.) The new Value Population will probably be added to the analytical type, being less emotional and more tactical.

In any event, be it reality TV or reality, for this upcoming Value Population, sitting back and relying on emotional or magical insights just won't cut it when the well-being of the entire planet is teetering on a day-to-day basis and you could maybe do something about it.

Work based on practical insights, family honor and loyalty to duty will likely be important to this Value Population. For them, it will probably be more about getting down to business and making something happen than about feeling good or having empathy for others' situations.

This group's mantra may well be, "You helped create these problems, so stop whining and start doing something to fix them." However, the bigger question might be, "Are there too many bosses and not enough workers to get anything really accomplished?"

While we can't possibly yet know how this will all turn out, we can acknowledge that, in 2008, the value-formation emphasis shifts from the cultivation of wisdom, curiosity, and freedom to the identification of prudent resource management and hard work. In the Owl value system, magic is king, yet, as we see exemplified by the events unfolding, to this new Value Population life will not be so much about expansion as it will be about getting things done and reaping the rewards or punishments for what we have sown in the past.

MARKETING TO VALUE POPULATIONS

In this third part of The Consistent Consumer, specific marketing implications and business applications of the Value Population material will be addressed and anchored in examples drawn from direct work with clients.

The first three chapters of Part Three cover selected consumer-focused research projects and presentations created for Near Bridge, Inc., clients. Chapter 23, "Core Customer Migration," looks into the world of upscale home improvement service providers through the eyes of California Closets and The Franchise Group. Chapter 24, "Reaching an Audience," outlines how understanding Value Population research helps clients, such as major entertainment providers like the National Basketball Association and the Miami Heat, better communicate and advertise to target audiences. Chapter 25, "Social Marketing," shows how organizations like Vegan Outreach can effectively use Value Population findings to create powerful and targeted collateral material that will have the largest impact on influencing behavioral change in specific target audiences.

Finally, Chapter 26 offers the highlights of an article that initially appeared in QSR Magazine, the leading trade publication of the American quick-serve restaurant industry. The chapter analyzes the impact that historical icons and consumer trends have on the quick-serve (fast food) restaurant industry and serves to illustrate the applications of Value Population insight to real marketplace issues.

23

CORE CUSTOMER MIGRATION

Not all consumer goods and services companies attempt to derive their mission from behavioral research data. Some are concerned with an aspect of the consumer that cannot be readily reduced to keystroke counts or computer-aided analysis. Such companies believe the mystery of the consumer is to be unlocked in the areas of deeply held attitudes and values—that it is neither silly nor superficial to consider that every shopper has a soul.

In 1978, California Closets invented the upscale residential customized storage industry. Today, the company is a nationally-franchised, $200 million unit of a billion-dollar Canadian consortium called The Franchise Company, and it remains the customized storage segment's sales leader. According to Edward Leaman, who serves as the company's Executive Vice President as well as President of The Franchise Company's Nomads and Growers marketing arm, California Closets' brand development was, has been, and will continue to be intuitive rather than research-led.

According to Leaman, California Closets' positioning as an "attitudinal brand" stems from an appreciation of the role that the home plays for today's consumer. In a world where individuality and personal expression are increasingly thwarted in the public domain, the home becomes the place where the consumer can most comfortably and effectively express his or her identity, thereby making it an arena in which a service company must endeavor to connect by "substantiating customers' feelings about themselves." In such a paradigm, explains Leaman, "one must market to the meaning a customized closet may have for someone—whether it's for life simplification or to create a sense of order or to enhance a feeling of personal security or to experience pride of possession—far more than one must dwell on the purely functional material and manpower considerations of building a closet."

In this context, what attracted Leaman and California Closets to the Near Bridge Value Population research was the fact that the material dealt in the identification and explanation of attitudes, or *values* in the Near Bridge lexicon. By emphasizing values migration—the phenomenon of cohort groups retaining their values throughout their collective lifespan and carrying them with them as they pass through different life phases—the Near Bridge material also promised some extremely useful insight into why today's core California Closet customer, a Techtician woman in her 40s with an annual household income in excess of $75,000, did not appear to have the same values as the Performer customer with the same demographic description from only a decade or two earlier. What adjustments in the marketing, sales, and installation processes, California Closets wondered, were thereby warranted?

Compounding and qualifying the urgency of this inquiry were the size and structural changes in the home improvement industry itself. No longer a "bijou business," to use Leaman's term, customized storage has become a $2 billion category in the still rapidly expanding $300 billion home improvement industry. In a brave new world of big-box, do-it-yourself retailers and in an era of burgeoning internet sales, was it prudent to confine one's marketing efforts to positive word-of-mouth and the pages of *Architectural Digest*?

The analysis performed by Near Bridge on behalf of California Closets concentrated on identifying the discrete set of values that differentiate Techticians, the "new" core California Closets customer, from Performers, the "original" core customer. See Figure 23.1. Unlike other generational analyses that lump the mid-1940s and 1950s post-WWII babies with children born from the late 1950s through the early 1960s (although finally suspecting there may be some lack of consistency, one now increasingly encounters the terms "late" and "early" applied to Baby Boomers), the Near Bridge matrix defines a rather sharp values break between the children of the 1950s and those of the 1960s. Under California Closets' direction, Near Bridge endeavored to identify how each of these groups approaches a luxury purchase, emphasizing such issues as the collection of information, feelings about what constitutes status, desirable retail environments, effective sales approaches, and, in the broadest possible sense, what each of these Value Populations is looking for in a premium brand. See Figure 20.2.

FIGURE 23.1

California Closets' Migrating Customer Base

	Performers	Techticians
Population	66 million	63 million
% of U.S. Population	23	22
Median Age (1978)	30.5	13.5
Median Age (2003)	55.5	38.5
Total Expenditures (2000)	$1.32 million	$1.45 million

Among the findings identified as particularly valuable by California Closets is the practical, heavily analytical, information-rich orientation of Techticians toward significant purchases. While scrutinized from a number of perspectives, this point is particularly well driven home by a comparison of shelter magazines and median readership ages. A Performer-oriented magazine such as *Architectural Digest,* that clearly positions itself as an aspirational lifestyle journal, is certainly appealing to a different set of values than the Techtician-oriented *Home* magazine, which pragmatically describes itself in terms of its contribution to asset investment and project utility and tends to run articles on dozens or even hundreds of ways of accomplishing a home improvement objective.

This insight similarly helps to explain, at least in part, the allure of the Internet and the importance of multichannel marketing to the Techtician shopper, whose luxury purchases often begin with extensive data collection relating to features. This infatuation with information often transpires before an appreciation of benefits and, only then, concludes with the satisfaction that a "smart" choice has been made. While time and stress factors can force a Techtician to make a decision before all the facts are in, this is hardly the normal course of affairs when a significant outlay of cash is involved—these people generally being the antithesis of the one-stop, one-source shoppers.

FIGURE 23.2

VP Shopper Value Matrix

Attribute	Performers	Techticians
Communication	Dramatic	Information Rich
Environment	Simulative	Orderly/Efficient
Proposition	Self-Referential	Analytical
Time Sense	Distracted/Involved	Methodical/Starved
Variety	Form	Function
Luxury	Exclusive	Consensual
Brand	Image	Promise of Delivery

It is this realization, says Leaman, that has helped him understand the appeal to Techticians of "ugly" big box stores such as Costco and Home Depot in terms of their broad product inventory rather than the niceties of the shopping environment that Performers prefer. He now acknowledges that information-seeking Techticians love such places as they simultaneously offer a large breadth of inventory and clearly defined product features. He further acknowledges that possession of this insight will be top of mind as California Closets for the first time contemplates a variety of strategic alliances and licensing agreements with retailers—appreciating more than ever that an approach to the Techtician consumer means being involved at as many relevant information intercept points as possible, whether there is an obvious traditional "quality" connection or not.

"When it comes to brand building, very few companies have real faith in their customers," observes Leaman. "They treat their brand as a little statue that you polish rather than as a response to a living and evolving set of circumstances. Brands don't matter to the customer with anywhere near the intensity that most companies think.

"I trust the customer more than anyone," says Leaman, "but you need to understand them and connect with them. It's not just about measurement."

24

REACHING AN AUDIENCE

What is bought before it is produced, cannot be touched or wrapped, and requires the consumer to go to the factory to get and use it—and once purchased, leaves nothing tangible to take home but memories? The answer? A sports or entertainment experience—and promoting it is one of the toughest challenges any marketing team can face.

No other industry has to so deeply and consistently resonate with a "consumer's soul" as does the sports and entertainment industry. Building a lasting brand around a living and continually changing product is difficult. If that is not challenging enough, the product has to be created and simultaneously consumed by a broad and demographically diverse audience, while meeting the needs of each demographic group and not offending the others.

Professional sports organizations are very familiar with these challenges. Leaders in these organizations are increasingly aware of the significant shifts in the values of their core audience and are now seeking new ways to more effectively understand, reach, and retain their target markets.

In an effort to counter flat or lagging season ticket sales, a tarnished public image of some players, diminishing corporate sponsorship, and a narrow retail product strategy, Bernie Mullin, the Vice President of Marketing for The National Basketball Association (NBA), invited Near Bridge to address these issues based on Value Population research. He was interested in knowing how he, the League presidents, and all the team marketers could better use this information to more effectively target the core values of the NBA's current and potential customer base.

Near Bridge presented its findings at the NBA's annual spring presidents' meeting. To better enable the attendees to quickly relate to the research, Near Bridge offered examples of legendary players whose personalities exemplified the emerging value set of each Value Population expressed in a sports context. These players personified the values of an emerging Value Population and became cultural icons of the era in which they played.

- *Performers: Bob Cousy, 1950–1963.* Bob Cousy was the heart and soul of six Boston Celtic championship teams, and his fans loved his zeal for the spotlight. He played the game of basketball with flare and passion and was flashy before flashy was cool (once famously being benched in college for showboating), constantly diving for loose balls and perfecting the showy behind-the-back pass. Cousy played basketball as if it were more than just a game and as if he were more than just a player. He was, rather, perhaps the first basketball player who appreciated that he was a prominent star in a hit show—and thereby a significant Performer icon.
- *Techticians: Wilt Chamberlain, 1959–1973.* Wilt Chamberlain personified skill under control and is arguably the most dominant player ever in NBA history. A marvel of statistical accomplishments, Wilt walked the talk and held many incredible NBA records such as: scoring 100 points in a single NBA game; averaging 50 points a game for an entire season; and, most incredibly considering his role as a silent but deadly intimidator, never fouling out in over 1,200 games. Unlike many of today's athletes who lose control and act out emotionally on the court, Chamberlain kept his mind in control of his actions and foreshadowed true Techtician values by always giving his best, measuring the results, and constantly improving. But what about winning? Merely icing on the cake.
- *Believers: Ervin "Magic" Johnson, 1979–1991.* Magic Johnson brought "vibe" to the game of basketball. The ultimate team player, he believed that personal passion for the game was best revealed by helping one's teammates perform better. In an era of weakening traditional aggressive male values and a growing mistrust for overtly "macho" leadership, Magic focused on group dynamics and personal relationships with his peers to win games. (Interestingly and representatively, this value did not always include his boss, as the concept of loyalty to the boss was "bogus"—and he proved this by getting one of his coaches, Paul Westhead, fired.) Above all else, Magic's selfless style and contagious smile reinforced the emerging Be-

liever message to fans, teammates, and opponents everywhere that even when championships are at stake, there is still room for looking good and having fun.

- *Transformers: Michael Jordan, 1984–1994.* The ascent of Michael Jordan to basketball prominence is a testimony to what power, skill, talent, and the desire to win can accomplish. Jordan demonstrated that institutions that survive and win (and that collect championships as regularly as clocks tell time) must be vested with endurance and an edge. Consistently rising to any challenge, Jordan was the chief sports icon in an era that brought black culture into mainstream America, and he will always be remembered for "effortlessly" flying through the air and into the country's TV sets and living rooms. Interestingly, as powerful a figure as he was, he still believed that tradition, with a little luck, was important, too, as he always wore his college basketball shorts under his NBA shorts. Jordan knew that winning required a strong team made up of competent players, but like Transformers today, he realized that sometimes, when times get tough, one cannot hesitate to drive the key and "take it to the hoop" all by oneself.

- *Owls: Shaquille O'Neal, 1992-2011.* It is hard to think of any athlete or entertainer better representative of the expansive values and great thematic breadth of the Owl era than the larger-than-life Shaquille O'Neal. Certainly his NBA career was extraordinary, including four championships on three different teams, 15 all-star appearances, and being the youngest player named to the NBA's "Greatest 50 Players of All Time" roster. Yet as compelling a presence as the 7'1," 325-lb Shaq was on the court, it is perhaps even more significant that he was contemporaneously larger than life in so many more endeavors than basketball. While competing at the highest level of his sport, Shaq successfully recorded four rap music albums, starred in several movies, seriously pursued a career in law enforcement, started an ambitious charity foundation, and earned two college degrees—including an MBA. Often affecting the persona of a philosopher-clown in interviews, Shaq has been called "the most gregarious personality in sports history." Particularly proud of the Superman tattoo on his left bicep, Shaq is the ultimate icon of a basketball era in which the arena could no longer contain the influence of the game—or its most popular player.

Early research for this NBA project revealed that ticket sales, corporate sponsorships, and retail strategy were each dominated by a single, but different, Value Population. The bulk of individual season ticket sales fell to the Techticians, the seven-figure corporate sponsorship decisions were made primarily by Performers, and a high percentage of sales of merchandise, video games, and apparel was being sold to Transformers. With this information and a newfound understanding of each of the Value Populations and their link to more effectively generating revenue, the NBA and its teams were shown how it is possible to focus marketing dollars more effectively on target audiences with values-based advertising campaigns.

As in any business, some of the key challenges the NBA teams face are continued revenue growth and profitability. In the context of this book, understanding Value Populations research allows the NBA to focus on this by including and specifically targeting multiple Value Populations in their ticket sales, sponsorship, and merchandising campaigns. For example, instead of relying heavily on season ticket sales to come mainly from Techticians, it can refine its marketing aim to include more emphasis on attracting Believers and Performers—significantly reducing single-source revenue exposure, upping attendance, and ultimately increasing profits.

A marketing campaign run by the Miami Heat, targeting season ticket sales, illustrates the effectiveness of this method. Like many other NBA teams, Heat ticket sales had been flat for three years as the market for sports and entertainment dollars in its trade area was highly competitive. Eric Woolworth, president of the Miami Heat, contacted Near Bridge and asked that his entire organization be trained on the concept of Value Populations. He wanted to use the resourcefulness of the entire organization to develop a highly targeted season ticket radio campaign suited to each Value Population.

Up to this point, the Heat strategy was heavily weighted toward a single, blanket campaign aimed at numerous local radio stations—a scattergun, one-ad-fits-all approach with little attention paid to segmenting their diversified audience. In other words, the same sales pitch went out to all the stations, regardless of the audience's demographic breakout. Because radio, unlike TV, allows for nearly instant and inexpensive modification of advertising, Woolworth wanted to change this strategy and use a targeted Value Population approach. With this strategy in mind, Near Bridge helped the Heat create new radio spots targeted at the different Value Populations.

In order to accomplish this, Near Bridge requested the Heat's marketing department to identify key area radio stations based on the specific age parameters of each Value Population. In order to increase the creative value of this material, the Heat's 160-person staff was first trained in the basics of the Value Population research and then divided into breakout groups with the instruction to create a 60-second radio spot directed at a specific radio station with a targeted Value Population audience.

An easy listening station with a Performer audience, for example, had an ad created for it that focused on the customer as king and emphasized personal service in Club Chivas, an exclusive place to watch the game. A rap station with a primarily Believer audience promoted a laidback, cool, and "chic" atmosphere where the "gang could hang."

As a result of this guided exercise, according to Kim Stone, Vice President of the Heat, "Not only did the breakout teams use the information to work together effectively, they developed spots that were so creative that they were used in our Fall advertising campaign ... We also saved money because we did not need to hire an expensive advertising company to create our spots that year. And, at the end of that campaign, and after working with Near Bridge, we had definitely sold more tickets."

More importantly, Stone said, "Looking at core values is way outside the box and makes immediate sense. Because of our new understanding of Value Populations, we now have a powerful way to more effectively reach our fan base."

25

SOCIAL MARKETING

Social marketing, although similar to cause marketing, is not quite the same. *Cause marketing* is a commercial activity by which businesses and charities or causes form a partnership with each other to market an image, product, or service for mutual benefit. Examples include such partnerships as: Avon Cosmetics and the Avon Breast Cancer Crusade; American Airlines—Miles for Kids in Need; and Barnes & Noble and the Anti-Defamation League "Close the Book on Hate" campaign.

Social marketing, on the other hand, is the use of commercial marketing techniques to influence behavioral change that will improve the well-being of a specific target audience or society as a whole. Examples include such issues as smoking cessation, recycling, sober driving, and eating a plant-based diet. What separates social marketing from commercial marketing is its fundamental motivation—to strictly benefit an individual or society rather than a marketer's organization.

Some examples of organizations that employ social marketing techniques include: The Centers for Disease Control and Prevention; local, state, and federal health agencies; The U.S. Environmental Protection Agency; nonprofit organizations, and in the case of this discussion, specifically Vegan Outreach, a 501(c)(3) nonprofit educational organization.

Vegan Outreach is "dedicated to reducing animal suffering by promoting a vegan lifestyle." Vegans do not purchase or consume products that contribute to that suffering. By not buying or using items such as meat, eggs, dairy and leather, vegans are, in effect, economically boycotting animal-based products.

In her book, *Hands-On Social Marketing: A Step-by-Step Guide,* Nedra Kiline Weinreich points out, "The first lesson in social marketing is there is no such thing as targeting the general public. To be most effective, specify the audience for your program as precisely as possible." It is in this vein that Near Bridge assisted Vegan Outreach in redesigning their *Why Vegan?* promotional booklet.

Vegan Outreach believes their message is best received and acted upon by young people. So, through widespread distribution of full-color illustrated booklets, titled *Why Vegan?* and *Try Vegetarian,* they aim their message at adolescents and college-aged youth. These booklets are handed out by many volunteers, from students to animal advocacy organizations, such as Farm Animal Reform Movement (FARM), Farm Sanctuary, In Defense of Animals, The Fund for Animals, People for the Ethical Treatment of Animals (PETA), and Viva!USA.

Because social marketers usually have a very strong personal connection with the issue they are promoting, they often create promotional material that resonates more with their own core values than those of their target audience. This was the case with *Why Vegan?* While the main targeted audience for Vegan Outreach is college students, which up until 2003 were primarily made up of Believers, the majority of the members of Vegan Outreach responsible for writing, compiling, and formatting the *Why Vegan?* booklet were Techticians. The booklet strongly reflected a Techtician slant—it was heavy on detailed information at the expense of being inviting—and for Believers, being inviting is not an option but a requirement.

Figure 25.1 shows the original "Techtician" booklet cover on the left. It is loaded with text, has a strong sense of knowledge signaling, and a heavy emphasis on detail is apparent. Techticians, who are more pragmatic than idealistic, operate from a place of intellect rather than emotion—and data and information sells.

Believers, on the other hand, whose values were developed during a time of social dysfunction and economic malaise, and who are much more oriented toward empathy and welcoming assistance, respond favorably to relationships, love, and harmony, and are much more apt to resonate with peaceful and inviting advertising rather than a "data download."

In the revised cover of the *Why Vegan?* booklet shown in Figure 25.1, the heavy data-rich overtones are gone, replaced with an inviting and friendly look. The font has been rounded and is less "aggressive," and the colors are much more playful. (In the original version, the colors were mainly a strong red and a deep purple, and in the revised version, they are lighter and more inviting tones of green, blue, yellow, and pink.)

FIGURE 25.1

Original and Improved Cover Designs

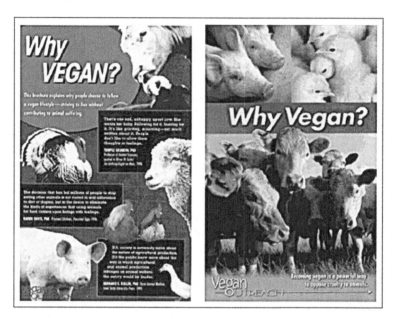

In this instance, it seems that one really can "judge a book by its cover." In addition to modifying the look and feel of the booklet to attract the target audience, the content method of persuading each Value Population also differs considerably.

Details, practicality, and a purpose all sell well to Techticians. Furthermore, Techticians deal poorly with hypocrisy, so if you want a Techtician to listen to you about becoming a vegetarian or vegan, you better be one yourself and "walk the talk." It is important to note that because Techticians will usually trust their own opinion over those of others, recruiting them as individuals and giving them the opportunity to make up their own minds is an effective strategy.

Believers, being fair-minded and much more socially oriented, require a promotion and recruitment technique that is much more group oriented. Believers deal poorly with aggression, are better motivated by consideration, and are best sold to with beauty and ease. It is important to remember that with Believers, if you get one, you get many—and the best bait to use to hook a Believer is another Believer. Once a promoted message catches on, step back and let the herd mentality take over—but don't stray far as Believers formed their values in a period of social and economic abandonment and will leave a cause as fast as they took to it.

Interestingly, Vegan Outreach's target audience, college-aged young adults, is currently in the process of a dramatic value changeover, from those of Believers to those of Transformers. The challenge Vegan Outreach faces is how to sell to both Value Populations at the same time—as the same material and promotion techniques will not work effectively for both Value Populations.

Unlike the Techticians, a little like the Believers, and more like the Patriots, Transformers feel the need for social interaction at the clan level, which they readily extend to close friendships. Because they are not expressly motivated by idealism, they need to see the personal advantage to them in order to be sold. It is best to sell to this group with clarity, action, and fun.

While Transformers will not be put off as much by the Believer-designed brochure as the Believers were with the Techtician-designed version, they will also not be strongly drawn to it because Transformers like an edgier look and stronger, bolder colors. The original fonts and the bolder red color of the Techtician version would be better received by Transformers; however, it would still be advisable to limit the language on the cover, as Transformers have grown up in an era where images take center stage.

When promoting to Transformers, one can sell to them in groups or as individuals. The real advice here is: don't single one out in front of the group, and don't pressure them in front of their friends. Because Transformers are strong willed and deal poorly with manipulation, forcing their hand will only invite trouble. Motivate them with a sense of responsibility but not guilt, treat them like grownups, and your message will go a lot farther.

In the end, one must remember that Value Populations hear messages differently. Effective messaging is assimilated best when it meets the target audience on *its* terms and not from the presenter's perspective. Social marketers need to stay emotionally distanced from the issues they are promoting, focus on the values of the audience they are targeting, and keep up the good work—as we all benefit from having a better world to live in.

C h a p t e r

26

AN INDUSTRY OVERVIEW
Quick-Serve Restaurants

This chapter offers highlights from an article that initially appeared in *QSR Magazine,* the leading trade publication of the American quick-serve restaurant industry. The intent of this chapter is to review the six Value Populations, offer a glimpse of how historic icons and consumer trends specifically impact an industry, and illustrate the applications of the Value Populations insight to real marketplace issues faced by the quick-serve industry.

PATRIOTS STAND ON TRADITION

Value Population Overview

Born: 1920–1937
Size: 7% of U.S. Population

With the Patriots, one encounters a Value Population "forced" to accept a uniquely complex, unknown, and dangerous future. Life is somehow more consistent, measured, local, and experientially familiar prior to the advent of mass industrialization and modern media, not to mention global depression, despotism, and war. While mass prosperity and personal freedom beckon in this new age, it is the collective pain that fate inflicts via global calamity, economic disappointment, and a rending of the established social fabric that most clearly leaves a mark. Subjected to the grim residue of war and want, the Patriots more than any other Value Population are about exercising caution; are about mistrusting the motives of others, keeping their hands on their wallets, and, most of all, attending to the rules and rituals of the families, friends, and social equals who validate and protect the Patriots' physical, psychological, and financial well-being.

Cultural Menu. The Complex and Sobering Aftermath of WWI; Prohibition; The Roaring 20s; The Jazz Age and The Age of Radio; Stock Market Collapse; The Great Depression; FDR's New Deal; The Rise of Foreign Dictatorships; and The Gathering Clouds of WW II

Some Key Personalities. Woodrow Wilson, Al Capone, Babe Ruth, Louis Armstrong, Mae West, King Kong, Franklin Delano Roosevelt

Primary Population Values (Partial List). Familiarity, Security, Affection, Abundance

Quick-Serve Restaurant History

Although most contemporary quick-serve-restaurant chains do little active courtship of Patriot customers, the birth of the fast-food industry is actually simultaneous with the start of the Patriot value-formation period. The nation's first drive-in restaurant, The Pig Stand, opens in Texas in 1921. Featuring a menu comprised entirely of a "Tennessee" BBQ pork sandwich and drinks, and offering carhop service, the chain expands to 120 units nationwide by 1934.

Even more noteworthy because it still remains very much in existence is the White Castle hamburger chain, founded in Kansas, also in 1921. Patriot values are plentiful in the brand new White Castle, whose *institutionalization* of the hamburger sandwich as America's chief culinary icon is built upon a creed of *uniformity,* ranging from product specifications to cooking to pricing to building construction to employee apparel. (White Castle is given credit for the creation of the military-looking paper hat.) Particularly indicative of Patriot values is that the chain has always remained a closely held family business.

Besieged by war, economic turmoil and modernism, and subsequently devoted to the self-protective strategies of group survival, Patriots put a very high value on loyalty, consistency, and the comfort of familiar surroundings. Their own moods may change, but they do not readily accept external variations that are thrust upon them. They are certain about what belongs where.

Todd Coerver, group director of operation services for Whataburger, offers a revealing glimpse of the Patriots' worldview. Whataburger, he explains, skews towards younger customers but does have "a great relationship with older loyal customers." He says that a number of Whataburger units are late-morning gathering places for local seniors, which he refers to as Coffee Clubs that have grown out of a long-ago, free-refill coffee mug promotion.

"We have a restaurant across the street from headquarters that really needs to be rebuilt," says Coerver. "But the Coffee Club heard we were thinking about remodeling, and one day I get a package in the mail that turns out to be a formally produced report. Basically, it says don't even think about remodeling until you meet with us, and it has sixty Coffee Club signatures followed by the number of years they've been coming to the restaurant—up to 40 years. The best part is that our tag is 'Whataburger: Just Like You Like It.' But printed on the cover of their report is 'Whataburger: Just Like *We* Like It.' I guess they were letting us know who really shepherds the brand."

Quick-Serve Restaurant Issues

Menu. The typical fast-food menu suits this group who is inclined towards sweetness, saltiness, and deep-fat frying as well as soft and thick textures; aggressively demand appropriate food temperatures; looking for comfort foods, but a lifetime of experience makes them finicky about perceived quality.

Service and Atmosphere. Easily scared into defensive posture by the unusual; crave familiarity and consistency in everything

Price/Value. Money has always been of massive importance to this group, and its cautious retention and investment is largely characteristic of this group; senior discounts are essential.

Nutrition. There are clearly health-based concerns in this age group, but there is also a strong sense of "treat"; born in an era of global plague and depression, this is perhaps the last modern generation that at least subconsciously links girth with health and happiness.

Marketing. Much mass retail image marketing to seniors includes grandchildren, but this is a generation that also values its place among its own contemporaries; images and messages should stress inclusion and safety; age-based, off-hours promos have appeal.

Employees. As the population skews older, the concept of the WalMart greeter should be kept in mind; peer presence works with this group as it establishes both a level of respect and a sense of cultural security.

Patriot Notables

1920. National prohibition of alcohol goes into effect. Speakeasies, commercial moonshine, and bootlegging come into existence. Alcohol becomes a key icon of generational rebellion. Ice cream parlors are designed to mimic saloon experience.

1931. Irma S. Rombauer's *The Joy of Cooking* is published; conscientious home cooking is codified as the book's sales eventually top 15 million.

1933. Wheaties, first introduced in 1924, invents the slogan "Breakfast of Champions" and becomes a national pioneer in the radio broadcast and promotion of baseball and other sports. The cereal company also introduces a popular radio serial, "Jack Armstrong—All American Boy."

PERFORMERS COURT THE WORLD'S FARE

Value Population Overview

Born: 1938–1957
Size: 21% of U.S. Population

Performers sometimes seem unduly self-involved, but perhaps they've earned the right. Born during and just after global war, heirs to the advent of "we will bury you" Communism and its attendant threat of nuclear annihilation, offspring of a Value Population [the Patriots] most notably characterized by caution and an obsessive allegiance to the prevailing practices of the clan, the Performer generation might well have emerged as a tribe of crushed, gray spirits quivering in the darkest corners of their own repressive nightmares. But be it a matter of fate or fortune or their own sheer numbers, the Performers take the exact opposite group tack—that of lighting their own inner flames rather than cursing the darkness. No other Value Population quite compares with their lust after life's sheer drama; for the belongings, feelings, and events that make an individual feel unique and very much alive.

Cultural Menu. The 1939 New York World's Fair Foreshadows The Future; The Wizard of Oz "Techni" Colors the World; World War II, Cold War, and The Atomic Age; The Baby Boom; A National Highway System; The Creation of Suburbia; and Television Arrives

Some Key Personalities. Adolph Hitler, John Wayne, Nikita Khrushchev, Senator Joe McCarthy, Walt Disney, Marilyn Monroe, Elvis Presley

Primary Population Values (Partial List). Freedom, Adventure, Creativity, Romance

Quick-Serve Restaurant History

It is not often that a discussion of the Baby Boomers, who begin to arrive *en masse* after WWII, looks back to the years just before the war. Socio-cultural analysis reveals, however, that the years 1938 and 1939 are a treasure trove of foreshadowing regarding the cultural blueprint of this vast population. The war is a grim interruption, but the key to the Performers is keeping in mind that their essence is a passion for beating back the grim reaper through taking delight in being alive.

Dairy Queen, which is born in 1938 and grows to more than 2,500 units before Ray Kroc opens his first McDonald's in 1955, tells part of the tale. Far more than dessert destinations, Dairy Queens become the community theatres of the heartland, the place where a car takes you so you can fraternize, flaunt, flirt, and fight about football. To understand the deep connection that the Performer Value Population has to dining out, even at quick-serve restaurants, is to keep in mind all of the books (Larry McMurtry's *Walter Benjamin at the Dairy Queen;* Bob Greene's *Chevrolet Days, Dairy Queen Nights*) and movies *(Texasville; Adventures in Babysitting)* that nostalgically evoke Dairy Queen as the place, as opposed to the family dinner table, where life's best stories unfold.

Away from the heartland, likely the most formative food event of 1938–1939 is the New York World's Fair, whose central exhibit is General Motors' Futurama. Beyond giving a prescient insight into the suburban/consumer/car-oriented/television society that will appear after the war, the fair captures the international cultural eclecticism that will eventually become a prized part of the American social fabric. More than 20 foreign restaurants are featured at the fair, and trend-setting New Yorkers open their hearts, minds, and mouths to the possibilities.

All these years later, Performers remain a population that seeks both culinary eclecticism and personal passion in their dining out experiences. Age and society have placed issues such as nutrition, speed, and convenience on the plate, but Wallace Doolin, president of la Madeleine, probably gets closer to the truth when he speaks of "quick casual" as a great segmentation opportunity with this group because of its broad culinary experience and sophistication, or when Jim Adams, the Chipotle spokesperson, acknowledges that today's 50-year-old customer is still looking for "fun, discovery, and adventure."

"A company like Panera understands that these are the perfect people to spend $8 for a 30-minute trip to Tuscany," observes David Groll, a veteran research and development chef who has worked on many national chain menus. "This group wants great breads, and veggie pestos, and high flavor profiles that are truly unique. They are looking for things that are *interesting.*"

Quick-Serve Restaurant Issues

Menu. Knowledgeable and experienced diners; quality, variety, and personal choice must figure into the menu mix; they savor the high-flavor profiles of international cuisines; open-minded but rarely fooled by pretentiousness.

Service and Atmosphere. This group grew up with a love for the restaurant experience; those quick-serve restaurants who can create comfortable and gregarious in-store environments may yet do well with a group that expects more from dining than the efficiency of a drive-thru.

Price/Value. In broad terms, this is a population of shoppers rather than savers; the current economic downturn coupled with the ambitious upscaling efforts of fast casuals may prove a financially, as well as gastronomically, happy match.

Nutrition. Aging, they are clearly interested in nutrition, especially with regard to heart health and youthfulness; this card can be overplayed, however, as many Performers were the guinea pigs for the early low fat/low salt days that generally meant terrible taste; want it on the menu, may not eat it.

Marketing. More into the story than the icon; like things to proceed at a pace rather than e-fast; they can be accessed through flattering images of themselves and affectionate portrayals of (their own) children.

Employees. Their personality-plus approach to doing business can be very effective around clients and customers (if not always coworkers); worldly, warm and courageous, they are often excellent in life-mentoring roles.

Performer Notables

1938. Lawry's Seasoned Salt is introduced. The colorful, flavor-enhancing mixture is a perfect taste (and visual) icon for the Performer population.

1941. M&Ms are created. This Value Population truly presides in the change from black and white to Technicolor.

1950. The first credit card appears. Appropriately enough, it is the card that eventually becomes the Diners Club card.

TECHTICIANS SAVOR THE SYSTEM

Value Population Overview

Born: 1958–1971
Size: 20% of U.S. Population

Techtician values derive from a complex mix of scientific rationalism, social idealism, and world-weary cynicism. Born into a world flush with scientific, social, economic and personal opportunity, the Techticians are ultimately subjected to a degradation of events. JFK invokes outer space as a metaphor for man's unlimited potential, but even a moon landing can't mask an era of political assassination, violent generational confrontation, self-serving economic and social proselytizing, and the ethical calamities of Vietnam and Watergate. Hoping for the best and prepared for the worst, Techticians now seem to be marked by nothing so much as their pragmatism and the belief that we all need to try just a little bit harder.

Cultural Menu. Mass Media—Commercial Jet Travel—Dawn of the Computer Age; JFK's "Camelot" Years Usher in Broadly Hopeful Social and Scientific Agendas; Americans Land on the Moon; Vietnam War Divides Nation; Assassination of Key Political Figures; Strong Economy Ultimately Sours

Some Key Personalities. John, Jackie, and Robert Kennedy; Martin Luther King, Jr.; The Beatles; Capt. James T. Kirk; Muhammad Ali; Lyndon Johnson; Richard Nixon

Primary Population Values (Partial List). Self-reliance, Pragmatism, Skill, Efficiency

Quick-Serve Restaurant History

Glen Bell, the founder of Taco Bell, freely borrows. So do Carl Karcher and John Gallardi, the founders respectively of Carl's Jr. and Der Weinerschnitzel. In the late 1950s, Southern California is fairly awash with soon-to-be-household-name fast-food entrepreneurs who recognize that Ray Kroc has latched onto something important. That something is a *system* comprised of a limited menu, uniform pricing, assembly line production, and self-service, all ultimately codified in McDonald's first ever system-wide operations manual ("the Bible") introduced in 1958.

The modern quick-service restaurant industry is itself a key icon of the Techtician value-formation period. Built upon such factors as: an emerging cultural fascination with speed; a belief in the consumer benefits of technology; the proliferation of suburban shopping; the growth of a youthful population out on its own with limited financial resources; the dynamics of national brand television advertising; the rapid conviction of Wall Street investors in the vast replicability of fast-food-restaurant systems; the proliferation of the national quick-serve-restaurant industry as the first modern "meal solution." To this day

Techticians prize efficient systems that resolve the requirements of a complex state of cultural affairs.

Significantly, advertising historians identify the year 1958 as the moment when women's magazines begin to tout the virtues of convenience products such as frozen vegetables and cake mixes in efficiently putting an attractive and wholesome meal on the family table. The issues of convenience and quality are both juxtaposed and intertwined in the value-formation period, with Techticians growing up to understand the difference between convenience and scratch cooking, accepting both for what they are and appreciating the role that each plays in a busy lifetime (explaining, perhaps, why so-called speed-scratch cookery is popular with chefs of this Value Population today). It is in the Techtician era that American regional cooking is first placed on a culinary pedestal, albeit at the unfortunately named Festival of Gas Pavilion at the 1964 World's Fair.

To appreciate the mature fruition of the Techticians, one needs only to connect the dots between the original Taco Bell (with no slight meant toward the ambitious company of today) and a company like Chipotle. Like the former was in its earliest days, the latter is a hip testament to functionality and minimalism, a model of operational efficiency deftly straddling the divide between mass production and attractive product. All of the creators and executives of Chipotle are in the Techticians Value Population, and they are fully aware, according to spokesperson Jim Adams, that the core values of the chain "reflect our values."

"We're selling burritos," says Adams, "so civilization is not riding or falling on what we do. But on the day when you are looking for something that tastes good, we want you to think of us. And on the days when speed is important, well, that's us too."

Quick-Serve Restaurant Issues

Menu. Gravitate towards upscale versions of regional and ethnic comfort food; seek authenticity in flavor profiles; understand superior ingredients and preparation; like to construct their personal version of perfection from cooking-style and garnish choices.

Service and Atmosphere. Speed and orderliness are essential here; particularly require efficiency and accuracy in the drive-through; expect minimally invasive but informed and well-trained service; value cleanliness and properly functioning equipment.

Price/Value. Human calculators; sometimes looking to make life a little simpler when they buy quick-serve food and therefore appreciate combo meals and simple uniform pricing policies; deeply experienced and informed as to what your competitors charge.

Nutrition. Very often a major preoccupation for both social cause and personal health reasons; fascinated by scientific details, they can rarely get enough information; "natural" and "organic" have significant appeal but so does premium chocolate.

Marketing. Many who market to this group allow edgy technical effects and cynical humor to take precedence over the product message; these have their place but so do the facts.

Employees. Detail- and service-oriented; far more hardworking than they are usually given credit for in generational analysis; powerfully competent with computers, they can be a little impatient with people who think at less than warp speed.

Techtician Notables

1963. The introduction of the self-cleaning oven, the birth of Weight Watchers, and the television debut of Julia Child capture many of the culinary crosscurrents of the time.

1966. Ronald McDonald airs in his first national television commercial, and McDonald's stock splits for the very first time. Fast food is vested as an industry of national importance.

1971. Starbucks opens in Seattle's Pike Place Market, and Chez Panisse opens in Berkely, California. The sincere and intelligent upscaling of the basic American food experience is on, although, soon afterwards, the chic inherit the earth.

BELIEVERS ESCAPE TO HAPPY MEALS

Value Population Overview

Born: 1972–1983
Size: 16% of U.S. Population

It is tempting to dismiss the Believers as victims of a bad patch of history. Their value formation takes place in an era of broad political, economic, and social distress, with the term "power outage" best describing the tone of the times. What makes the Believers vital, though, are the values they develop to cope with the issues posed by a time of such cultural malaise and distress. These qualities include empathy, forbearance, and, perhaps most importantly, a real faith that rescue is always a possibility. The essence of the Believer value-formation period is that, at its darkest hour, the Ronald Reagan administration comes along and things just get better. Grace, Believers seem to inherently know, can arrive only if one makes room in the spirit for its possibility.

Cultural Menu. Vietnam War Ends With U.S. Troops Withdrawal; Watergate Ushers In Period of Weak Political Leadership; Oil Embargo and Energy Crisis; Inflation and Recession; Broad Social Dysfunction; Iranian Hostage Crisis; Feminist Culture Ascends

Some Key Personalities. Gerald Ford, Jimmy Carter, John Travolta, Helen Reddy, Patty Hearst, Ayatollah Khomeini, Darth Vader

Primary Population Values (Partial List). Affinity, Patience, Diplomacy, Faith

Quick-Serve Restaurant History

They may seem impossibly quaint and goofy these days, but the Hamburglar, Grimace, and Mayor McCheese are originally born, in the early 1970s, out of a sort of historical necessity. The same holds true for McDonald's national roll-out of the Happy Meal in 1979. Be it a brilliant marketing insight or an act of corporate philanthropy, the folks at McDonald's seem to understand that society has at least temporarily moved its children to a low rung on the social totem pole and that these children are very hungry for some consideration and a little escapist fun.

Whether it is such social problems as broken homes and the excesses of the disco era, or economic problems such as energy shortages and high unemployment, or political problems such as Watergate and the Iranian hostage crisis, one quickly comes to realize that the Believer value-formation period is dominated by physical, spiritual, and cultural exhaustion. It is useful to recall "Fred the Baker," the Dunkin' Donuts advertising pitchman introduced in 1981, who wearily sleepwalks back and forth to work intoning the litany, "Time to make the doughnuts." In such a milieu, simple pleasures come to matter a lot.

Menu changes and innovations throughout the period are instructive. Runaway inflation drives the cost of premium protein to untenable heights, and the restaurant world is suddenly flooded with "gourmet" hamburgers (instead of prime rib), fried veggie appetizers (instead of shrimp cocktails), salad bars, and the minimalist high-style offerings of nouvelle cuisine. Positioning dwells on freshness, fun, and garnish aesthetics that make life seem just a little less oppressive and colorless.

While quick-serve restaurants are certainly an everyday-since-birth fact of life for Believers, as much convenience as destination, the key to this Value Population is that they are still after that sense of escape. Tim Hackbardt, Vice President of Marketing for Del Taco, shares a relevant insight as he discusses the chain's key 18 to 34-year-old male demographic: "[Our key demographic] is looking for very large portions at very inexpensive prices. But when you sit down and ask them what they like about Del Taco, every one of them has a story about something cool that has happened in their lives at a Del Taco at 2 AM in the morning. They are still creating those memories."

Quick-Serve Restaurant Issues

Menu. Not much big meat focus (with the exception of steak house celebrations); into appetizers, fruits, veggies, and foods served with some artistic flourish; often happily fad-oriented yet gravitate towards the social security of brands; many are without even rudimentary home cooking skills.

Service and Atmosphere. Require a total lack of discomfort and hostility in the "vibe"; respond well to contemporary aesthetics and empathic service; like friendly social scenes.

Price/Value. Born into real economic duress, one might expect price to be everything, but this is a group who can be up-sold with literal and conceptual "freshness"; group-oriented and comfortable with taking on debt, they somewhat easily share money with peers.

Nutrition. Significant body consciousness here, and dietary sensitivity is high; nevertheless, there is also a tendency to try out different behaviors, and one might well think of the Believers as "cigarette smoking vegetarians."

Marketing. Many marketers have appropriately fixed on the strong social orientation of this population; nevertheless, frequent emphasis upon gross humor may not be as effective as an emphasis on kindness and empathy; orientation to children will prove important (painful memories versus wanting to do better).

Employees. Tricky; Believer women formed their values during an era of feminist empowerment and seem generally both capable and ambitious; young men of the era had less effective role models and often seem to equate diligent commitment with the life of Fred the Baker; "luck" is sometimes the plan.

Believer Notables

1973. Miller Lite is born to the slogan: "Everything you always wanted in a beer. And less." Company begins long campaign to put macho spin on feminist-era product.

1979. Coke airs the legendary Mean Joe Green ad in which the fierce

Pittsburgh Steeler tosses his game jersey to a kid in thanks for a Coke. It is a totally on-target tearjerker.

1982. Wolfgang Puck opens Spago. Little pizzas are made available in designer flavors.

TRANSFORMERS: "WHERE'S THE BEEF?"

Value Population Overview

Born: 1984–1995
Size: 17% of U.S. Population

Although still in their late teens and twenties, it is safe to assume that Transformers will aggressively lay claim to a share of the world's wealth and power. Whereas the Believers who preceded them appear to have accepted peace as a path through turmoil, the Transformers have received their value conditioning in an era that endorses a far more energetic, bold, and competitive approach towards personal survival and self-satisfaction. Created in a complex time of personal and economic power resurgence amidst dangerous chaos, built by the speed and perception-bending qualities of the computer age, and fraught with streetwise intelligence about what separates winners and losers, the fate of the already exquisitely adept and savvy Transformers is very likely to be written on their terms.

Cultural Menu. Return To Strong U.S. Political Leadership; Economic Boom; Cold War Ends—USSR Dissolves; Wall Street Rules; Black Culture Ascends; Geological and Humanmade Disasters; Chaos Theory; Aids Epidemic; Personal Computer Proliferation

Some Key Personalities. Ronald Reagan, Bill Clinton, Michael Jordan, Arnold Schwarzenegger, Oprah, Ivan Boesky.

Primary Population Values (Partial List). Power, Clarity, Perseverance, Fidelity

Quick-Serve Restaurant History

Transformers will simply not be victimized. Even if the oldest of them is now 28 (2012), there is broad spiritual kinship with Clara Peller, the aged actress who first famously stood at the order counter of a Wendy's competitor in 1984, stared at a miniscule beef patty on an oversized bun, and demanded to know "Where's the beef?" Peller's plea captured the historical moment to perfection, as the resurgent Reagan era bred a new sort of red meat mentality in a nation that had become gastronomically distracted by exotic fruits, tiny vegetables, and the effete preciousness of nouvelle cuisine.

The key here is more towards attitude than menu. Not long after the Wendy's campaign launched, Burger King brought in "Herb the Nerd," a poor nebbishy soul who had never eaten a Whopper, to pitch its corporate wares. The campaign was a monumental failure as the era of pulling for, or identifying with, the underdog was quite simply over.

Ultimately, the Transformers are about obtaining and exercising power. While there are many implications for quick-service restaurants in this observation, chief among them may be that this is a generation of kids who, if not ready to be perceived as adults, will just not tolerate the condescension and manipulation frequently aimed at children. They may accept the bribe of a free toy with their meal, but they also are quite aware that Dad's getting a bigger burger.

"I actually do believe that today's ten-year-old is a lot more sophisticated," offers Joe Adney, Senior Director of Marketing for Baskin Robbins. "It is amazing how much they tend to mirror adult tastes versus kids of 20 or 30 years ago. I'd definitely say that the current group of 12-and-ups tends to brand emulate their parents."

Scott McCullough, Director of Marketing for Fuddruckers, takes it even a step further. His observation is that the Fuddruckers' produce and toppings bar concept appeals to today's adolescents because it confers control of the dining experience to them.

"What a wonderful thing it is for a teen to order a 2/3-pound burger and pile on the toppings," says McCullough. "It is a huge thing to them to have authority over these decisions. They love affirming their identity."

Quick-Serve Restaurant Issues

Menu. An expanded concept of "traditional" foods includes the likes of focaccia, fajitas, and noodle bowls, but Transformers favor the familiar and seem generationally indisposed to the purely avant-garde; early signs point to adult tastes in spices, dipping sauces, and portion sizes; "new traditionalist" label fits.

Service and Atmosphere. Advantage to quick-serve restaurant is that this group pretty much expects food to be ready when they want it; disadvantage is that they will not accept being faceless patron fodder for "the system."

Price/Value. Born into the era of the value meal and preternaturally savvy about money, this group is being programmed to expect a bargain.

Nutrition. The jury is still out; this is the first generation to receive comprehensive education regarding the personal and social benefits of proper nutrition, but they are suspicious of nutritional authority being wielded as a political and economic power.

Marketing. They frequently respond to the bold, sexy, and sometimes violently competitive icons of their generation; must not be talked down to or suspect that they are being "handled."

Employees. Seriously ambitious, they fully intend to work their way to the top and will employ practice, perseverance, and cunning to get there; they will respect authority only if it is competent and willing to coach.

Transformer Notables

1987. The California Raisin Board introduces the claymation raisins. Black culture goes mainstream on the sports pages, the stage, and the street.

1990. The first Jamba Juice opens. A nation begins turning towards energy additives and nutriceuticals to help produce an edge.

1993. The Food Network premiers. Simultaneously, the culinary mano a mano that is to become the network's biggest phenomenon, *Iron Chef,* premiers in Japan.

OWLS TAKE A BITE OUT OF EVERYTHING

Value Population Overview

Born: 1996–2007
Size: 13% of U.S. Population

Whatever they are to become in their maturity, it must be stipulated that above all else the Owls are children of globalization and the Internet Age, the first Value Population to live from birth with easily accessed universal communications and limitless interpersonal and cross-cultural connections. As has already been discussed in great detail in this work, the evolutionary implications of such a proximate and intertwined world are enormous and growing. Two things, though, are immediately apparent. The first is that nothing on this earth is too remote to be considered excluded from an Owl's potential knowledge and experience. The second is that the effect of this universal competition for consciousness is an often brutally noisy and conflicted world quite capable of fostering both figurative and literal indigestion. Will the Owls have a stomach for partaking of such a world? It may very well be the point of their existence.

Cultural Menu. The "Information Superhighway" Opens to All Travelers, A Tech Boom Drives a Strong (Consumer) Economy and an Unprecedented Stock Market Surge, Impeachment of Bill Clinton and Establishment of Fox News Ushers In Unprecedented Era of Ideological Contention, Bitter 2000 Bush/Gore Presidential Election Adjudicated by Supreme Court, Tech Boom Implosion, Terrorist Bombing of World Trade Center, War in Afghanistan & Iraq, Major Incidences of Political & Business Corruption, Real Estate Boom & Bust, Economic Recession

Some Key Personalities. Bill Clinton, George W. Bush, Al Gore, Dick Cheney, Rush Limbaugh, Michael Moore, John Stewart, Tiger Woods, Will Smith, Will Ferrell, Alanis Morissette

Primary Population Values (Partial List). Truth, Adventure, Humor, Creativity, Magic

Quick-Serve Restaurant History

When one looks at the food themes and trends of the Owl value-formation period, there is little that isn't represented. American culture is flooded with globally sourced ethnic ingredients and cuisines at the same moment mom's meatloaf and macaroni & cheese are hailed as essential comfort foods. Fresh, natural, and organic are the rage in an era that witnesses unparalleled growth in the availability and consumption of industrially processed foods. Vegetarians and vegans significantly elbow their way to the table amidst a classic crowd of steak-craving carnivores.

Perhaps the dietary range of the period is best expressed as a function of nutritional partisanship. On the one hand is a strident anti-obesity, pro-health sentiment represented by such memes of the era as Atkins-style low-carbohydrate diets, Eric Schlosser's muckraking exposé *Fast Food Nation: The Dark Side of the All-American Meal* (book 2001, movie 2006), and Morgan Spurlocks' McDonald's-bashing film documentary *Super Size Me* (2004). On the other is a period that unapologetically celebrates the partaking of giant hamburgers, over-stuffed burritos, and fresh-from-the-oven doughnuts as near-sacred cultural rites.

Even in culinary areas that are not strictly gastronomic, there are broad selections regarding speed and style of service, atmosphere, and method of transaction. As in so many other areas of Owl era culture, communications technology opens up entirely new and vast systems of identifying, selecting, and engaging with one's food sources and with other consumers. By the end of the Owl era, there are, according to the website Technorati, more than 30,000 active food blogs, and a Google search for the term "food" yields just shy of 2 billion hits (twice as many as "God").

Observing specifically from a QSR viewpoint, it is appropriate to point out that the period is one that witnesses the advent and flourishing of the "fast casual" restaurant trend, an appropriately oxymoronic moniker for restaurant concepts that include Chipotle, Panera and Pei Wei, among many others. The key to these concepts and their considerable influence on more traditional fast food venues is observable in their eclectic menus, their strong flavoring profiles, their exotic ingredient sourcing, their earnest nod to fresh and healthy food choices, and their more comfortable dining environments. All of this represents augmentation to an attractive price/value proposition and a limited service platform, not a replacement of that proposition or platform.

Given all that we have observed in their value-formation period so far, we can pretty safely assume that Owls are far more likely to be omnivorous experimenters than picky dogmatists when it comes to culinary matters. In 1999, Tim Ryan, who is currently president of America's preeminent culinary college, The Culinary Institute of America, coins the term "alternivore" to capture his sense of emerging food trends. It's no longer that most people are vegetarians or carnivores, he argues, they are at various times both; i.e. people are increasingly comfortable with culinary eclecticism and opportunism, rather like owls.

Quick-Serve Restaurant Issues

Menu. We are probably safe in assuming that the Owls will be collectively rather open-minded and adventurous when it comes to food selection. Surely, economic considerations will drive some choices, as will personal tradition and taste preferences, but it is hard to imagine the members of this Value Population rejecting en masse any earnest and reasonably appealing culinary effort without at least a trial. Some Owl gourmets there will certainly be, but far more likely to be iconic is the all-appreciative gourmand.

Service & Atmosphere. Eclectic needs are likely, although exotic and authentic are two terms likely to come up often. Unlike Techticians, this Value Population is not just looking to quick-serve restaurants for efficiency and price, and the fast, casual trend towards investing in comfortable dining areas where socialization is possible is likely to continue. Of course, WiFi connectivity and high-definition screens will be standard—if they aren't already.

Price Value. Again, fluctuating circumstances will drive different considerations. The Owls have been brought up in era of "dollar menus," and given the immediate economic outlook they are not likely to be throwing money away on overpriced food or vapid culinary promises.

Nevertheless, the Owls will appreciate that you can't always get a lot for a little—unless you use a two-for-one coupon or hit the all-you-can-eat buffet. Some quality splurges are likely, but culinary fakers won't get a second chance.

Nutrition. As they will with every issue on their plate, they will ask the question, "What is true?" Vanity and the emotional arguments of social activists will only drive them so far into the fat-free zone. Owls are not the sorts to willingly deny themselves when they are hungry, as there is always something interesting to eat—not necessarily nutritious—if you look hard enough.

Marketing. It's not just that a proliferation of alternative media and technology-driven marketing channels fracture the message delivery system once and for all during the Owl value-formation period. As is acknowledged by restaurant companies and consumer analyst groups alike, it is the very notion of a mass market that essentially bites the dust in this era. "Affinity groups" becomes a popular buzz term, and the Owl era beckons in a time when it is important to identify limited groups of people who are passionate about something, rather than larger groups who are bored with it all. Interestingly, Owls may actually turn out to be "big picture" thinkers, but the great sin of marketing in their heyday is likely to be messaging that makes easy assumptions about a collective point of view.

Employees. Owls are likely to bring a lot of nice attributes to the job, including perceptiveness, a sense of humor and a genuine desire to do some good in the world. Unfortunately for an industry such as the quick-serve restaurant that relies so much on tight systems and repetitive processes, however, there is little denying that the easily bored and free-thinking Owls are going to be disinclined to get in line simply for a paycheck. Processes, no matter how perfect, are just not a draw here. Understanding why the work is important in a larger social sense is what matters most of all.

Owl Notables

1998. McDonald's makes a commitment to emerging fresh and foreign trends by taking a significant stake in "Fresh Mex" burrito chain, Chipotle. By 2001, they are the majority holder. While the investment is later dissolved, the trend to broadening culinary horizons is noteworthy as the company also dabbles in pizza (Donato's in 2001), Italian food (Fazoli's in 2001), and fresh and natural sandwiches (Pret a Manger in 2001). Meanwhile, competitor Wendy's buys Baja Fresh (2002), and Jack in the Box captures Qdoba (2003).

1998. Red Bull energy drink enters the U.S. market, scientific journals suggest that the lycopene in ketchup may be an anti-carcinogen, and *Food Processing* magazine names "functional foods/nutraceuticals" as the year's number-one processed food trend. The notion that food can be a delivery system for biological and mental enhancement agents (both natural and manufactured) is likely to maintain considerable appeal for the open-minded and experientially inclined Owls.

2000. There is no food more iconic in the Owl period, both as a menu item and as the key product in a meteoric business rise and fall, than the Krispy Kreme Original Glazed doughnut. An almost ethereal combination of freshly baked dough, hot air, and sugar glaze, the product's expansion from its southeastern American roots into New York City (1996) and then the rest of the nation touches off a media and sales frenzy that floods the cultural consciousness with the joy of sticky calories and the even sweeter possibility of owning a Krispy Kreme franchise. More contagious than a bad flu season, the highpoint of the craze is the 2000 issuing of stock on the NASDAQ (soon transferred to the NYSE) that very quickly yields a valuation of nearly a half-billion dollars, a figure close to 40 times annual net corporate income. The demise of the product's popularity and the company's financial reputation is swift and brutal, but the story of regional expansion, media frenzy, fortunes made and lost, and a product that, by volume, is mostly air definitely makes the Krispy Kreme doughnut a meme that screeches Owl value formation.

OPENING NEW AVENUES:
Managing Talent and Finding Trends

While the first three parts of this book focused on describing and applying Value Population research to better understand and connect with customers, Part 4 broadens this approach and opens new avenues from which the reader can additionally benefit: internally toward workforce management and externally toward the early identification of trends.

In Chapter 27, "Attitudes at Work," the benefits of lasting values will be discussed as an effective tool for attracting, training, motivating, coordinating, compensating, and retaining a strong workforce. Furthermore, the recognition of the "intergenerational mix" of Value Populations within the workforce provides a constant object lesson as to how the corresponding Value Populations outside an organization, i.e., the customers, may be best understood and conceptually approached on a values basis.

In Chapter 28, "Attracting Trends," a proprietary method developed by Near Bridge, Inc. that uses cutting edge thinking in regard to chaos theory to uncover and predict trends is discussed and an example of its use with two Near Bridge clients, the United States Potato Board and the Foodservice and Packaging Industry, is presented.

The final chapter of this book, Chapter 29, "The Age of Meaning," offers executives and entrepreneurs additional ways to use Value Population research to increase their market penetration and financial profitability.

Chapter

27

ATTITUDES AT WORK

With a broadly reported decline in job loyalty and a projected decrease in skilled workers creating a dangerous double whammy for business, it is particularly important that business professionals pay close attention to what motivates, grows, and retains workers. Because of this, more and more companies today understand that they are not only marketing to external customers but to internal ones as well.

Current demographic trends confirm that we are entering into an era that will be characterized by the most generationally and ethnically diverse workforce in American history. Value Population research is of enormous value in identifying the personality marketers (Performers), the efficiency experts (Techticians), the natural team players (Believers), the power-hungry challengers (Transformers) and the broadminded disruptors (Owls).

Motivation and collaboration are the keys to a well-oiled workforce, and Near Bridge Value Population insights will certainly help anyone who has to negotiate the human resources "minefield."

In the following pages, we explore the attitudes of the Value Populations with regard to their orientation toward work, including such areas as: styles, motivation, talent, relationships, and rewards. At the end of each section is a set of key workplace attributes intended to provide the reader an overview of the Value Populations attitudes within the work environment.

PATRIOTS: THE PLEDGE OF ALLEGIANCE

Now in their 70s, 80s and 90s, Patriots are unlikely to be in the employment ranks. Yet, many businesses still act as if the work-related values of the Patriots are the values of more contemporary groups, and, therefore, it is important to at least briefly consider their orientation to work and the workplace because theirs is the lingering paradigm.

As a result of a confluence of factors—the First World War and its attendant manufacturing requirements; large-scale immigration; and the emergent mass popularization of such consumer goods as the automobile, the radio, and the telephone—the Patriots are the first truly modern and mass industrialized population. It is in the Patriot value-formation period when broad society encounters the struggle between the dehumanizing requirements of assembly line work and the emotional needs of human beings. Due to value formation during a Global Depression, the fierce motivational force of money and general material security is also never far from conscious consideration.

As has already been suggested throughout this book, the resolution of Patriot needs lies in the cultivation of material rewards and the establishment of a useful personal role within a group definition. Fear of want, an understanding that life is hard, a shared bearing of burdens, and the security of "creed-based collectivism" are rolled up in this population. In this group, there is an especially strong gravitation to the one-man-in-charge, drill sergeant archetype—strong and blustery leaders whose mission is to vigilantly protect the well-being and the creed of the group, gregariousness and graciousness be damned.

Not surprisingly, much of the business theory that emerges in the Patriot value-formation era pertains to mass production, from quality control to social implications. Notions of "scientific management" begin to proliferate, extolling such virtues as efficiency, trained skills, and sacrifice of the individuality to the system—a workplace philosophy with profit benefits to the owners and overtones of dependability, and therefore security, to the workers. The problem here, as eloquently pointed out in the classic Charlie Chaplin movie Modern Times (1936) and referenced earlier in this book, is that a workplace based solely upon "scientific principles" is quite capable of beating the humanity right out of you.

Along these lines, perhaps the most useful theorist when it comes to an appreciation of Patriot workplace values is George Elton Mayo, a Harvard Business School professor who, between the years 1927 and 1932, conducted a series of studies at the Western Electric Hawthorne Works in Chicago. His research involved isolating teams of assembly line workers and monitoring their productivity as they were subjected to variables relating to the fatigue and monotony of their work. These isolated teams were monitored by an observer who explained to the groups what was transpiring and solicited their input and reactions regarding the particulars of the study.

What Mayo discovered, in a series of conclusions that have collectively come to be known as The Hawthorne Effect, is that the specific study variables (break periods, working hours, work weeks, work techniques, and environments, etc.) had far less a predictable impact on productivity than the simple fact that the groups were being formed, observed, and consulted. What apparently motivated the groups (and productivity did rise in almost every case regardless of variables) was observation by a superior and the bonding dynamics of the group itself.

While the privations of the Depression era witnessed a corresponding rise in fear-based workplace motivation, there is little denying that a group ethos, coupled with meaningful personal stature within the group, is the key principle of productivity.

The security orientation of the Patriots may be amply evidenced in their present-day concern with retirement plans and Social Security, but the Patriot value keynote has been and always will be group participation, group loyalty, and group approval. Patriots are very loyal workers and do well in positions that work to serve the organization as a whole. When marketing work to Patriots, security of their job must not be breached. In the end, the best way to motivate Patriots is through clear direction, strong leadership, safety for the group, and a pledge of "One Nation under God, indivisible, with liberty and justice for all." See Figure 27.1.

FIGURE 27.1

Key Patriot Workplace Attributes

Big Metaphor: — Military

Work Nature: — Defensive

The Leader: — Drill Sergeant

The Follower: — Soldier

Key Strength: — Loyalty

Fear / Vulnerability: — Loss of Security

Conflict Technique: — Defensiveness

Resolution Technique: — Assurance

Tends to Avoid: — Innovation

Training: — Group Instructions

Rejuvenation: — Rest

Reward Beside Dollars: — Security

Coin of the Realm: — Money

PERFORMERS: I'VE GOTTA BE ME!

The landmark insight for anyone who wants to understand a Performer boss, colleague, or employee is contained in the work of Abraham Maslow, a founder of the field of humanistic psychology. It is in Maslow's article, *A Theory of Motivation* (1943), that he first introduces the notion of a "hierarchy of human needs." In it, Maslow sets forth the premise that after a human being satisfies basic survival needs such as food and shelter, and after addressing such security needs as group belonging, and even after experiencing love, a human being can find greatest fulfillment in the exaltation of his or her individuality through "peak experiences" leading to self-actualization and personal transcendence.

To the Patriots, such a worldview flies in the face of the centrality of the collective and to the Techticians, who will be considered next, humanistic psychology is plainly self-indulgent, unscientific, and inefficient. Yet, to accept the Performers on their own terms is to accept the fact that, to them, direct personal experience is a great, maybe the greatest, good. Noisy, restless, profligate, pontificating, overly-dramatic, and self-referential though they may sometimes be, at this point in their advanced career lives, Performers are becoming increasingly more prized for the real wisdom that has accrued through lives that have been far more active than passive, and far more bravely intuitive than safely tactical.

A December 2003 *USA Today* article reported, "In the battle for jobs during this jobless expansion, workplace veterans over 50 have caught up to and may soon surpass their younger rivals when it comes to finding new positions in the shortest amount of time. The median search time for unemployed executive-level staffers 50 and older has dropped 10 times faster than that of younger job seekers." While Performers are easily bored and demand considerable attention, their breadth of experience translates into very attractive big picture capabilities. Particularly, a lifelong interest regarding what others outside "the tribe" think and do is paying dividends for smart companies in a global environment. Naturally gifted in such interpersonal disciplines as sales and marketing, enthusiastically oriented toward consideration of foreign cultures, and generally able to go with the flow when the unexpected occurs, this group may find mentoring of both younger colleagues and consumers a perfect marriage of personal needs and the needs of the American economy.

In a February 6, 2004, press release, The Home Depot, the world's largest home improvement retailer, and AARP, the leading membership organization for the 50+ population with over 35 million members, announced a national partnership to attract, motivate, and retain eligible older workers as part-time and full-time associates in new and existing stores across the country.

"This hiring partnership with AARP is a great opportunity for The Home Depot to attract qualified, knowledgeable, and skilled individuals to work as associates in our stores," said Bob Nardelli, Chairman, President and CEO of The Home Depot. "AARP has a broad national reach with the mature workforce making it a powerful resource and an ideal organization for Home Depot to partner with for a national hiring initiative. At The Home Depot, we believe knowledge, experience, and passion never retire."

Bob Nardelli is on to something with both his description of key Performer qualities and his "never retire" observation. When one considers the broad financial ramifications of downturns in the economy coupled with the Performers' sense of material entitlement, and when one acknowledges that the prevailing Performer sense of "retirement" is one of active engagement rather than restful retreat, it becomes clear that Performers have every intention of working later into life than any previous population.

A 2003 Towers Perrin study, "Redefining Retirement in the 21st Century," provides additional insight into this phenomenon. Although retirement has traditionally involved a period of leisure following a 30- to 40-year career, 78 percent of employee respondents said they expect to continue working in some capacity well into their retirement years. Of these respondents, 64 percent expect to work part time, while 57 percent plan to change occupations. Significantly, 35 percent of those employees who expect to continue working into their retirement years said they would continue working for financial reasons, while more respondents—43 percent—said they would work chiefly to stay involved and active.

Ultimately, the Performers are a group who will continue working because of material needs but also, and far more importantly, because of the continued possibilities for personal discovery and fulfillment. Performers are terrific leaders of a cause and do well in positions requiring strategic thinking and enthusiasm. They are very well suited for sales and marketing positions and make excellent recruiters and human resource managers. When marketing work to Performers, *personal dignity* must not be compromised. Sincere praise and appreciation goes a long way here as well. See Figure 27.2.

FIGURE 27.2

Key Performer Workplace Attributes

Big Metaphor: — Theater
Work Nature: — Strategic
The Leader: — Star
The Follower: — Actor
Key Strength: — Curiosity
Fear / Vulnerability: — Personal Disrespect
Conflict Technique: — Self-importance
Resolution Technique: — Concern
Tends to Avoid: — Detail Work
Training: — Interactive
Rejuvenation: — Travel and Adventure
Reward Beside Dollars: — Status
Coin of the Realm: — Enthusiasm

TECHTICIANS: IT ALL ADDS UP

No less of a shift in workplace consciousness than that from the Patriots to the Performers takes place when one moves from the Performers to the Techticians. The most obvious dividing line here is information technology. The average Techtician worker has more faith in the abilities of his computer to rationally and efficiently model reality than in the insights and agendas of his human colleagues to create a rational and efficient reality—particularly the non-Techtician ones.

As discussed in the previous section of this book, Techticians formed their values in a hopeful era characterized by vast scientific advances and a belief in mankind's ability to adapt this science to the broad political, economic, social, and environmental benefit of mankind. Sadly, due to the Vietnam War era and its society-wrenching value conflicts between Patriots and Performers, Techticians have apparently come to the somewhat cynical conclusion that only the science, and not the big picture social agendas, has any real clarity and objective truth.

At the risk of oversimplification, Techticians are really "skeptical pragmatists" at heart. They are Dilberts to the pointy-haired bosses, Mr. Spocks to the Captain Kirks. Mistrustful of abstraction, particularly in such attitudinal business areas as marketing, these are the individuals who deify data and measurement. What matters most are circuitry and task, the efficient organization and flow of information for the solution of specific issues, not ruminations regarding the greater society or the corporate master plan.

A key to understanding the Techticians' value system is their belief that most any business issue can and should be addressed with a spreadsheet, a flow chart, or a formula. For example, Greg Diamond, Techtician, founder, and managing partner of Clovis, a staffing firm in Gaithersburg, Maryland, uses a formula to decide whether it is more cost-effective to hire an employee or hire a temp as was pointed out by Chris Pentilla in *Entrepreneur Magazine,* July 2004.

Even in sports such as baseball, as Michael Lewis adeptly describes in his book, *Moneyball,* professional scouts increasingly rely on the laptop over the clipboard with legal pad to do their jobs. *PC Magazine* has identified a segment of largely Techtician-age knowledge workers they call "The New Geeks." Basically, these workers are bringing their computer-based statistical backgrounds into fields other than traditional IT. Steve Lohr wrote the following in the July 2004 *PC Magazine:*

> Andrew Davenport, a 36-year-old researcher at IBM, has a background that is both deeply technical and academically rigorous. His field of expertise is mathematical optimization, and his Ph.D. in computer science was in optimization constraint programming, followed by postdoctoral research ... Davenport is one of the New Geeks, people who are technically trained but also have the ability and inclination to work comfortably in other disciplines like business, the sciences, and the social sciences. They personify the future of computing as its impact spreads further. Computing has already helped transform everything from the way scientists plumb the mysteries of biology, chemistry, and physics to the way Detroit designs cars and Hollywood makes movies. As it moves increasingly beyond traditional calculation, computer science is inevitably becoming more interdisciplinary, introducing the computing arts to a wider circle of people.

The downside to the Techtician approach to work, at least in the eyes of other Value Populations, is that Techticians most often would rather be correct than useful. People skills and relationships tend to suffer when data is made king, as data-based conclusions foster rigid attitudes about objective truths and right or wrong answers. An example of the attitude and tone many Techticians bring to work is found in the title of a recent book by organizational consultant John Hoover, *How to Work for an Idiot.* This title clearly articulates the frustration Techticians feel when confronting Performer bosses—who may be more dramatic, self-referential, and intuitive rather than practical, self-effacing, and logical.

When in the service of a leader who has a coherent vision,

Techticians can be remarkably swift and capable in realizing and appreciating the specifics of a strategy or plan. What is particularly interesting, though, is that Techticians are now becoming the corporate leaders, the culture creators, and the visionaries of workplace organizations. When one considers the Techtician predilection toward micromanaging, and a worldview in which data collection is never quite complete, it does not necessarily add up that members of this group, whose loyalties are task oriented, will be able to effectively set strategy over the long haul.

Ultimately, Techticians tend to stay around as long as their jobs make not just dollars but *personal sense.* Work that is well-defined on a task level, where new career-enhancing skills may be acquired, and loyalty is defined by contribution rather than longevity, is the motivational ticket for this group. Techticians often handle pressure well, although often with cynicism, and have a cultural-biased disposition for positions requiring analysis such as engineering, manufacturing, material control, accounting, and program management—and when working with Techticians, for God's sake (and yours), keep your meetings short and your technology up to date! See Figure 27.3.

FIGURE 27.3

Key Techtician Workplace Attitudes

Big Metaphor: — *Control Room*
Work Nature: — *Tactical*
The Leader: — *Administrator*
The Follower: — *Service Provider*
Key Strength: — *Industriousness*
Fear / Vulnerability: — *Outdated Skills*
Conflict Technique: — *Sabotage*
Resolution Technique: — *Interest*
Tends to Avoid: — *Conceptual Work*
Training: — *Self-administered*
Rejuvenation: — *Continuing Education*
Reward Beside Dollars: — *Personal Development*
Coin of the Realm: — *Information*

BELIEVERS: THE CULTURE CLUB

Much about the Believer Value Population is frustrating to those who subscribe to the protestant ethic that "life's rewards come from hard work." Unlike the Techticians, Believers do not easily resonate with the merits of duty, details, and discipline. Believers are convinced that objectives have an inconsistent relationship with outcomes and often avoid stress by assuming that "grace" will prevail.

Considering the various traumas of the Believer value-formation period—energy shortages, economic malaise, challenges to family morals, weak leadership—history has taught this group that the most important thing they can do in life is to pick their friends, associates, and significant others well. Then, even in the most oppressive of environments, one will have like-spirited allies to make the hard times seem easier. Beyond that, all one really needs is faith that "the ship" is eventually going to come in.

As a group that defines itself through peer relationships, there is at first glance something vaguely reminiscent of the Patriots here. However, Believers are far less willing to go along with authority just because of a title on the door and far less likely to accept relentless pain as the price of a paycheck. They are also far less accepting of oppressive cultures that are imposed upon them by "accidents" of tradition or birth. Yet, ironically, participation in a coherent culture *is* of the essence.

A fertile area for studying Believer work-related values is the retail industry, whose store-level jobs are for the most part presently held by Believers. Despite enormous general turnover rates (close to 50 percent per year), some companies such as Starbucks and Petco are doing an exceptional job of worker retention. These companies understand that workers of Believer age are adamant about work being an extension of personal values.

In the May 2004 issue of *California Jobs Journal*, Michael Kinsman writes that Petco, with more than 650 stores and more than 15,000 employees, retains employees by viscerally engaging them in their work at the value level. "Turnover is all about the right hire," declares spokesman Don Cowan. "It really begins for us in function and fit. Do they have the skill sets we need, and how do they fit in? The fit here is about how they fit in the culture." Consequently, Petco seeks to hire people who like animals and relate well to them. "We have living, breathing animals," Cowan stresses. "We want to keep people engaged by hiring the kind of people that will relate to them."

John Izzo, author of *Values-Shift: The New Work Ethic and What It Means for Business*, does an excellent job of addressing some of the realities and implications of the Believer-age population in the workplace. He notes that this is an age group that expects to find social fulfillment at work, with spontaneous celebrations, job-related friendships and even marriages rapidly proliferating at this time. A study of recent college graduates, reports Izzo, reveals that for two thirds of this group, "work life will never be more important than personal life." This suggests that wise employers will recognize this attitude about timely recognition, relationships, and fun and will build it into the corporate culture.

An unusual corporate freebie that some companies have adopted for their single employees is dating agency membership. Rachel Basger, business development director at the dating agency Club Sirius, explains in a May 2004 *Managing Information Strategies Magazine* article, "Some people have the view that people in a relationship are happier, more productive, and easier to retain. As a result, some companies have membership as a perk for staff who are relocating, as otherwise they can get lonely in the evenings. They want them to have a good balance between work and life."

Similarly, one catches an interesting glimpse of a Believer value manifestation in the *blogging* phenomenon. Blogging, the creation of personality-intensive online diaries, is a business communications strategy with great appeal for Believers, who need to feel a human connection with others about their work.

A June 2004 *Business Week Online* article reported that executives are increasingly encouraging employee blogs as a way to personalize customer transactions with an otherwise faceless behemoth. Microsoft has been one of the biggest evangelists. In 2005, it had about 100 corporate bloggers. Today, 1000's have blogs and nearly every employee has a Facebook and/or Twitter account. They post pictures of company refrigerators—there's one that has all Coke and one that has all Pepsi—and spout off on everything from the death of Boots the cat to naming Microsoft's new operating systems." Furthermore, says *Business Week Online,* Microsoft Chairman William H. Gates III is so certain that corporate blogging is the next gold rush in communications that "he's practically handing out the pails and shovels by enabling any employee to create a blog within two seconds." Microsoft does not teach employees to blog, but it does allow employees to hold meetings to talk about them. The blogs carry disclaimers, but other than that, "our unspoken policy on blogging is: Don't be stupid," says Microsoft product manager Adam Sohn.

It is interesting to contemplate how members of this group will eventually fare as leaders. While there is definitely some aversion to conflict and distaste for exercising authority that is often integral to action, the members of this Value Population may accomplish much through peer consensus building in a generally supportive culture.

As followers, Believers are in a very difficult position. While Techticians struggle with Performer bosses who don't seem to care about the details and seem to focus too much on the drama of the situation, there is a natural order in a boss who is strategic and a subordinate who is tactical.

Unfortunately for business, no such natural order is found as Techticians, who just want to get things done, tend to be unemotionally direct in their management style and now manage Believers who want to build consensus among all of the players before a decision is made.

Fortunately for the Techtician manager who understands this issue, there is a solution—consultative management. Unlike consensus management, which is often slow because it seeks complete group approval to resolve issues, consultative management, a more efficient and often a more effective process, encourages the voices of all to be heard but gives final authority of the decision to the manager. Consultative management meets the needs of both Value Populations, as Believers get to be heard and Techticians get abundant information and the ability to move forward quickly.

Because Believers are truly team players, they do well in positions requiring strong emotional support and interaction such as human resources, training, customer support, and call center operation. Never motivated by fear, Believers prefer flight to fight in difficult situations; and in the Believer world, the quality of the work will always be linked to the quality of the relationships. See Figure 27.4.

FIGURE 27.4

Key Believer Workplace Attributes

Big Metaphor: — *Social Club*

Work Nature: — *Communal*

The Leader: — *Consensus Developer*

The Follower: — *Team Player*

Key Strength: — *Charm*

Fear / Vulnerability: — *Peer Conflict*

Conflict Technique: — *Passive Resistance*

Resolution Technique: — *Appreciation*

Tends to Avoid: — *Conflict*

Training: — *Group Participation*

Rejuvenation: — *Socializing*

Reward Beside Dollars: — *Inclusion*

Coin of the Realm: — *Relationship*

TRANSFORMERS: THE ART OF WAR

Having now entered the workforce in a powerful way, Transformers are taking their work lives very seriously. As has been discussed earlier in this book, Transformers already tend to see life as a competition for increasingly limited resources. For Transformers, the business avatars are likely to be individuals such as Lee Iaccoca, who in his 1984 autobiography writes that the most important qualities in a job candidate are "fire in the belly" and "street smarts," and the Sun-Tzu quoting fictional capitalist Gordon Gecko, who in the 1987 movie *Wall Street* puts forth the proposition that "greed captures the essence of the evolutionary spirit."

One of the great misperceptions in today's marketplace is that Transformer teens were essentially like the social, flirty, financially blithe, trend-following Believer teens who have just vacated their adolescent years. While some life-phase echoes of Believers do linger, Transformers are infinitely more particular when it comes to statements of personal style, group dynamics, price/value relationships, and the perception of what matters in securing a successful future. Most importantly, to consumer marketers and future employers alike, the Transformers are fierce rejecters of manipulation.

It is worth noting that Believers spent their teen years in the boom economy of the 1990s, attending high school and college during a period of robust employment opportunities and apparently stress-free career paths. No such illusions exist for the Transformers, who are now battling to obtain/keep the entry-level jobs and menial employment positions that are now increasingly occupied by older workers pushed down the employment ladder

"Kids are doing worse this year than last," says Andrew Sum, the center's director. "The job growth hasn't filtered down. If anything like this happened to the adult workforce, you'd call it a depression. It's that severe."

The implications of this state of affairs are intriguing. On one hand, Transformers are likely to acknowledge that entering the employment arena is going to be difficult, requiring the cultivation of skill, courage, foresight, persistence, responsibility, useful contacts, and the ability to endure tradition and authority as a right of passage. On the other hand, this situation is making them more astute, avaricious, and angry, such that given their value predispositions are coming to regard business as a battlefield in a way that is only slightly metaphorical—making them the perfect "corporate soldiers" or renegade corporate terrorists. Transformers will bring training, concentration, generally solid instincts, a bias for taking action, and easily identifiable motivations regarding money and power into the work arena. More and more reports speak to what may well be a rare cohort confluence of skill, savvy, and ambition. The best and brightest of them will have a lifelong appreciation for the twin virtues of preparation and patience—and an innate grasp of technology that has been developing from birth.

According to the results from Kaufman Foundation survey of 5,077 young adults in 2010 showed that 41% of young adults between the ages of 18 and 24 years old want to start a business or already have started one.

While young adults find the idea of starting their own business alluring, such dreams appear to be firmly grounded in reality. The young adults also showed that they were aware of the challenges and risks involved in a start-up, the necessary preparation to be successful, and trade-offs between working for others and being self-employed. Indeed, some companies are already starting to transform*er* themselves. For example, per *QSR Magazine,* July 2004, Dan Cathy, CEO of Chick-fil-A, volunteered during an executive roundtable that his company is now doing more and more management-track recruitment of "mission capable" teens, some as young as 15 and 16. Parents are involved in the interview process, and grades, as well as character, must be exemplary. "They bring competence, character, and chemistry," says Cathy, "and they put passion into it."

Transformers understand that apprenticeship is part of the game—but not forever, and they will quickly expect to move up in the organization, or even run it, once they have mastered the required skills. They will do well in almost any position that requires savvy thinking, heightened competition, and winning results such as legal, sales, and product design. Transformers are motivated by responsibility and power and ultimately may prove to be the most business-oriented of all the Value Populations. See Figure 27.5.

Understanding, anticipating, and meeting the needs of current and potential customers is the fundamental role of marketing, but to be successful in this quest requires many people working in unison. Understanding the workplace attitudes of different Value Populations gives marketing executives a competitive advantage in that it allows them to create stronger and more balanced marketing organizations, effectively recruit and retain good employees, reduce the friction between team members, and better motivate their teams. So in the end, they can spend less time managing their people and more time searching for ways to uncover or, better yet, attract trends.

FIGURE 27.5

Key Transformer Workplace Attributes

> *Big Metaphor: — Street Gang*
> *Work Nature: — Assured*
> *The Leader: — Champion*
> *The Follower: — Challenger*
> *Key Strength: — Courage*
> *Fear / Vulnerability: — Marginalization*
> *Conflict Technique: — Engagement*
> *Resolution Technique: — Compromise*
> *Tends to Avoid: — The Weak*
> *Training: — Competency-based*
> *Rejuvenation: — Competition*
> *Reward Beside Dollars: — Responsibility*
> *Coin of the Realm: — Power*

OWLS: THROW OUT THE RULES

Because right now this is a job. If I advance any higher, this would be my career. And if this were my career, I'd have to throw myself in front of a train.

John Krasinski as Jim, The Office (2005)

By this time in our discussion of the Owls, one thing should be very apparent. This is not likely a generation that will buy into any existing system simply on the basis of that system's entrenchment or because of the passion of individuals who support that system. As potential employees, particularly on the entry and staff levels, the Owl insistence upon coming to their own conclusions about "meaning" may well create some workplace issues.

It's hardly that the Owls will reject organization outright, or that they will fail to understand the vast majority of humankind gets to participate in the material rewards of society by having careers or holding some sort of job. It's not even that temperamentally, as discussed in the earlier Owl chapters, that Owls are likely to be ill suited to the sort of mental repetition and physical confinement that characterizes so much of today's technology-driven systems work. What is really going to be hard to erase from the collective value-formation consciousness of the Owls is the profound Owl-era influence of institutional capital interests and the mantra of "increased shareholder value," a cut-to-the-chase economic prioritization that tends to place 'ordinary' employees far towards the back of the line that leads to the payoff window.

Quite demonstrably, the Owls have been value formed in an era that increasingly rewards investment far more than labor, one in which: accounting becomes as much a dark art as a science; competency-challenged top executives receive increasingly outlandish compensation packages while workforce salary growth is at best stagnant; traditional short- and long-term employment benefits are eliminated for the good of the balance sheet; and millions of jobs are expeditiously shipped overseas (with the government's support) if the result is an enhanced quarterly report to Wall Street. Arguments about the methods and goals of capitalism aside, it's just that the "little guy" (which now seems to include a sizable chunk of the middle class in addition to the lower) has little reason for being loyal to a company or even an entire system that increasingly treats them, quite frankly, like financial fodder. In this context, both the economic and human rewards of work and career, as most cogently portrayed in much of the Owl-era television and movie culture, are increasingly marginalized.

"Would I leave this company?" representatively ponders Rainn Wilson as the character Dwight Schrute on the hit television show *The Office* (2005–). "Look, I'm all about loyalty. In fact, I feel like part of what I'm being paid for here is my loyalty. But if there were somewhere else that valued loyalty more highly, I'm going wherever they value loyalty the most."

Quite noteworthy are the many Owl-era hit movies such as *Gone in 60 Seconds* (2000), *Oceans 11* (2001), *Fast and Furious* (2001), *The Italian Job* (2003), and *Inside Man* (2006) that involve an "inside" robbery or a heist or a con job in which the perpetrators are not only the 'cool' characters with whom the audience is asked to identify, but who are also generally successful in the commission of their crimes. This is certainly not to paint an entire generation with criminal intent, but it is clear that there is a lot of empathy for characters who attempt to short-circuit a system stacked against them with a bold big-dollar gamble (a feeling consistent with the immense growth of stock day-trading, sports wagering and casino gambling in the Owl period). In *Scorched* (2003), a little-known but eminently instructive film, three employees of a low-paying rural bank independently decide to rob their employer on the same day after one of them gets a 55-cent/hour pay raise—all three are portrayed sympathetically and all get away with their larceny.

This admittedly daunting analysis is harped on here, because Owls are not going to just blithely buy into the "common" build-a-career perspective or unquestioningly play by someone else's rules, particularly when they find themselves merely low paid producer-pawns in a reality not of their own design. And here, please let it be understood that the Owls are likely to bring potentially prodigious talents to the workplace, among them curiosity, creativity, candor, entrepreneurial spirit, and an inclusive communal temperament that will be an essential attribute in an increasingly multi-cultural global workforce. Ultimately, it's not so much that the Owls will be ill-prepared to make a contribution to commerce, but that the enterprise culture that might fully incorporate all of these values probably just doesn't exist quite yet—at least not in the "shareholder sovereignty" world of Owl-era big business.

Of course, the question presents itself as to whether an Owl-friendly corporate culture can (or should) exist and what it might be like. Georgetown University business school professor Robert M. Grant, author of the acclaimed *Contemporary Strategy Analysis*, visits this issue in his work. He persuasively describes the need for flexible learning-based organizations in which "emotionally intelligent" leaders are primarily keepers of a cultural flame rather than unassailable decision makers, rules are simple and kept to a minimum, situational adaptability and voluntary project/personnel linkages are encouraged, and strategy, rather than being something delivered from above, emerges from open-mindedly and bravely searching at the creative edge of chaos.

All of the preceding may be something of a pipe dream, but it does truly speak to the Owl values' essence. "Life is a search for meaning," observes Grant, and that dynamic, unfettered quality of search will likely be everything to the Owls. Work satisfaction, and most everything else in the Owl life, will derive its meaning from discovered rather than delivered wisdom.

And finally, it is worth reiterating here that the Owls are the first Internet-since-birth Value Population. This gives them a tremendous and unprecedented cultural advantage with regard to both low-price-of-entry, web-based business creation and intimate awareness of employment opportunities anywhere on the globe. Add to this the easy accessibility of the once closely held strategic and tactical business information that is now freely available on the Internet, and it is highly likely that the Owls, when all is said and done, will prove to be both an entrepreneurial and highly migratory workforce.

Of course, just like the members of every Value Population that has preceded them, the Owls may be forced by economic circumstances to just take a job. It seems a certainty, though, that they will not be conned into thinking they are doing something wonderful unless they are actually doing something wonderful. And wonderful, the Owls will likely be aware, is something they may have to do on their own. See Figure 27.6.

FIGURE 27.6

Key Owl Workplace Attributes

Big Metaphor: — *University*

Work Nature: — *Curious*

The Leader: — *Sage*

The Follower: — *Explorer*

Key Strength: — *Broad-Mindedness*

Fear / Vulnerability: — *Micromanagement*

Conflict Technique: — *Candor*

Resolution Technique: — *Honesty*

Tends to Avoid: — *Certainty*

Training: — *Concept-based*

Rejuvenation: — *Off the Grid*

Reward Beside Dollars: — *Freedom*

Coin of the Realm: — *Meaning*

Chapter

28

ATTRACTING TRENDS

By now it should be clear that Value Population analysis focuses on consistent *lifelong* values rather than *transitory* mass behaviors—or trends. As temporary and conditional as trends may sometimes be, however, they are certainly the stuff of which opportunities are made, and forecasting, or better yet attracting trends, is a profitable marketing strategy.

While many consulting groups and advertising agencies are in the business of forecasting trends, most of this "trend prediction" is not so much predictive as it is an early recognition of already observed behaviors. Generally, there is little acknowledgment that in our very complex and kaleidoscopic world, trends most often just emerge randomly and spontaneously. Value Population analysis contends that a systematic approach to evaluating change in terms of consistent values is of much greater worth to marketers than simply capturing random events that are already sliding into the past.

CHAOS THEORY

Chaos Theory helps to explain this systematic approach with its notion of the *strange attractor.* Not as well known as the "butterfly effect," i.e., the power of the tiniest force to elicit extraordinarily profound and random disruptions in a system over time, the somewhat diametrically opposed "strange attractor" principle deals with the tendency of a chaotic system to spontaneously organize itself around what are at first seemingly random and arbitrary points within the system.

Why, it is reasonable for professional marketers to ask, do consumers become so suddenly and passionately, albeit temporarily, enamored with oddities? Why are boy bands and Britney Spears the center of the cultural universe for a season and then old news? What makes carbohydrates such a pillar of healthy living one year and such a pillory the next?

Near Bridge addresses this phenomenon of the random and spontaneous emergence of short-term trends through an understanding of macro value factors we term *Trend Attractors*™.

UNIVERSAL TREND ATTRACTORS™

Issues such as globalization, security, technology, education, poverty, and the environment are all examples of *Universal Trend Attractors*. Despite the daily random chaos of life on our planet, these are some of the issues around which we all form our *present* basic understanding of civilization and through which we express some of our deepest values. While each Value Population is predisposed toward certain and unique valuations of these issues, every one of these issues touches the value matrices of every Value Population.

Thus, the first principle in Trend Attractor analysis is to identify how the apparently spontaneous emergence of trends may or may not be integrated with each Value Population's relationship to Universal Trend Attractors. Is a given new product merely stylish, or does it address in some fashion the primal value structure of the group(s)? Does a particular pitch merely call for a passing glance, or does it subliminally connect with consumers at their greatest depth of understanding regarding the way society itself must be perceived and understood?

Trend power and longevity are largely related to how deeply ingrained a phenomenon is with the individual value interpretations that the Value Populations make with the Universal Trend Attractors.

SITUATIONAL TREND ATTRACTORS™

A subsequent Trend Attractor phenomenon occurs in the valuation of specific trend phenomena. Whenever a company or an industry addresses the development of a strategic response to a trend, they are actually confronting a set of *Situational Trend Attractors*. As will be illustrated in the project example that follows shortly, Situational Trend Attractors are the macro factors around which we presently form our basic understanding of a particular industry, product, service, or cultural phenomenon.

Thus, for example, if we are looking at an increase in wine consumption among American consumers, we are considering all of the Situational Trend Attractors surrounding wine. These may range from issues of connoisseurship to issues of health to issues of social responsibility to issues of leisure, etc. In most cases, the closer the relationship a Situational Trend Attractor has with a variety of Universal Trend Attractors, the more powerful factor it will be in qualifying the importance of a trend.

In the Near Bridge system, identifying Situational Trend Attractors and putting them through the filters of the various Value Populations yields practical insights into the market forms that messages, products, and services should take with each Value Population in the successful capitalization of a trend. Intriguingly, a company or an industry may well define a set of Situational Trend Attractors independent of a specific trend phenomenon and, by pushing these Situational Trend Attractors through the Value Population lenses, can identify and quantify, or more powerfully, create likely trends!

WORKING WITH TRENDS

A pair of projects undertaken by Near Bridge for nonaffiliated trade organizations, the United States Potato Board and the Foodservice and Packaging Institute, helps to clarify this Trend Attractor approach. Both of these organizations directed Near Bridge to consider their primary products in a specific context. For the United States Potato Board, it was potential at-home potato usage in the context of a growing number of smaller one-person and two-person households. For the Foodservice and Packaging Institute, it was the role of single-serve disposable packaging in the context of a rapidly burgeoning take-home meal phenomenon.

In both instances, it became clear that there were some significant overlapping issues. For example, in the broadest sense of "trend," both assignments entailed an evaluation of a consumer's decision to dine at home rather than to eat in a restaurant; and that being the case, there is an inherently similar set of Trend Attractors, both Universal and Situational, brought to bear on the diverse particulars of the assignments.

While the significance and strength of a particular Trend Attractor is not always of equal importance in the separate projects, nor do they necessarily figure with equal prominence in the values of the various Value Populations, here is a list of some of the Trend Attractors and some of the questions that were raised during these projects:

- *Time and convenience.* In this case, this Trend Attractor is Situational as well as Universal. Nearly everyone reports time stress these days. But given some discretionary recuperation time, is the member of a particular Value Population likely to fill it up with chores or to pursue pleasurable activities—or to just "give it a rest?"
- *Menu entitlement.* Today's consumers are exposed to an enormous amount of culinary variety and choice, including cuisines, cook styles, customized ingredients, garnishes, and price points. When dining at home, which of these are likely to be more important? Is variety itself a two-edged sword to some Value Populations?
- *Social situation.* The United States Potato Board project stipulated one-person and two-person households, but is this meal part of an evening of work, an evening of romance, or an evening of collapsing in front of the television set—and are these activities looked at similarly by each Value Population?
- *Health and nutrition.* No dining occasion is devoid of dietary birddogging these days. Being healthy and staying healthy, or at least staying thin, is a top priority. But how does nutritional prudence and sound dietary practice vary between the Value Populations?
- *Safety.* Admittedly, this is more of an issue to the membership of the Foodservice and Packaging Institute than to the United States Potato Board. But, in either case, how differently does each Value Population define and understand safe practices regarding food transit, storage, and preparation?
- *Environmental impact.* To companies that manufacture single-serve disposables, the issue of environmental impact looms large. But are there Value Populations so cause-oriented toward this issue that they even wonder if a potato peel is bad for the environment?
- *Brands.* Such a big buzzword these days! But what does a brand or label portend for different Value Populations—a guarantee of quality and timesaving convenience, or the feeling of romance and escape?
- *Fun factors.* Current "trends'" in the home improvement industry suggest that more and more people regard their home as the one place left where they can have fun and still safely pursue creative personal expression. How does this figure into the Value Populations view of at-home dining?

- *Service.* Surveys indicate that service is still the number-one area of concern for retail customers. As a packaging issue, the implications are multiple, including speed of service, materials dependability, and information labeling. Regarding at-home dining, does the perception of poor service in restaurants encourage greater eating-in frequency consistently in all Value Populations?
- *Fuel gauging.* Here is a good example of a Situational Trend Attractor that "suddenly" emerges. Until it becomes empirically clear that a rise in fuel costs depresses an industry's sales, insiders pooh-pooh the impact of an extra few dollars worth of gasoline on consumer discretionary spending. Aided by a burst of media attention, however, the twin issues of price and perception are suddenly on everyone's mind. How do the different Value Populations deal with the economic impact of a ride to the store?
- *Price/Value.* Arguably, this issue is, and will always be, the key to a consumer's soul. The less obvious questions are, how do the Value Populations differ in their orientation toward money and how does this affect their purchasing decisions?

"VALUING" TREND ATTRACTORS

While confidentiality and space requirements must limit the discussions of all the findings and recommendations associated with these two projects, here is an overview of some of the findings related to the previously mentioned Situational Trend Attractors in regard to Value Population values.

Performers

This Value Population strongly resonates with the Situational Trend Attractors of *Menu Entitlement* and *Fun Factors*. There is an expectation that dinner will have entertainment value, even if that entertainment is provided by the television. Performers gravitate to food that is internationally inspired, uniquely seasoned, colorful, and novel. They are often talkers and flirts, and they tend to value the social content of a meal as much as the sauce.

Recommendations:
- Recipes that can be described as "romantic" and "sexy" are top shelf with Performers.
- Performers, as the Value Population first exposed to TV dinners, have some desire that food be packaged and presented as a novelty.

Techticians

Techticians have an inordinate sensitivity to the Situational Trend Attractor of *Time and Convenience,* having little patience for things that are unnecessarily complicated or take longer than seems reasonable. Dining experiences are, for the most part, vested with a desire for intelligence, stretching beyond efficiency to such Situational Trend Attractors as *Health, Environmental Impact,* and most certainly *Price/Value.*

Recommendations:
- At home, Techticians are particularly comfortable with healthy side dishes served alongside grilled items—enjoying the opportunity to master this relatively straightforward and expeditious cooking technique that also lends itself to further personal "perfecting" through discretionary seasoning and sauces.
- Regarding take-out packaging, Techticians expect spill-proof and sanitary materials—up to the task of temperature and texture retention.

Believers

Social Situation and *Brand* are two of the Situational Trend Attractors that loom large in the Believer worldview. If it looks good, it must be good. To Believers, a desirable brand, be it restaurant or packaged goods, is one that guarantees the delivery of "edible chic." It is important to keep in mind that this Value Population collectively has little culinary training, so *Safety* and *Convenience* and *Time* will always be part of the equation—even if they do not realize it.

Recommendations:
- Socially, Believers tend to be far more concerned with "trendy" aesthetics than tasty dishes and expect to look at something stylish on their plates.
- When Believers are by themselves, they are very likely to pursue some extremely easy and personally restorative indulgence—with take-out and/or a microwave oven featuring prominently in their choices.

Patriots and Transformers

The scope of work undertaken for the United States Potato Board was confined to the three Value Populations listed above. Similarly, the Food-service and Packaging Institute project acknowledged that the Patriots are not a key consumer group driving the take-home restaurant meal trend. However, it is interesting to consider some similarities between Patriots and the Transformers.

Although widely separated by age, these two Value Populations share a child-centric theme and certain culinary echoes—related to a similarity in attitude regarding the selection of what is personally pleasing and plentiful versus any marketing concept of what one "should" like. Thanks to life-phase considerations, while Patriots may always ask for their food to be hotter and Transformers never think their food is "cool" enough, both of these groups share a primal appreciation for food as emotional sustenance.

In the end, the age-segmentation process inherent to Value Population analysis is only one set of lenses appropriate to the discussion of Trend Attractors. Clearly, an analysis of Trend Attractors can also benefit from traditional demographic breakouts such as consumers' income, gender, education, ethnicity, location, and life phase. However, the Trend Attractor/Value Population approach is of particular benefit in that it simultaneously embraces a consistent set of values while allowing for life to unfold in its often unpredictable ways.

To observant marketers, that concept is universally attractive—and highly profitable.

29

THE AGE OF MEANING

In the early 1980s, John Naisbitt's classic work *Megatrends* proclaimed that a profound shift had occurred in the nature of human affairs. According to Naisbitt, the world had demonstrably shifted from an Industrial Age to an Age of Information. Global society had become a realm in which "we now mass-produce information the way we used to mass-produce cars" and in which "everything comes in thirty-one flavors."

What is sometimes overlooked in Naisbitt's seminal work is that he also foresaw the negative as well as the positive implications of this new information age. Indeed, there is certainly both awe and appreciation expressed regarding the data-driven society exploding around him. But Naisbitt also astutely observed that "we are drowning in information but starved for knowledge."

The concepts expressed in *The Consistent Consumer* are driven by the desire for data to evolve into something more cohesive and sustaining than "fact candy." While marketing may yet have much to derive from quantitative techniques, the beauty of addressing lasting values versus episodic behaviors is that values speak to clarity and longevity, and thereby offer real knowledge and the ability to apply it to daily business situations.

Proceeding from this knowledge of values, it becomes feasible to develop products and services, write marketing campaigns, institute hiring and training strategies, and create corporate cultures that partner with the future rather than simply pass through it. So many industries might benefit from this broad-perspective, values-based approach. Consider the following:

Apparel Industry

Styles seem to always change from generation to generation. For example, the clothing tastes of teenage Believers were radically different from those of Transformer teens. Transformer girls were far less into the flirtatious, skimpy, "Britney Spears" look and very much wanted the discrete option of dressing conservatively and not to be so overtly sexually objectified—a fact missed by many apparel manufacturers and retailers.

Service Businesses

In service businesses, there is generally high personal contact with the individual customer. To "get the contract," it is important to quickly understand how to meet the customer's needs and how to interact with the customer appropriately. Whether you're running a cleaning firm or a repair business or a travel agency or a network marketing company, it's important to know, for example, that Techticians will generally go over your work with a fine-toothed comb and Patriots will be very upset if you overrun the price estimate or threaten their private physical or emotional environments. Performers, on the other hand, are less sensitive to these issues and generally like it when service people have entertaining personalities and show some true personal passion for their jobs.

Restaurant Management

Value Population research can address many issues in the restaurant management industry. Consider menu development, where Value Population principles can literally be applied to the subject of taste. With Performers, whose sense of self-determination is large, one has to include opportunities for personalized ingredient and topping options. Techticians will "grill" you if something represented as "authentic" is anything but authentic. Believers tend to opt for pleasing visual aesthetics and anything that the "in-crowd" has elevated to cult status this month.

Financial Products and Services

Anyone who sells a financial product or service can use Value Populations information to effectively improve their customer service and their close rate. Think about all the financial instruments available to an investor, ranging from stocks and bonds to hard assets to savings accounts to aggressive derivative products and so on. Generational insight into risk tolerance and financial sophistication is of incredible value to someone doing financial planning. It's not just a matter of older individuals being more conservative, because a monetary mindset is also based on the core values created in one's youth.

Real Estate Agents

It's common sense that homebuyers are looking for value and the potential for resale profit, but residential real estate brokers need to understand that most people looking for a home are also looking for something to love. For Techticians, who generally like to stay busy around the house, home offices, sophisticated kitchens and landscape gardens are desirable features. Believers are more interested in balancing community life with a sense of sanctuary. Also essential to real estate agents is an understanding of the Transformers, who expect to be consulted in major family transactions and will have real influence over their parents in the home-buying "deed being done."

Strategic Planning

It used to be a popular workplace practice, whether one was talking about products or personal career paths, to seriously address five-, ten-, or even fifteen-year road maps. While some organizations still do strategic long-range planning, there is increasing cynicism about the usefulness of these "guestimated" timelines. Values, as has been seen in this book, are a way of readdressing long-range issues within a context of consistency and durability over long periods of time. Rather than asking the consumer, the client, or the colleague what they will be doing in ten years, Value Population demography suggests that a more useful question is, "In ten years, what will you value?" The answer is likely to be, "Pretty much the same thing I value today."

In Part One of this book, our attention was on the reasoning behind values-based demographic profiling and the method used to identify Value Populations. In Part Two, we introduced the Value Populations and outlined the significant events, cultural artifacts, and lasting icons associated with each. We also provided a glimpse of "who" might be the next Value Population. Part Three moved into the direct application of this material with real businesses that have successfully used Value Population research to increase their marketing impact and business profitability.

Finally, in Part Four we outlined how values can and should be an important part of any business strategy—from organizational structure to personnel management to employee motivation to trend identification and creation.

To this end, the authors hope that the reader accepts *The Consistent Consumer* on its intended terms—not as a mature work of the Age of Information but as an earnest early contribution to the Age of Meaning.

KEN BELLER is the president and CEO of Near Bridge, Inc. An award-winning author and accomplished international business leader, Ken has lived and worked in 20 countries across North America, Europe, and Asia. Throughout his career, he has successfully developed, implemented, and run multicultural and cross-functional initiatives for some of the world's leading companies, including General Electric, Daimler Benz, Applied Materials, and NASA.

STEVE WEISS is the director of trends research for Near Bridge, Inc. He is an award-winning journalist with over 25 years experience as a marketing and management consultant to the food service industry. His work has been profiled in *Nation's Restaurant News, Restaurant Hospitality*, and *Restaurant Business magazines.*

LOUIS PATLER, Ph.D. is the president of The B.I.T. Group, a strategic and organizational development company. An award-winning author, speaker and consultant, Louis brings pioneering technologies for identifying emerging business, education and consumer trends, organization culture/integration solutions, generational differences among workers and consumers, and strategic initiatives to Fortune 500 companies, multinational corporations, and foreign governments. England's BBC-TV, SKY-TV and Canada's CBC-Radio praised him as one of America's new breed of business thought leaders.

ABOUT NEAR BRIDGE

Near Bridge specializes in linking employee and customer values to the bottom line. Their groundbreaking research into sociocultural value formations reveals the hidden factors that motivate people of different generations and provides practical ways to engage and empower employees and turn customers into raving fans.

They challenge clients to look beyond using just "state-of-the-art" programs, processes, and technology to grow and manage their businesses and recognize that it is people and their values that consistently drive meaningful and lasting change.

Based on their ground-breaking research, their training programs, speaking events, and consulting expertise, Near Bridge help clients discover and implement innovative solutions to important business issues such as product positioning, customer communication, and employee engagement and productivity. For more information, visit their website at:

www.NearBridge.com

Q–R

S

CPSIA information can be obtained at www.ICGtesting.com
Printed in the USA
BVOW08s1953210814

363675BV00003B/5/P

9 780980 138290